CW00545547

Morbid Symptoms

Morbid Symptoms

Anatomy of a World in Crisis

Donald Sassoon

VERSO

London • New York

First published by Verso 2021
© Donald Sassoon 2021
Hope (1886), George Frederic Watts, presented to the Tate 1897 (see p. 237)

All rights reserved

The moral rights of the author have been asserted

1 3 5 7 9 10 8 6 4 2

Verso
UK: 6 Meard Street, London W1F 0EG
US: 20 Jay Street, Suite 1010, Brooklyn, NY 11201
versobooks.com

Verso is the imprint of New Left Books

ISBN-13: 978-1-83976-145-4
ISBN-13: 978-1-83976-148-5 (US EBK)
ISBN-13: 978-1-83976-147-8 (UK EBK)

British Library Cataloguing in Publication Data
A catalogue record for this book is available from the British Library

Library of Congress Cataloging-in-Publication Data

Names: Sassoon, Donald, 1946– author.
Title: Morbid symptoms : an anatomy of a world in crisis / Donald Sassoon.
Description: First edition hardback. | London ; New York : Verso, 2021. |
 Includes bibliographical references and index. | Summary: 'In this
 geopolitical study, historian Donald Sassoon paints an unforgettable
 picture of our galloping descent into political barbarism, mixing blunt
 exposé and classical references with an astonishing array of data' –
 Provided by publisher.
Identifiers: LCCN 2020037913 (print) | LCCN 2020037914 (ebook) | ISBN
 9781839761454 (hardback) | ISBN 9781839761485 (ebk)
Subjects: LCSH: Geopolitics – United States. | Geopolitics – Europe. |
 Political corruption – United States – History. | Political
 corruption – Europe – History. | United States – Politics and government. |
 Europe – Politics and government.
Classification: LCC JC319 .S347 2021 (print) | LCC JC319 (ebook) | DDC
 327.101 – dc23
LC record available at https://lccn.loc.gov/2020037913
LC ebook record available at https://lccn.loc.gov/2020037914

Typeset in Sabon by MJ & N Gavan, Truro, Cornwall
Printed in the UK by CPI Group (UK) Ltd, Croydon CR0 4YY

La crisi consiste appunto nel fatto che il vecchio muore e il nuovo non può nascere: in questo interregno si verificano i fenomeni morbosi piú svariati.

Antonio Gramsci

Contents

List of Figures and Tables

Acknowledgements

Thanks to various friends who read the manuscript, made suggestions, and corrected mistakes: above all, Marina Lewycka, but also Lauro Martines, Ilaria Favretto, Vassilis Fouskas, Stella Tillyard, Leonardo Clausi, Paul Auerbach, and my old friend Ivo Galante. Thanks also to Sam Cohn for guidance on Machiavelli and the morbid symptoms of the fourteenth century.

Preface

I became aware at a very young age that history (unlike maths) was not the same everywhere. It happened that I started my primary school in Paris at a time when every French schoolchild was told that 'our' ancestors were the Gauls. The textbook we used contained a picture of the Gallic leader Vercingetorix (the inspiration for the famous comic-strip character Asterix, created in 1959), who had defied the Roman conquerors. He was defeated by Julius Caesar at the battle of Alesia, and then taken to Rome as a prisoner, paraded through the streets, and executed. We were all full of sympathy and pity for the man in chains dragged behind the chariot of the nasty conqueror.

A couple of years later, in 1954, my parents moved to Milan and I found myself in an Italian primary school. Reassuringly, the multiplication tables were the same, but in the history section of our textbook there was no mention of the Gallic hero. I asked the teacher about Vercingetorix. After a moment of hesitation, she said 'Ah, si, *Vercingetorige*', adding 'oh, just one of the many barbarians crushed by the might of Caesar's Roman legions'. I was impressed: a national hero in France was almost unknown in Italy, a neighbouring country, where the brute who had him in chains was celebrated.

That was the best history lesson of my life. Since then I have remained suspicious of national assumptions, not from any great personal merit, but from my life experience. As a Jew, born in Egypt, with a British passport (obtained presumably for colonial reasons by my ancestors), educated in France, then in Italy and later in the

UK and the US, I found it easier than most to avoid falling prey to national mythologies, including Jewish ones.

Though I have always tried to write for a wide audience, my previous books conformed to what would be regarded as 'respectable' by the academy. History, after all, is a subject of general interest and eminently approachable, unlike most sciences and the more recondite and specialised spheres of literary criticism, philosophy, sociology, or economics.

When people ask me 'what is the purpose of history?' I answer, according to my mood, that history has no purpose at all, that it is just fun, like music or drawing, or, more seriously, that history is something no society, not even the most primitive ones, can do without, since the questions 'where do we come from?' and 'what happened in the old days?' are asked in virtually all societies. Answers are sought and are either found or invented; hence stories, fairy tales, myths, religions ... and history. More recently, that is to say since the nineteenth century, many historians have generally stopped pandering to the powerful and celebrating their deeds, and tried to provide answers based on solid evidence and a dispassionate analysis of sources. It is of course difficult to be balanced, to abandon one's prejudices and be fair, but one tries, if not always successfully. To achieve this does not simply depend on personal disposition. There must be an environment in which the historian can pursue his or her task without fear. It is obviously easier to be a historian in a democracy than in a society like Stalinist Russia or Nazi Germany, though one can be a good scientist in both. The Soviet Union had good historians, but they were clever enough to steer clear of recent history. The dangers of not taking the correct line on Peter the Great were not as great as those of not taking the correct line on Stalin.

In modern democracies, historians are freer – though they do not count for very much (a price well worth paying for freedom). People get their history mainly from novels, films, and television. Politicians often use history as one does a supermarket trolley, picking and choosing whatever seems useful. Historians, with the exception of the few who have mastered the art of communicating on the small screen, must be content to provide the raw material for filmmakers and novelists. Most are thrilled if their books are used in this way. In countries where an emphasis is placed on what the French call the *roman national*, the founding narrative of the state, there may be problems, but on the whole 'revisionism' (the term for challenging the orthodoxy) is allowed and occasionally prized. The new Irish or Israeli historians, for example, though sometimes subject to vigorous and occasionally vicious criticism from other historians and from some politicians, have not been shot or deported and have not lost their jobs. If anything, trying to 'liberate' the Irish or the Israeli Jews from the founding myths of their respective states has made some of them famous, and deservedly so, since it was a brave thing to do. As a result, it soon became possible to write about the Irish famine as having mainly social and economic causes, and not as something deliberately engineered by the British or callously ignored by them. In Israel it became possible for the so-called 'new historians', scholars such as Benny Morris, Avi Shlaim, and Ilan Pappé, to write that some 700,000 Palestinians were ethnically cleansed in the course of the 1948 war and had not left of their own free will – as I was told, years ago, in my Jewish school.

In Britain in the nineteenth century, the Whig interpretation of history prevailed, with its benign view of national progress through reform, but today no longer. There are no remaining national British myths of great importance. There are, of course, many who believe that Britain won the Second World War almost single-handedly, or that British colonialism was uniquely benevolent, or that England/Britain was the first democracy in the world, but few serious scholars believe that any of this is the case. In Britain it is easy to be an unruffled and composed historian. There are hardly any risks. But this doesn't mean I don't have to try to control my political passions, even if I am not always successful. There are ways of attempting to be self-critical. When I write history I like to imagine that, perched on my shoulder, there is a little nagging man who spouts advice in an irritating manner. He reads everything I write in a hyper-critical mode, saying things like 'This does not mean anything. Be clearer'; 'This sentence is too long. Shorten it'; 'How do you know that? Where is your evidence?'; 'This is not very original. Someone must have said it before.' Sometimes I listen, sometimes I don't, but if one aspires to be a decent historian, one tries to listen seriously. This book, however, though written by a historian, does not try to be 'balanced'. It is not a history book. It is a polemic – informed by history, of course – and, compared to some of my earlier books, quite short.

1

The Old Is Dying

In a Fascist prison cell in Turi, southern Italy, in 1930, a year after the Great Crash of 1929, eight years after Mussolini's March on Rome, and three years before Hitler's rise to power, the leader of the Italian Communist Party, Antonio Gramsci, penned this famous reflection:

> The crisis consists precisely in this: the old is dying and the new cannot be born; in this interregnum a great variety of morbid symptoms appear.[1]

Are these words still relevant to describe our present situation, more than eighty years after Gramsci's death? We are not in the 1930s. Fascism is not at the door. Liberal democracy is extant in more countries than ever before. Unemployment may have increased compared to the golden years of the post-war boom, but the global downturn of 2007–8, however serious, was nowhere as catastrophic as the Wall Street Crash (though the long-term economic consequences of the coronavirus pandemic maybe prove to be worse than those of 1929). Gramsci explained that the crisis – in which the old was dying but the new was not yet born – was what he called a 'crisis of authority', with the dominant classes losing ground, the consensus buttressing their rule fading, and their ideological grip on the masses slipping away. These masses, Gramsci observed, no longer followed traditional ideologies; they were becoming progressively more cynical and sceptical. They no longer trusted the elites, and the elites knew it. Yet the 'new' remained unpredictable. Marxists traditionally saw crises as opportunities for radical change. Gramsci, so much closer to us, is less optimistic. The conjuncture he was describing was an 'interregnum' teeming with 'morbid symptoms', not a potential revolutionary situation. He did not exclude a return to the old, though he hoped – with what he called an 'optimism of the will' as opposed to the 'pessimism of the intellect' – that the morbid symptoms might offer an opportunity for progress.

The chief characteristic of the interregnum between old and new is uncertainty. It is like crossing a wide river: the old riverbank is left behind, but the other side is still indistinct; currents might push one back and drowning cannot be ruled out. Unable to anticipate what will happen, one is overcome by fear, anxiety, and panic. A critic might point out that when Gramsci wrote those words an undesired 'new' had already appeared: Italian fascism, a 'morbid symptom' certainly, but also a new form of state that enjoyed some popular consensus. The old liberal state had evaporated; the hopes engendered by the Russian Revolution had been dashed and the expected continent-wide revolutions had failed to materialise.

In the wake of the Great War, and the uneven spread of the so-called 'Spanish' flu which killed between 17 and 25 million people worldwide, the revolutionaries who hoped to replicate the achievements of the Bolsheviks had been thoroughly routed.[2] The Hungarian revolution led by Béla Kun in 1919 had been violently suppressed. In Austria, soldiers' and workers' councils ('soviets') led by communists failed to destroy the nascent bourgeois republic. In Germany, the Spartacist revolt of 1918–19 had been bloodily suppressed by the Freikorps, a right-wing paramilitary organisation, in partnership with the social democratic president of Germany, Friedrich Ebert. The Spartacist leaders, Rosa Luxemburg and Karl Liebknecht, were murdered. In Italy the *biennio rosso* (the two red years, 1919–20), as the factory occupations and the peasant turmoil of those years came to be known, ended in failure. Mussolini was appointed prime minister while his followers descended on Rome (on 28 October 1922). A few years later the Fascist dictatorship was established.

Nothing as radical as that occurred in the UK, France, or in the US. In 1920 in Britain, dockers refused to load ships headed for a military intervention against the Bolshevik regime. In 1926 there was a general strike but it lasted only nine days, while the miners continued their struggles for months. Starved into submission, they returned to their mines. The British establishment remained as sturdy as ever. In France the currency depreciated, governments came and went, but there was little unrest after the wave of strikes of May 1920. In 1921, in the US, one of the most significant outbreaks of labour unrest in American history occurred, involving some 10,000 armed miners in West Virginia (the 'Battle of Blair Mountain').[3] The army intervened and quelled the strike, killing dozens of miners, before things reverted to the customary pattern of US violence. Few in America are aware of this episode, which is hardly ever mentioned in novels, songs, or films.

The left had been defeated everywhere, but much of the old had gone – the Tsarist regime, the Austro-Hungarian Empire, the Ottoman Empire – and there was some 'new': the birth of the USSR, of Yugoslavia, Hungary, Austria, Turkey, and the Irish Republic. Soon the US would embark on the New Deal. In China the nationalist government led by Chiang Kai-shek, having defeated various warlords and killing, in 1927, hundreds of communists (Chiang's erstwhile allies), successfully established control over most of China.

In the wake of the October Revolution no other communist regime emerged, with the single exception of Mongolia. Communists were banned, persecuted or unable to emerge from political insignificance, except in Germany (where they were soon destroyed by the Nazis) and France. On the eve of the Second World War authoritarian right-wing governments dominated most of Europe. In 1923 in Bulgaria, a military putsch morphed into the dictatorship of King Boris. In Albania, a local chieftain, Ahmed Zogu, having seized power in 1924, turned himself into King Zog in 1928, with no fear of ridicule. The country was already well established as a police state when, after the Second World War, the communists under Enver Hoxha turned it into an even more repressive regime.

By 1935 Poland too had become a de facto military dictatorship. In 1932 in Lithuania, Antanas Smetona, who had taken power in

1926, established a one-party system. In 1929 King Alexander was at the head of an authoritarian regime in Yugoslavia. In 1934 in Estonia it was Konstantin Päts's turn to become a dictator. King Carol II obtained full powers in Romania in 1938, as a dictator in all but name. In the same year, in Latvia, Kārlis Ulmanis, an anti-Semite, had staged his own coup d'état. Throughout the inter-war period (and up to 1944) Hungary was ruled by Admiral Miklós Horthy, who, like Mussolini, introduced anti-Jewish legislation in 1938.

There were dictatorships in Western Europe too: Fascist Italy, obviously, then Nazi Germany, Francisco Franco's Spain, António de Oliveira Salazar's Portugal, and Ioannis Metaxas's Greece. In the 1930s in Finland, under pressure from the quasi-fascist Lapua movement, the government promulgated a series of anti-communist laws banning communist publications, and arresting leading communists and socialists. In Austria Engelbert Dollfuss assumed dictatorial powers in 1933 only to be murdered by pro-Nazi elements a year later. A dictatorship lasted until Hitler's annexation of the country in 1938.

Pre-1945 Europe was in thrall to right-wing authoritarianism.

In jail, Gramsci did what intelligent revolutionaries should always do: reflect on the causes of their defeat. He was also writing in the shadows of what then appeared to be a major capitalist setback: the Great Crash of 1929. For some, it was as if the long-awaited and long-predicted crisis of capitalism had finally manifested itself. Yet the left was unable to stage a comeback. The situation of the working classes was dire.

In the 1930s, unemployment rates were truly horrific: 17.2 per cent in Germany, 22 per cent in the US, almost 20 per cent in Canada and in Australia, 16 per cent in Austria, and 15 per cent in the UK.[4] Just prior to the coronavirus pandemic, unemployment, especially youth unemployment, was also an issue. The unemployment average in the EU was 8 per cent (but 20 per cent for the young). In the eurozone it was a little higher: 9.4 per cent. It was a very serious issue in Spain (17.4 per cent, 40 per cent for the young) and in most of the Balkan countries (though Croatia with 11.5 per cent was on a par with Italy). But in the majority of the former communist countries unemployment was around the EU average, ranging from 9.4 per cent in Latvia to 3.2 per cent in the Czech Republic. Matters were not so good in Cyprus (11.9 per cent), Portugal (11.2 per cent), Italy (11.6 per cent; 30 per cent for the young), and France (9.9 per cent; 20 per cent for the young). Greece was a special case with unemployment at over 23 per cent (40 per cent for the young). Finland was just above the EU average, Sweden just below. Canada and Ireland had just over 6 per cent unemployment; Israel, Russia, Australia, and New Zealand just over 5 per cent; the US, Great Britain, China, and Switzerland less than 5 per cent; Germany 3.8 per cent, Japan 2.9 per cent, and Singapore only 2.1 per cent.[5] It was a mixed picture, and unemployment certainly played into the hands of xenophobic parties. However, when we consider that in some east European countries the far right is strong and yet joblessness is not particularly pronounced, there does not seem to be a close correlation between the surge of extremist parties and the overall unemployment rate.

Thus, though nothing like the 1930s, the employment situation was not good before the coronavirus pandemic, and of course it is too early to assess what consequences it will have. Yet we too were already facing 'morbid symptoms': democratically elected authoritarian rulers in much of Eastern Europe, in Hungary (Viktor Orbán), and in Russia (Vladimir Putin), but also in the West and elsewhere, such as the unspeakable Trump in the US and Benjamin ('Bibi') Netanyahu in Israel, constantly under investigation by the police for corruption.

There is the loss of popular support for the established parties which have ruled Europe since 1945, mainly the traditional social-democratic left, but also traditional conservative parties, and, above all, the rise of xenophobia in much of the West.

Then there is the disintegration of the 'European dream', the idea that the challenges ahead would be faced by a strong, secure, and integrated Europe. In 2004 Jeremy Rifkin, a guru eternally in the news and usually wrong, announced that Europe was 'quietly eclipsing the American Dream'.[6] By 2020 the UK had withdrawn from the EU; Spain continues to face Catalonian separatism; Greece fears even harder times ahead; Belgium is finding it difficult to form governments and hold the country together. In Italy the emerging parties are Eurosceptic.

This book focuses mainly on the West, but there are 'morbid' social and political symptoms everywhere: Narendra Modi in India, a country which is growing economically while massive poverty still prevails, and where, according to official statistics for 2016, 'a woman was raped every 13 minutes ... a bride was murdered for dowry every 69 minutes, and 19 women were attacked with acid every month'.[7] Then there is Recep Tayyip Erdoğan in Turkey – initially praised by all and sundry, including the *Financial Times* and the *New York Times*, now reviled and not unjustly – while in Turkmenistan we are faced with Gurbanguly Berdymukhamedov, re-elected president for the third time in 2017 with 98 per cent of the popular vote (in a previous life he had been the leader of the Turkmen Communist Party).

In Brazil there is Jair Bolsonaro, nostalgic for the good old days of the dictatorship, homophobe, racist, misogynist, defender of torture, etc., thus ticking every right-wing box. In South Africa there was Jacob Zuma (a polygamist accused but acquitted of rape, eventually forced to resign by his own party, and investigated for corruption); his successor, Cyril Ramaphosa, a former union leader who became a millionaire, was on the board of Lonmin, the British mining company that called in the police to quell a strike, causing the death of thirty-four striking miners and injuring seventy-eight in Marikana in August 2012.

In the Philippines there is the dangerously psychotic Rodrigo Duterte, praised by Donald Trump for the extrajudicial killing of drug users.[8] According to official statistics, more than 4,000 people – some say 8,000 – have been killed in anti-drug operations since Duterte became president, which led to an investigation by the International Criminal Court. Yet, enthused by Duterte's example, Sri Lanka's president, Maithripala Sirisena, announced that it too would begin hanging drug dealers, ending a near half-century moratorium on executions. Over the past decade in Mexico, the so-called drug wars have cost the lives of 230,000 people (13,000 in 2011 alone).[9] More than 130 candidates and party workers were killed during the July 2018 election campaign, probably because of their stance against the drug cartels.[10] President Andrés Manuel López Obrador (known as AMLO), who campaigned against corruption, has an uphill task.

In Myanmar, the Nobel Peace Prize winner Aung San Suu Kyi remained culpably silent while murderous pogroms and ethnic cleansing against the Muslim Rohingyas were taking place, with 6,700 killed in just one month in 2017 according to Médecins Sans Frontières.[11] The war in Afghanistan, the longest in US history, continues, having seen tens of thousands killed, with more to come unless the 2020 US-Taliban accord holds. Iraq is not yet at peace. The Arab Spring that raised so many hopes in the hearts of so many has ended in disaster: in Tunisia, where it all started, popular dissatisfaction has not abated after nine changes of government and few serious reforms. In Egypt, a bloodthirsty dictatorship led by the Western-backed Abdel Fattah el-Sisi (another leader praised by Trump, who called him 'my favourite dictator') makes one almost nostalgic for the days of the previous dictator, Hosni Mubarak. In Libya, in spite or because of Western 'humanitarian' intervention, civil strife has torn the country apart. Syria, having suffered extraordinary casualties (just under 500,000), is now in what one hopes are the final stages of a terrible civil war, with the Assad regime still in power. In Yemen, the neighbouring Saudi regime is conducting a pitiless war that has engendered a massive humanitarian crisis.

In the West we think that Muslim terrorists mainly kill westerners, but they have killed a far larger number of Muslims. The countries most affected by terrorism are Iraq, Afghanistan, Pakistan, Nigeria, and Syria. In Nigeria, the jihadist Boko Haram group has murdered tens of thousands and displaced 2.3 million from their homes. It has even targeted 'moderate' mosques such as that in Kukawa, killing almost 100 people in July 2015. In Pakistan between 2000 and 2019, according to the South Asia Terrorism Portal (SATP), there were over 63,000 fatalities as a result of terrorist violence.[12]

In October 2017 in Mogadishu, the terrorist group Al-Shabaab killed some 300 people using a truck bomb. The news was relegated to page six of the *Financial Times* and page ten of the *Daily Mail*. As the British-Somali novelist Nadifa Mohamed observed, comparing this reaction to the coverage of the terrorist attack at the Bataclan theatre in Paris the previous year: 'London, my home city, [has] not marked this atrocity the way it has those in western cities: no flags at half-mast, no illumination of the London Eye in the blue and white of the Somali flag – not even a tweet from mayor Sadiq Khan.'[13]

A month later in Northern Sinai, armed militants killed over 300 worshippers including twenty-seven children during Friday prayers at the Rawda mosque. On 28 December 2017, a suicide bomb attack in Kabul killed forty-one and injured hundreds, but by the following day there was barely a mention of it on the BBC website: the top story was a fire in New York which had killed twelve people.[14] In July 2018 a suicide bomber killed at least 128 people at a campaign rally in south-western Pakistan, again with minimal coverage in the Western media. And while the murder of fifty Muslims by a far-right terrorist in New Zealand in March 2019 attracted widespread coverage, the killing, in the same period, of well over 100 Fulani herders (all Muslims) in central Mali was barely reported. There are plenty of morbid symptoms in the West, but it's far worse elsewhere.

2

The Rise of Xenophobia

Xenophobia has expanded as the global movement of people has expanded. Europeans – including those often willing to support 'humanitarian' intervention (which usually involves bombing raids in war-torn countries) – complain that they are being 'swamped' by refugees. Yet only 17 per cent of forcibly displaced persons worldwide are hosted in Europe (16 per cent in the US), against 30 per cent in Africa, 26 per cent in the Middle East, and 11 per cent in Asia and the Pacific.[1] Between 2014 and 2017, 22,500 migrants died while trying to reach safety, half of them attempting to cross the Mediterranean. For the period 1993–2018, more than 34,361 deaths can be attributed to the 'Fatal Policies of Fortress Europe'[2] – which is more than all those killed by terrorism in Europe since January 1970 (11,288 fatalities, a figure which includes Russia, the foremost victim of terrorism in Europe).[3]

Most of those killed or injured by terrorists in Western Europe since 1970 were not murdered by jihadists but by members of various separatist groups (Irish nationalists, Ulster Protestant paramilitaries, Basque separatists), or by neo-fascists and extreme leftists in Italy. In Northern Ireland, during 'the Troubles', 3,720 people were killed (almost half under the age of twenty-five) and 47,541 were injured.[4] The peak year for terrorist incidents in Western Europe was 1979, well before the term 'jihadist' had been coined.

In the popular imagination the word 'terrorist' conjures up a Muslim, yet the deadliest mass shooting *by an individual* in Europe occurred in Norway in 2011, when Anders Behring Breivik, a far-right Islamophobe, killed seventy-seven people (mainly young

Labour Party supporters). In the UK the worst mass shootings by individuals were not carried out by Muslims or terrorists but by an unemployed antique dealer (in Hungerford in August 1987 when sixteen people were killed), a taxi driver (in the June 2010 shooting in Cumbria in which twelve people died), and a former shopkeeper (who killed twelve children and their teacher at Dunblane in Scotland in March 1996). The worst terrorist incident in Western Europe occurred in December 1988, when a bomb planted on a Pan Am jumbo jet exploded over the Scottish town of Lockerbie, killing all 259 passengers and crew plus eleven on the ground. Libya accepted responsibility, though many claim that it did so purely to avoid UN sanctions. The person held responsible, Abdelbaset al-Megrahi, was convicted in 2001 (and died in 2012), but controversies continued and, on 11 March 2020, the Scottish Criminal Case Review Commission concluded that a miscarriage of justice may have occurred.[5]

Terrorists pursue a political goal using 'purposeful' violence directed against military targets or, more often, innocent civilians. This is not so different to what the military historian Frederick W. Kagan (of the 'neocon' American Enterprise Institute) suggested when he wrote: 'War is not about killing people and blowing things up. It is purposeful violence to achieve a political goal. The death and destruction, though the most deplorable aspect of war, are of secondary importance. The pursuit of the political objective is all, in fact, that separates killing in war from murder.'[6] Osama Bin Laden would not have disagreed.

Before 9/11, the greatest single loss of American civilian life in a non-natural disaster occurred in the 'Reverend' Jim Jones's jungle outpost in Guyana in November 1978, when more than 900 men, women, and children who had followed Jones were murdered or induced to commit suicide. Jones was neither a terrorist nor a Muslim but one of the many cult leaders who seem to thrive in the US, similar to David Koresh, leader of the 'Branch Dravidian' in Waco, Texas. The Waco siege of April 1993, and the eventual assault by the FBI, resulted in the death of seventy-six people including twenty children.

The deadliest terrorist attack in the US before 9/11 was carried out by Timothy McVeigh, who on 19 April 1995 blew up a federal building in Oklahoma City killing 168 people and injuring 680 others. McVeigh was not a Muslim or a Mexican or an Arab. He was a gun-loving graduate from a military school in Georgia and a multi-decorated veteran of the 1991 Gulf War who, like many Republicans, was opposed to 'big government'.

The deadliest mass shooting by a single individual occurred in Las Vegas on 1 October 2017. At least fifty-eight people were killed and over 500 more wounded. Had the killer claimed to be a Muslim, the attack would have been classified as a 'terrorist' incident, and many commentators would have attributed the 'problem' to Islam – as was the case with Omar Mateen, the lone perpetrator of the Orlando massacre in June 2016, in which forty-nine were killed. Had the Las Vegas killer been a 'refugee', many would have been clamouring to keep refugees out and send those already in the country 'back home'. However, he was a white, sixty-four-year old retired accountant, born and bred in the US.

A month after the Las Vegas shooting, in Sutherland Springs, Texas, a former member of the US Air Force (also white) killed twenty-six people in a Baptist church. Of course, on neither occasion was there an outcry against retired accountants or former members of the Air Force. And there was relatively little alarm. Donald Trump simply said the Baptist church attacker was insane and that he was glad someone else had a gun to shoot him. The Texas Attorney General suggested that churches should employ professional armed security guards for their protection (though the killer had himself been a security guard).[7] A number of senators and politicians expressed their sorrow and horror at the Las Vegas tragedy, including Senator John McCain, a Republican presidential candidate in 2008 who had received $7.7 million from the National Rifle Association (NRA), who 'prayed' for the victims; Marco Rubio, who sought the presidential nomination in 2016, who 'prayed for all the victims and their families' while being a beneficiary of the NRA to the tune of $3.3 million; Senator Richard Burr, whose 'heart was with the people of Las Vegas' and who received $6.9 million; Senator Roy Blunt, who was 'saddened by the tragic loss of life' yet received $4.5 million; and Senator Thom

Tillis who sent his 'deepest condolences' but accepted $4.4 million, and on and on and on.[8]

In February 2018 another mass shooting occurred at a school in Florida, in which seventeen pupils were murdered by a former student. It was the eighth mass shooting so far that year. This drew further prayers and condolences from mainly Republican senators and congressmen whose campaigns and expenses had been heavily subsidised by the gun lobby. Trump's surreal 'solution' was to arm the teachers. The economist Nouriel Roubini tweeted in exasperation: 'Republicans with criminal blood on their hands "pray" for victims of gun violence while pocketing daily millions of dollars of murderous NRA money that blocks sensible gun control laws and lets massacres occur daily. Bloody murderers.'[9] A couple of months later, on 18 May, a further ten children were shot dead in a Santa Fe school by a disgruntled student (neither a Muslim nor a terrorist), who, it was claimed, aimed at the students he didn't like.[10] In October an attack on a Jewish synagogue in Pittsburgh resulted in eleven dead. The killer was a white middle-aged man who hated Jews because, or so he thought, they help Mexican migrants. A few weeks later at Thousand Oaks, California, an Afghan war veteran, white and non-Muslim, killed twelve people. On 31 May 2019 in Virginia Beach a disgruntled city employee (who had also served in the military) killed twelve of his colleagues. In August 2019, at a Walmart in El Paso, on the border with Mexico and with a largely Latino population, a young white supremacist shot dead more than twenty people and left many more injured – one of the deadliest incidents in Texas's history and in a city with one of the lowest crime rates in the US (contrary to what Trump mendaciously declared in his 2019 State of the Union address).[11] Less than twenty-four hours later another white male killed nine people (including his sister) in Dayton, Ohio. And so it goes on and on.

In the United States – where, proportionally, there are more guns in civilian hands then there are in Yemen, where there is a war on – 64 per cent of all homicides are gun-related, in comparison with 4.5 per cent in the UK.[12]

 භ

You know there is a problem when the misdeeds of a minority force an entire community to feel under siege. In the north of England, in towns such as Rochdale and Rotherham, a series of scandals involving minors who were raped, abused, and exploited by gangs of Asian men, mainly British of Pakistani origin, received, quite rightly, widespread coverage. In August 2017, this led Sarah Champion, Labour MP for Rotherham and shadow minister for women and equalities, to write an article in the *Sun* complaining that 'For too long we have ignored the race of these abusers and, worse, tried to cover it up. No more. These people are predators and the common denominator is their ethnic heritage.'[13] In a BBC follow-up interview she added, mixing self-pity with the mantle of righteousness, that 'The far-right will attack me for not doing enough and the floppy left will have a go at me for being a racist.' She later resigned from the opposition front bench, apologising 'for the offence caused by the extremely poor choice of words in the *Sun* article'. A few days later, on 13 August, the *Sun* columnist Trevor Kavanagh added fuel to the fire in a hysterically Islamophobic article claiming that 'Sweden fears it is losing its identity as a nation', 'Germany is fighting a wave of rape and other sex crimes', and that Britain had a 'Muslim Problem' – capitalised, and hence reminiscent of the Nazi 'Jewish Problem' (the capitalisation was later changed on the website). Among many others, the article was denounced by the Board of Deputies of British Jews as well as more than a hundred MPs. In London two months earlier, an Islamophobe incensed by the sex exploitation scandals and a dramatisation of them on television, had driven a van into a crowd of people, some wearing traditional Islamic clothes, killing one and injuring several others. He was, it turned out, a loner and an alcoholic with 'mental health issues' who had been out of work for a year. Hating Muslims must have given him a purpose in life. In a way he was the equivalent of a jihadist. When the incident happened, an imam stepped in to save him from the anger of the crowd.[14]

One can imagine the fully justified outcry there would be if anyone dared to claim that 'powerful Jews have a problem with sexual harassment', bearing in mind the sex assault allegations involving the former IMF director Dominique Strauss-Khan, the

film director Woody Allen, the actor Dustin Hoffman, the conductor James Levine, the retailer Philip Green, and the convictions of
the American financier Jeffrey Epstein, the film director Roman
Polanski (for unlawful sexual intercourse with a thirteen-year-old
in 1977), and, last but certainly not least, the Hollywood producer
Harvey Weinstein, recently convicted for rape.

In fact many powerful men, of whatever ethnic origin, seem to
have a 'problem with sex'. As revealed in the *Financial Times*, in
January 2018 a men-only 'charity' gala (now in its thirty-third year)
held at the Dorchester Hotel in London was attended by 360 men
in black tie. A mix of businessmen, property tycoons, film producers, financiers, and the odd politician, they were joined by 130
specially hired hostesses who had been instructed to wear skimpy
black outfits with matching underwear and high heels, and made to
sign a non-disclosure agreement. Many of these women – some of
them students earning extra cash – were groped, sexually harassed
and subjected to lewd and vulgar comments and repeated requests
to join diners in bedrooms. Some men repeatedly put their hands
up the women's skirts; one exposed his penis during the evening.
Fundraising included prizes such as a night at a strip and lap-
dancing venue for up to 100 guests. The task of finding women
was entrusted to an agency specialising in hostesses, who were paid
£150 for the evening and had to be 'tall, thin and pretty'. One experienced hostess admitted that quite a few of the men were likely to
be 'arseholes'. This in the financial centre of the world, where so-
called 'masters of the universe' and 'captains of industry' behaved
like pathetic, sex-starved young louts, who needed their egos mas-
saged and who probably thought it would be fun.[15] Even some
aid workers, such as those working for Oxfam, used prostitutes in
places such as Haiti, after a terrible earthquake in 2010 which killed
160,000 people, injured 300,000, and left 1.5 million homeless.[16]

The vast majority of sex offenders in the UK are white males,
according to the head of the Crown Prosecution Service in the
north-west of England, Nazir Afzal (himself a Muslim), who has
campaigned against forced marriage, female genital mutilation, and
honour killings. Sue Berelowitz, deputy Children's Commissioner
for England, explained that sex offenders 'come from all ethnic

groups and so do their victims – contrary to what some may wish to believe'.[17] If one looks at child sexual abuse as a whole there is no evidence that the perpetrators come disproportionately from one ethnic group. They are, however, overwhelmingly men.

Despite the recent apparent upsurge in racism, we should remember that in Britain it was worse in the 1950s and 1960s. In 1950, the Labour government under Clement Attlee set up a review into how 'to check the immigration into this country of *coloured* [my emphasis] people from the British Colonial territories'.[18] In August 1958 there were 'race riots' in London's Notting Hill, sparked by right-wing white youth, then commonly referred to as Teddy Boys. A year later, Oswald Mosley, leader of the British Union of Fascists in the 1930s, stood in the 1959 general election in Kensington North on behalf of his 'new' Union Movement, (he had wisely dropped the 'Fascists') calling for the forcible repatriation of Caribbean immigrants (who, he claimed, brought diseases with them). His share of the vote was a not insignificant 7.6 per cent. At the 1964 election, won by the Labour Party led by Harold Wilson, the Conservative candidate for the Smethwick constituency, Peter Griffiths, ran an overtly racist campaign, with his supporters chanting the slogan, 'If you want a nigger for a neighbour, vote Labour.' Griffiths refused to disown them: 'I would not condemn any man who said that. I regard it as a manifestation of popular feeling.'[19] He won the seat from Labour with a swing of 7.2 per cent – against a pro-Labour national swing of 3.5 per cent.

In 1968, the Labour government passed the Commonwealth Immigrants Act which reduced the rights of citizens of Commonwealth nations to settle in the UK. It was obvious from clauses in the Act to do with the origins of grandparents that the aim was to keep out people of Asian descent who were being persecuted in some African countries as a result of a policy of 'Africanisation'. Weeks later, Enoch Powell, the Conservative shadow defence secretary, warned that immigration from Britain's former colonies would lead to apocalyptic violence on the scale of the recent race riots in the US. In his famous 'rivers of blood' speech (in which the words 'rivers of blood' were never actually used), he quoted a constituent who had told him that soon 'the black man will have the whip hand over the white man', employing the rhetorical device of quoting someone else saying something which one does not wish to say directly.[20] Powell could have mentioned, but did not, the numerous racist incidents in which blacks had been beaten by whites. The incidents he mentioned in a second, less famous speech, were almost all false.[21]

Powell's hypocrisy was made all the more evident by the fact that he had never complained about black immigrants when he was minister of health (1960–63), during which period the health authorities continued to recruit much-needed personnel from former colonies to work in the National Health Service. As health minister he was a disaster: he refused to hold a public inquiry on thalidomide, a drug taken by pregnant women to relieve morning sickness and which eventually caused, worldwide, more than 10,000 cases of children being born with malformed limbs, including some with severe brain damage. Powell's senior medical adviser had been briefed by Distillers, the company making the drug.[22] To cap it all, he also refused to introduce tests for cervical cancer which could have saved many lives, as they already had in the United States.[23]

Even his 'rivers of blood' speech is inaccurate: to show off his knowledge of the classics he quoted from Virgil's *Aeneid*: *As I look ahead, I am filled with foreboding; like the Roman, I seem to see the River Tiber foaming with much blood.* He is wrong: it is not a Roman who foresees blood. There were no Romans at the time. It was the (Greek) God Apollo speaking via his priestess, the Sibyl of Cumae, who is Greek (Cumae or Cuma was a Greek colony near Naples), and she tells Aeneas (a refugee from Troy, who would not have got anywhere near Rome if Enoch and his followers had their way), 'I see wars, horrible wars, and the Tiber foaming with much blood' (*bella, horrida bella / et Thybrim multo spumantem sanguine cerno'*, Book VI). This is about invasion and conquest – a far cry from whatever threatened Enoch's Wolverhampton constituency which, by a wonderful irony of history, returned, in 2017, Eleanor Smith, a Labour MP who is black with an African Caribbean background.

Following his 'Rivers of Blood' speech Powell was sacked from the shadow cabinet by the Conservative leader Edward Heath. He received support from unexpected quarters: 1,000 dockers led by Harry Pearman (a Christian anti-communist) marched with slogans such as 'Don't Knock Enoch' and 'Back Britain, Not Black Britain', protesting against the Powell's 'victimisation'.[24] They were soon followed by meat porters from Smithfield market while the conservative *Times* (then edited by William Rees-Mogg) called Powell's speech 'evil' (22 April 1968). Powell received thousands of letters of support. Needless to say, the fact that he was wrong in this as in much else, and that he changed his mind frequently, did not dent the admiration of his many supporters and hagiographers. One of them, Simon Heffer, author of a very lengthy and positive biography of Powell, wrote an article about him in the *Daily Mail* with the headline 'A prophet yet an outcast: 100 years after his birth Enoch Powell has been vindicated on a host of crucial issues'.[25] The word 'vindicated' is hardly uncontentious: Powell was an opponent of British entry into the European Union and a fervent monetarist – in other words a path-breaker for morbid symptoms.

The fact that the *Daily Mail* was at the forefront of the whitewashing of Powell is hardly surprising, since it constantly produces articles disparaging refugees, often claiming that many are not refugees at all, and reporting inaccurately in May 2017 that 'around 6.6

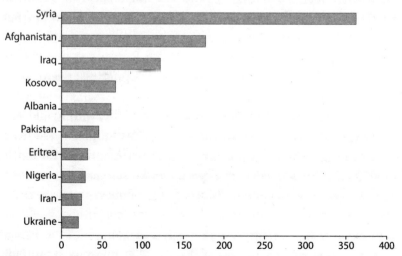

Figure 1 Top 10 origins of people applying for asylum in the EU: First-time applications in 2015, in thousands

Source: BBC, 'Migrant Crisis in Seven Charts', 4 March 2016.

million refugees in North Africa, Jordan and Turkey are waiting to come to Europe'.[26] Most refugees seeking protection in Europe are from Syria and Afghanistan (see chart), and they are nowhere near 6.6 million in number.

The *Daily Mail* has a track record of peddling fake news (such as the forged Zinoviev letter which it published just before the general election of 1924 with the headline 'Civil War Plot by Socialists' Masters') and of reporting negative comments about foreign refugees: on 20 August 1938 it reported positively on a British magistrate's complaint that the way 'stateless Jews from Germany' were 'pouring in from every port of this country is becoming an outrage'.[27] A few years earlier (15 January 1934), the *Daily Mail* had hailed the British Union of Fascists with an editorial written by its owner, Lord Rothermere, headlined 'Hurrah for the Blackshirts'. A week later the Labour-leaning *Daily Mirror* ran the headline 'Give the Blackshirts a helping hand.' The author of this article was the very same Lord Rothermere, who happened to own the *Mirror* as well. Anti-Semitism in various forms was alive and well in the higher reaches of the Labour Party well before the recent furore sparked by paranoid anti-Corbynism. In a 1922 pro-Zionist pamphlet, written on his return from Palestine and published by the Jewish Socialist Labour Confederation Poale-Zion, Ramsay MacDonald, the future Labour prime minister, distinguished between good Zionist Jews and

> the rich plutocratic Jew, who is the true economic materialist. He is the person whose views upon life make one anti-Semitic. He has no country, no kindred. Whether as a sweater or a financier, he is an exploiter of everything he can squeeze. He is behind every evil that Governments do, and his political authority, always exercised in the dark, is greater than that of Parliamentary majorities. He has the keenest of brains and the bluntest of consciences.[28]

In 1929, Sidney Webb, one of the main architects of the Fabian Society, expressed satisfaction at the fact that there were 'no Jews in the British Labour Party', while 'French, German, Russian Socialism is Jew-ridden. We, thank heaven are free', adding that this was probably the case because there was 'no money in it'.[29] Such anti-Semitism was only too common at the time: though she hated fascism, Virginia Woolf (whose husband was Jewish), wrote the kind of stuff which today can only provoke disgust: perturbed at sitting next to Sir Philip Sassoon, whom she described as an 'underbred Whitechapel Jew', she reflected: 'How I hated marrying a Jew – how I hated their nasal voices and their oriental jewellery, and their noses and their wattles' (though she added: 'what a snob I was: for they have immense vitality, and I think I like that quality best of all'.)[30]

The Second World War did not significantly change British xenophobia. In 1948, in an article headlined 'Let Them Be Displaced' attacking a scheme to find employment in the UK for displaced persons (i.e. refugees), the *Daily Mirror* thundered: 'Other countries have taken the cream and left us most of the scum ... They add to our discomfort and swell the crime wave. This cannot be tolerated. They must now be rounded up and sent back.' In 1949, the organ of the socialist 'intelligentsia', the *New Statesman* (edited by the revered Kingsley Martin), called for a rigid selection of Ukrainian refugees, in order 'to exclude the illiterate, the mentally deficient, the sick, the aged, the politically suspect, and the behaviourally disruptive. [We should] clear out the rubbish amongst those who have already come.'[31]

In France, immigration (without which France and the West as a whole would be a dismal place) has given rise to an alarmist literature which has resuscitated ancient racist tropes. Stephen Smith, an American who writes in French, claimed in his *La Ruée vers l'Europe. La Jeune Afrique en route pour le Vieux Continent* that by 2050 100 million Africans are likely to have crossed the Mediterranean; Alain Finkielkraut, in his bestseller *L'Identité malheureuse*, lamented the dangers that immigration would bring for French identity (as if that had ever been a stable construct); while Renaud Camus, a former socialist now on the far-right, in his *Le Grand remplacement* (published in 2011 by a small pro-Israeli publishing house), denounced the 'plot' to replace the 'real' French population with that of Africa.[32]

Today there is money in Islamophobia the way there isn't in

anti-Semitism. It is difficult to imagine nowadays a bestseller ringing the alarm about the alleged power of the Jews, but there are plenty of books warning of the threat Muslims present to 'European values' (such values, presumably, do not include Nazism and Stalinism). The Islamophobic genre is hardly original in its claims that there are too many Muslims, that soon they will take over everything, and that the West is doomed unless 'we' react. The celebrated Italian journalist Oriana Fallaci – in her bestselling and widely translated *La rabbia e l'orgoglio* (*The Rage and the Pride*, written in reaction to 9/11 and published in Italy in 2004) and her *La forza della ragione* (*The Force of Reason*, also 2004) – has produced texts full of hysterical insults towards 'the sons of Allah'. The title of Melanie Phillips's *Londonistan: How Britain Is Creating a Terror State Within* (2006) says it all (Phillips is another journalist who, like Fallaci, has journeyed from left to right). A more recent exemplar of this genre was *The Strange Death of Europe: Immigration, Identity, Islam* (2017) by the British journalist Douglas Murray. The historian Niall Ferguson, in an article in the *New York Times*, wrote that 'A youthful Muslim society to the south and east of the Mediterranean is poised to colonize – the term is not too strong – a senescent Europe.'[33] *America Alone: The End of the World as We Know It* (2006), by the Canadian journalist Mark Steyn, lamented the 'fact' that soon Muslims will outnumber the whites: 'they breed with gusto'.[34]

Steyn can relax: Muslim Americans (currently 1 per cent of the population) have an average of 2.4 children over the course of their lives. 'Normal' Americans have an overall average of 2.1 children.[35] According to the Pew Research Center, by 2050, the US Muslim population is projected to reach 8.1 million, or 2.1 per cent of the nation's total population, significantly lower than the percentage of Muslims in Britain, France, or Germany today.[36]

This is hardly breeding 'with gusto'. If anyone is breeding 'with gusto' it is the American Orthodox Jewish community, with four children per couple (unlike non-orthodox Jews, who, on the whole, are liberals and vote Democrat).[37] Nor is this just an American phenomenon. In Britain, home of some 270,000 Jews, the ultra-orthodox (whose birth rate far exceeds that of all other groups) will make up 30 per cent of all Jews by 2031 and a majority twenty years later, leaving behind the somewhat stereotypical image of the progressive, intellectual, enlightened Jew.[38]

In *America Alone*, Steyn confidently predicted that Europe will be overwhelmed by Muslims, who reproduce at a faster rate than non-Muslims.[39] Such demographic fears are ancient, and the statistics employed to stoke them are often fake. The Muslim population of the EU was still only 4.9 per cent in 2016. According to the Pew Research Center there are three possible scenarios for the percentage of Muslims in Europe in 2050:

1. 7.4 per cent if there is no immigration;
2. 11.2 per cent under 'normal' migration;
3. 14 per cent if present trends, boosted by the refugee crisis, continue.[40]

It is not just Muslims who supposedly represent a threat to the US. There are Mexicans too, 'rapists' as Donald Trump infamously called them. This is the logic behind the 'wall' on the Mexican border that Trump promised to erect. He is hardly an innovator here, since he follows in the footsteps of the 'liberal' President Clinton. In 1994 the Clinton administration's Operation Gatekeeper was designed to make it more difficult and dangerous for illegal Mexican immigrants to cross the border, forcing them to journey across the desert and mountainous terrain. The result was hundreds of deaths.[41] In 1996 Clinton signed the Illegal Immigration Reform and Immigrant Responsibility Act, establishing the huge deportation system that has endured to this day. Nor should one ignore the support given by Hillary Clinton to the coup in Honduras in 2009, when she was secretary of state in the Obama administration, a coup which contributed enormously to the wave of refugees and immigrants from Honduras.

Between May and June 2018 a strict application of existing rules meant that some 2,342 children of illegal immigrants were separated from their families and sent to mass detention centres.[42] The spectacle of children in steel cages, crying and demanding to see their parents, horrified many Americans, but not Trump. Writing in the *Washington Post*, Laura Bush, wife of former president George W. Bush, denounced the cruelty and immorality of this zero tolerance application of the rules.[43] She was joined, apparently, by Melania Trump, who declared that she 'hates to see children separated from their families'. Judging for once that he had gone too far, 'The Donald' caved in and made an unusual (and perhaps temporary) U-turn, notwithstanding his firm belief that undocumented immigrants 'aren't people. These are animals.'[44] On Fox News, Ann Coulter, a far-right commentator who owes her fame to her outrageous comments, declared that the children crying were 'actors'.[45]

Some of these immigrants from Central American countries are labelled, somewhat disparagingly, 'economic migrants' rather than refugees, as if the desire to emigrate to improve one's life were somehow shameful, and as if it were not the case that such immigrants made America what it is today. Rejecting those escaping famine, war, or persecution is even more shameful, and Britain's record in welcoming refugees is reprehensible (though not as bad that of Japan, which in 2017 accepted only 20 of the 20,000 applications for asylum it received).[46] The record of the US, a country with 300 million inhabitants, is also dire. In 2015, under Obama's presidency, it admitted 2,192 Syrian refugees; in 2016 the number went up to 15,479; but in 2017, under Trump, it plummeted to 3,024. By April 2018 the US had admitted that year only *eleven* Syrian refugees, even though, moved by the plight of those (allegedly) gassed by the Assad regime, it bombed Syrian military facilities.[47]

While the British tabloid press likes to depict a country swamped by asylum seekers, the reality is quite different. By 2015 there were an estimated 123,000 refugees in the UK – around 0.2 per cent of the population.[48] By contrast over 647,000 refugees have fled from Myanmar to Bangladesh (one of the poorest countries in the world) since 25 August 2017.[49] Hysteria about refugees is common in the press, but politicians play the game too: David Davies, a Welsh Conservative, and Jack Straw, former Labour home and foreign secretary, also descended into the gutter when they demanded that child refugees in Calais be given a teeth test to determine their age.[50]

By far the most important voice to emerge in Europe against the anti-refugee hysteria has been that of the German Chancellor and

Christian Democratic Party leader, Angela Merkel. Exhibiting an integrity seldom seen on the official left, or indeed anywhere else among Europe's leaders, Merkel, at the height of the refugee crisis, decided to open the border, welcoming more than a million refugees. It was an opportunity for Germans to look good. As Thomas Meaney wrote: 'For a brief season, Germans were besotted with their own magnanimity, handing out bottles of water and stuffed animals to Syrians', unlike the French who made sure that they festered in the Calais 'jungle' (a policy followed by the socialist Hollande as much as by the centrist Macron), or the British who hardly accepted any, or the Hungarians who fenced themselves in.[51] Merkel's popularity began to dwindle after sexual assaults (including over twenty rapes or attempted rapes) on women in Cologne and other cities allegedly by North African men during the 2015–16 New Year's Eve celebrations.

Negative views of Muslims are almost inversely proportional to the number of Muslims in a country. In Hungary (the most Islamophobic country), negative views of Muslims are held by 72 per cent of the population (of which Muslims make up 0.1 per cent), in Italy by 69 per cent (3.7 per cent), and in Poland by 66 per cent (0.1 per cent). Negative views are lowest (around 28–29 per cent) in countries with the highest Muslim populations: France (7.5 per cent), Germany (5.8 per cent), and the United Kingdom (4.8 per cent).[52]

According to a YouGov survey, British people are more persuaded of the benefits of immigration than any other major European nation. Almost half of Britons think immigrants are either positive or neutral for the country, and 28 per cent believe the benefits of immigration outweigh the costs, compared with 24 per cent in Germany, 21 per cent in France, and 19 per cent in Denmark. By comparison, 50 per cent of Italians believe the net impact of immigration is negative, as well as 49 per cent of Swedes, 42 per cent of French, and 40 per cent of Germans. Britons were relatively less hostile to refugees.[53]

The growth of anti-immigrant parties in Europe cannot be explained by concerns about the economy alone. In Spain, Ireland, and Portugal anti-immigrant politics is relatively subdued. The success of such parties elsewhere in Europe is linked to ideological factors such as the perception of an attack on national identity, exploited by politicians in what the historian Richard Hofstadter famously described as the 'paranoid style' in his classic essay on the American radical right in McCarthy's time.[54]

In the US, paranoid Islamophobia is given intellectual credence by so-called think-tanks which claim to be non-partisan, such as the right-wing Gatestone Institute (its chairman was John Bolton, former US ambassador to the United Nations, and then, and not for long, national security adviser to Trump). Its website hosts articles claiming that Europe has Muslim 'no-go zones' and 'microstates governed by Islamic Sharia law'. The idea of no-go zones originated from terrorism 'expert' Steven Emerson, who claimed that Britain's second city Birmingham was 'totally Muslim', a place 'where non-Muslims just simply don't go'. He later abjectly apologised ('a terrible error ... I am deeply sorry'). By then his claim had become such a major story that it led Prime Minister David Cameron to describe Emerson, quite correctly, as 'a complete idiot' (*Daily Telegraph*, 12 January 2015). The same could be said of Pete Hoekstra, the Trump-appointed ambassador to the Netherlands (and himself an immigrant from the Netherlands), who had claimed in 2015 that the country had no-go zones and that politicians and cars were being set on fire by radical Islamists. On Dutch TV he denied having made such claims ('fake news', he said). The clips were then played back to him.[55] Not only do they lie, they don't remember that they lie.

The bestselling doomsters were simply repeating the old tropes that prevailed around 1900, when the modern literature of alarm emerged: everything was doomed; the barbarians were at the gates; our values were in danger. Perhaps they are, but not necessarily from Muslims: in the US a (small) majority of US Muslims back same-sex marriage, while opposition to it is now limited almost entirely to white evangelical Christians and Jehovah's Witnesses, most of whom supported Donald Trump.[56]

The theme of doom is exciting. After the First World War, the 'decline and fall' genre became fashionable, popularised by writers such as Arnold Toynbee with his multi-volume *A Study of History* (1934–61), and Oswald Spengler's bestselling *The Decline of the West*, published in 1918 though written before the war. Xenophobia was rife among the educated classes. Max Weber (that paragon of liberalism, but always more a nationalist than a liberal), alarmed at the arrival of Polish workers, advocated closing the eastern frontier. 'From the stand-point of the nation', he wrote, 'large-scale enterprises which can only be preserved at the expense of the German race deserve to go down to destruction'.[57] More recently, Samuel P. Huntington (he of the 'clash of civilizations') had 'theorised' (if that is the word for banal prejudices taken seriously only because he was a Harvard professor) the incompatibility of multiple identities in a single nation and the threats presented to 'the West', above all by Muslims (presumably all of them, whether in Indonesia, Pakistan, Morocco, Iraq, Albania, or Nigeria) – and, indeed, by non-Protestant Christians, since his last book, *Who Are We? The Challenges to America's National Identity* (2004), warned against the cultural threat posed by immigration from Latin America.[58]

In Germany today, xenophobia is not just the prerogative of the outer fringes but of rising parties such as Alternative für Deutschland (AfD). The politician Thilo Sarrazin, a member of the Social Democratic Party (SPD) and former member of the Executive Board of the Bundesbank, gave an interview to the German cultural magazine *Lettre International* (September 2009) in which he referred to the large number of Arabs and Turks in Berlin who, according to him, did little else except sell fruit and vegetables and produce 'little headscarf girls' while living on benefits and refusing to integrate (he was even able to cite statistics for such 'refuseniks': 70 per cent of Turks and 90 per cent of Arabs).[59] In 2010, Sarrazin used his newly acquired notoriety to publish a book, *Deutschland schafft sich ab* (Germany Abolishes Itself), full of hostility towards immigrants, which quickly became a bestseller with 1.5 million copies sold – apparently the bestselling hardback non-fiction book in post-war Germany.[60] A second book, called *Hostile Takeover: How Islam Hampers Progress and Threatens Society*, has encountered publishing problems. Much of Sarrazin's mish-mash of pseudo-science, reminiscent of the eugenic theories of the past, was widely criticised by scientists everywhere, including Angela Merkel (who has a science background). Liberal thinkers, such as the jurist Christoph Schönberger and the political theorist Herfried Münkler, thought that Germany could lead Europe precisely because its past had vaccinated it against various types of modern populism, unlike France (Le Pen), Italy (Lega), and Greece (Golden Dawn).[61] They were too optimistic. Views until recently regarded as illegitimate in Germany have started to become acceptable. In the September 2017 elections, the AfD, seen not long ago as a minor right-wing fringe party, won 12.6 per cent of the popular vote, becoming Germany's third-largest party. It did particularly well in East Germany where there are few immigrants, and is not simply a party of the 'left-behinds': 39 per cent of its supporters have a higher than average income.[62] AfD was initially founded by mainstream figures opposed to the Greek bailout programmes. One of its founders, Konrad Adam, was the culture editor of the highly reputable conservative daily *Frankfurter Allgemeine*. Its deputy spokesman in 2014 was Hans-Olaf Henkel, who was a member of Amnesty International and president of the Federation of German Industries from 1995 to 2000. He quit in 2015 when the party morphed into an all-out xenophobic party. Alice Weidel, the party's co-leader and a former Goldman Sachs banker whose role model is Margaret Thatcher, is also a Eurosceptic, and perhaps something of a feminist since she deplored the fact that only 18 per cent of AfD voters were women.[63] As if to confound those who think that the far right is necessarily homophobic, she came out as a lesbian, with a partner originally from Sri Lanka and two adopted children; yet officially the party she leads is against gay marriage and defends the traditional family.[64]

In Italy racism is decidedly less complicated and more vulgar, and not just among some football supporters. (Racism is endemic throughout European football, with black players subjected to abuse and 'monkey chants'. In England in the 1970s and 1980s the refrain 'There ain't no black in the Union Jack/Send the bastards back' would echo throughout the stands.)[65] The football boss Carlo Tavecchio became infamous for lamenting that 'banana-eaters' (i.e.

African players) were now playing in Italy.[66] Notwithstanding such remarks (and his criminal record for tax evasion, etc.), Tavecchio was elected president of the Italian Football Federation in 2014 and re-elected in 2017. He resigned in November that year because Italy failed to qualify for the 2018 World Cup. In politics matters are even worse. On 13 July 2013, vice-president of the Senate Roberto Calderoli, a leading member of the xenophobic Lega Nord (Northern League) party and formerly a minister in Silvio Berlusconi's government, declared that the minister for integration, Cécile Kyenge (who was born in the Democratic Republic of the Congo), reminded him of an orangutan. Kyenge, a member of the centre-left Partito Democratico, was regularly insulted in public and a banana was thrown at her during a public speech she was giving. Calderoli was acquitted by the Senate on the charge of spreading racial hatred, with the aid of votes from the Democratic Party, and withdrew nearly all the 500,000 amendments he had tabled on the Democratic Party's proposed constitutional reforms. Calderoli is not new to such disgusting comments. In 2006 he had said that the French football team had lost to the Italians because their team was full of 'negroes, Islamists, and communists.'[67] One wonders what he thought in 1998 when France beat Italy. In 2018 Calderoli was still vice-president of the Senate, and his party, the Lega, signed a cooperation pact with Putin's party, United Russia, as have other far-right European parties.[68] In 2019 he was handed an eighteen-month prison sentence for defamation and incitement of racial hatred, but given the peculiarities of the Italian legal system, it is unlikely that he will ever see the inside of a jail.

Berlusconi himself, of course, wasted no time in playing the immigrant card. During the 2018 electoral campaign he announced that immigration 'is a very urgent question' because 'there are now in Italy 600,000 immigrants who have no right to stay here', and who represent a 'social bomb about to explode since they are ready to commit crimes'. A couple of weeks earlier he had claimed that the number of illegal immigrants had been 476,000. Apparently he had forgotten that more crimes were committed in Italy when he was prime minister (2008–11) than in the previous five years, when the number of immigrants increased remarkably.[69] These comments were Berlusconi's reaction to the shooting by Luca Traini, a Northern League activist, which resulted in the wounding of six African immigrants in Macerata in southern Italy. The 2018 elections were dominated by the immigration issue, even though the main problem was unemployment, especially youth unemployment. The results were a victory in percentage terms for the Eurosceptic and anti-immigrant Movimento Cinque Stelle (Five Star Movement), but the centre-right coalition won the largest number of seats, though not a working majority. The leading party within this coalition was now the far-right Lega, which outdistanced Berlusconi's Forza Italia, and this party, in alliance with Movimento Cinque Stelle, formed a government. Not for long, however, since Matteo Salvini, leader of the Lega, assuming he could force a new election and outdistance the Movimento, was ousted by the Movimento itself, which simply switched sides and forged a shaky alliance with the centre-left Partito Democratico.

In France the leader of the Front National (known since July 2018 as the National Rally), Marine Le Pen, has been careful to distance herself from the more extreme racist comments she uttered in the past, until reminded, as she was by Christiane Amanpour in an interview on CNN (20 February 2017), that she had warned in 2012 that immigrants 'would steal your wallet and brutalise your wife'. The abject racism is now left to some of her candidates, and few doubt that the main appeal of the Front National is xeno-phobia and Islamophobia. This paid off: one-third of the country which gave birth to the Declaration of the Rights of Man and of the Citizen (1789) voted for her in the second round of the 2017 presi-dential elections – obviously thinking that the *droits de l'homme et du citoyen* should not be extended to those who are not 'really' French.

But it is not just a matter of the Front National. The wave of Islamophobia in France is a serious matter, and the 'left' is hardly innocent. Plenty of intellectuals took the opportunity to praise anyone who expressed distaste for Islam, particularly after the insane attack on the journalists of the satirical weekly magazine *Charlie Hebdo* on 7 January 2015 by two Muslim terrorists, in which twelve people were killed and eleven injured. A banal novel, *Soumission* by Michel Houellebecq, described a France 'legally' taken over by Islam. It was soon a bestseller. The author, whose deliberately provocative anti-Islam insults ('It is disgusting to read the Koran', etc.) added to his notoriety, was soon celebrated by 'distinguished' intellectuals and assorted gurus: Alain Finkielkraut, author of a book against anti-Semitism and a member of the Académie Française, the philosopher Bernard-Henri Lévy, Emmanuel Carrère, and Hélène Carrère d'Encausse, a historian of the USSR and permanent secretary of the Académie Française, among many others.[70]

In the summer of 2016, French police patrolling beaches in Nice fined a Muslim woman for not wearing a swimsuit. She was fully dressed and had her hair covered, though not her face (since April 2011 covering one's face in public has been forbidden in France, as it is in the Netherlands and other 'liberal' European countries, though such silly laws are difficult to enforce).[71] On 28 July 2016 the mayor of Cannes David Lisnard, (who belongs to the centre-right party Les Républicains) forbade the wearing of the so-called burkini (a kind of swimsuit which covers most of the body but is light enough for swimming). France was ridiculed with the Twitter hashtag #WTFFrance (What The Fuck France). The mayor's justification was that not wearing a 'normal' swimsuit was against the principles of '*Laïcité*' (one should point out that no Catholic nun walking the beach in full religious regalia has ever been fined). Marine Le Pen joined the struggle with a new definition of 'Frenchness': *La France ce n'est pas le burkini sur les plages. La France c'est Brigitte Bardot.*

So-called *laïcité* has increasingly become a cover for Islamophobia, while retaining its allure as the founding myth of modern France. It is supposed to be about the separation of Church and State, but conventional morality, in France as elsewhere in the West, is full of taboos and dogmas, holiday rituals, and sanctioned days of rest which owe their origins to religion, and *la France laïque* shuts down on Easter Monday, Ascension Day, Pentecost, the Assumption of the Blessed Virgin Mary (*l'Assomption*), All Saints' Day, and, of course, *Noël*. Jews and Muslims have to put up with this *laïcité* on their holy days. Besides, the law of 31 December 1959 ensures that the French secular state (that is, the taxpayer) finances over 8,000 faith schools, almost all Catholic, with their 2 million pupils (17 per cent of the total) and their 140,000 teachers.[72]

In the name of *laïcité* more than ten municipalities along the French Riviera banned the burkini, created in 2003 by an Australian of Lebanese origin, and which in Britain could be bought at Marks and Spencer. This ridiculous *affaire* did not stop with a few unprincipled mayors trawling for votes in muddy waters. Laurence Rossignol, the socialist minister for women's rights, joined the righteous struggle against the 'burkini', which she regarded as a symbol of the oppression of women. She was soon supported by Manuel Valls, the fairly right-wing socialist prime minister, who in 2012 had defended the right of Jews to wear the kippah.[73] Like the Taliban, the Iranian ayatollahs, and other exponents of a totalitarian conception of society, Rossignol, Valls, and others wanted to tell women what to wear. Electorally speaking they were on to something: according to an IFOP poll, 64 per cent of French people were against the wearing of the burkini on beaches, and only 6 per cent were favourable to it, the rest remaining indifferent (*Le Figaro*, 24 August 2016). Sanity was restored by the Conseil d'État (the top administrative court) which, knowing more about human rights than various socialist ministers, declared the ban invalid, a decision welcomed by *Le Monde* as a victory for the rule of law (*l'état de droit*).[74]

The sanity did not last long, however, at least among France's right-wing politicians. Dismayed at the poor performance of François Fillon, candidate of Les Républicains (the heirs to Gaullism) in the 2017 presidential election, his party elected as his successor a far-right candidate, Laurent Wauquiez (with a staggering 74.6 per cent, though only 42 per cent of the members voted). Wauquiez had stood on an anti-immigration platform which, the Républicains hoped, would attract some of the Front National voters. He called for 'a right not ashamed of being on the right' (*une droite qui ne s'excuse pas d'être de droite*).[75] Like Fillon, Wauquiez is a staunch Catholic who opposes welfare, the shorter working week, same sex-marriage, and even IVF. He explained that homosexuality was not compatible with his 'personal values'. By contrast Marine Le

Pen is 'liberal' on gay rights, a move seen as a further attempt to attack Muslims on the widely held assumption that Islam is particularly homophobic.

French hysteria over symbols of commitment to the Muslim faith has continued even under the Macron government. In May 2018, Maryam Pougetoux, the student leader at the Sorbonne, gave a television interview wearing the hijab. She would have been safer in a bikini. She was attacked not just by the usual trolls, but by the minister of the interior, Gérard Collomb (a former socialist and a freemason), who was 'shocked' that a student leader would wear such a religious symbol. *Charlie Hebdo*, the magazine victim of terrorism and alleged proud defender of republican freedoms, sank even lower in the racist mud by publishing a 'satirical' cartoon depicting the nineteen-year-old Maryam Pougetoux as a monkey.[76]

In 2017 the European Court of Justice ruled that employers could prohibit staff from wearing religious symbols. The case was first referred by the Belgian courts when, in 2006, a receptionist for the Belgian branch of G4S, the UK security company, was fired because she wanted to wear a headscarf. Though Muslim women were the main target of the ban, the prohibition meant that, in theory, an employer could also prevent Jewish men from wearing a kippah, Sikh men from wearing turbans, and Christians from wearing crosses. Meanwhile the ban on appearing in public with one's face covered is deplored by Amnesty International, upholding the obvious liberal principle that 'all women should be free to dress as they please and to wear clothing that expresses their identity or beliefs.'[77] In Bavaria, by contrast, a new law was introduced by Markus Söder, minister-president and a leading member of the Christian Social Union, decreeing that a crucifix should hang in the entrance of all public buildings, the so-called *Kreuzpflicht* (crucifix obligation). A similar initiative was undertaken in Italy by Salvini, leader of the far-right Lega and then interior minister. Both encountered the firm disapproval of the Catholic Church. In Bavaria the bishop of Würzburg, Franz Jung, the Cardinal Reinhard Marx, archbishop of Munich, and other prominent members of the Catholic Church, who obviously know more about the principles of *laïcité* than the Bavarian state premier, deplored the move.[78] In Italy the Catholic journal *Famiglia Cristiana*, supported by bishops and Jesuits, condemned the move with the front-page headline 'Vade Retro Salvini', thus comparing Salvini with Satan.[79]

Alarmist cries in France about the end of Western civilisation and the arrival of 'hordes' of immigrants are nothing new. In 1880 Gustave Le Bon, the theorist of the psychology of the crowd, believed it was a waste of time to try to impose Western customs or to transform Muslims into Frenchmen. In 1889 he published *Recherches anatomiques et mathématiques sur les lois des variations du volume du cerveau et sur leurs relations avec l'intelligence*, in which he 'proved' that the larger the skull the greater the intelligence, and that Parisians have (of course) larger skulls than provincials, men larger skulls than women, etc.[80] Presumably if you moved from Marseilles to Paris your brain would increase in size.

In 1886, in his bestselling *La France juive*, Édouard Drumont explained that the Jews would never miss an opportunity to cheat. One should be on the lookout for their 'famous nose', ears that stick out, the flat feet, and 'the moist and soft hand of the hypocrite and the traitor'; and, of course, they smell.[81]

More recently, 'scientific racists', such as Richard Lynn and Tatu Vanhanen in their *IQ and the Wealth of Nations* (2002), have claimed that a country's average IQ is the crucial variable in explaining differences in per capita income. So, presumably, if Malawi discovers the world's largest reserves of oil, thus increasing its per capita income, it's because its inhabitants have a high IQ; until that happy moment it might remain rather low. Charles Murray and Richard Herrnstein, in their bestselling *The Bell Curve* (1994), claimed that whites were more intelligent than blacks. Race 'science' is old hat. The sub-text is that it is a waste of time to educate blacks. They used to say that about women. Some still do.

Fear of 'race' sells. A century after Le Bon, in 1973, Jean Raspail, a right-wing Catholic who went on to win the Grand Prix du Roman of the Académie Française in 1981, published a successful novel, *Le Camp des Saints*, which imagines that 1 million immigrants from the Indian sub-continent arrive in France. Frightened, the 'true'

French run away faced with this threatening mass. In 2011, when thousands of North Africans did seek refuge in Europe, the novel was republished and sold 20,000 copies in a few days.[82]

Laws against practising Muslims have proliferated throughout Europe. In Switzerland a popular referendum in 2009 amended the constitution in order to prevent the construction of minarets (just as in Saudi Arabia one cannot build churches). One can still construct high-rise buildings as long as they are not minarets. In 2014 another Swiss referendum decided (by a narrow majority) to limit the number of immigrants. Previous referendums on the same issue had failed. But that was before fear of *Uberfremdungsangst*, or 'over-foreignisation', had reached new heights.[83]

In the US in 2015, even before the advent of Donald Trump, there was a sharp increase in hate crimes directed against Muslims and Arabs, which reached their highest level since 2001. And though hate crimes against other groups (LGBT people, Jews, blacks, whites, etc.) have also increased, those directed at Muslims and Arabs have increased proportionately more.[84]

In comparison, Victorian Britain was a relatively tolerant place. Though there was plenty of morbid antagonism against those who were foreigners, refugees, immigrants, poor or just different, between 1823 and 1905 (when the Aliens Act was passed) no foreign refugee was expelled. Political exiles such as Karl Marx, the French socialist Louis Blanc, the Hungarian nationalist Lajos Kossuth, the Italian nationalist Giuseppe Mazzini, and the anarchist Felice Orsini lived more or less happily in London (though when Orsini went to France and tried to blow up Napoleon III, he was arrested and executed. He should have stayed, quietly, in Kentish Town ...).

Migrants have long been disliked. If they failed and were jobless they were regarded as scroungers. If they were successful they were disliked even more, since their success caused envy. This fate afflicted Jews almost everywhere, but also the Germans, the Greeks, and the Armenians in (respectively) the Tsarist, Austro-Hungarian, and Ottoman Empires; the Chinese in much of South East Asia; and the Gujarati and Punjabi Indians in East Africa (they were expelled from Uganda in 1972 and widely discriminated against in Kenya).

Insults against those who were 'different' came from all quarters. In 1880 in Italy the Jesuit journal *Civiltà cattolica* explained that the Jews were 'eternal insolent children, obstinate, dirty, thieves, liars, ignoramuses', that they abused the freedom they had been granted, managing to take 'control not only of all the money ... but of the law itself in those countries where they have been allowed to hold public offices'.[85]

In the US, non-white immigrants felt the blows of American xenophobia. The Declaration of Independence stated that 'We hold these truths to be self-evident, that all Men are created equal', but in California and across much of the western United States special taxes were levelled on the Chinese, who were also denied the right to own land or even to testify in a court against whites.[86] Such discrimination was established in law by the Chinese Exclusion Act of 1882 (repealed only in 1943), and was supported by the American Federation of Labor (AFL). Samuel Gompers, the AFL leader (and a Jew from London's East End), declared in 1905 that 'the caucasians are not going to let their standards of living be destroyed by negroes, Chinamen, Japs, or any others'.[87] Henry George, the radical reformer and author of the bestselling *Progress and Poverty: An Inquiry into the Cause of Industrial Depressions* (1879), railed against the Chinese: 'their moral standard is as low as their standard of comfort', they were 'filthy in their habits', and 'incapable of understanding our religion' or 'our political institutions'.[88]

In Australia too, white supremacist beliefs were regarded as normal. In 1901, the White Australia Policy limited immigration to whites only via a 'dictation' test in any European language (the Australian Labour Party explicitly wanted to exclude Asians and Africans). It was completely abolished only in 1973.

In France at the Congrés Ouvrier of Lyons of 1878, a delegate referred to the Arabs as '*ce peuple ignorant et fanatique*', and in the socialist daily *L'Humanité* (7 August 1913) Maurice Allard, a socialist and anti-clerical MP, referred to 'primitive and grotesque blacks' with whom he claimed to have far less in common than with the Germans.[89] Xenophobia in the trade unions was rife, reflecting the worries of many French workers about the influx of Belgian and Italian workers (in 1886 there were over 1 million foreign workers in France).⁹⁰ Between 1881 and 1893, some thirty Italians were killed in the south of France in what can only be described as a series of pogroms.⁹¹

Immigration did not need to be massive to give rise to racist prejudice. In Britain between 1908 and 1911, Joseph Havelock Wilson, a Liberal MP and leader of the National Sailors and Firemen Union (NFSU), waged a campaign against Chinese labour in British shipping.⁹² Yet in 1911 there were hardly any Chinese in the UK, and fewer were working on British ships than Scandinavians.⁹³

Immigration controls are a modern invention. Throughout most of the nineteenth century, emigration (much of which was *from* Europe) was uncontrolled. By the end of that century there were restrictions in many countries, as governments asserted their right to exclude people from crossing borders.

Today there are throughout Europe solidly entrenched parties whose main raison d'être is hatred of immigrants and foreigners. And they are not all 'fringe' parties; some are in power. In former communist countries the problem is particularly serious. Poland has the Law and Justice Party; Latvia, the National Alliance; Slovakia, the Slovak National Party, Lithuania, the Order and Justice Party. There is also a proliferation of nationalist parties busy reinventing a past of victimhood or lamenting lost battles, such as the battle of Kosovo of 1389 where the Ottomans prevailed over the Serbs, or the 1620 Battle of White Mountain where Catholics defeated Protestants in the Czech lands; or else celebrating victories such as that of Charles Martel against the Arabs at Tours (or Poitiers) in 732, which allegedly saved Christian Europe from the Moors when in fact all he did was to stop some of them looting the local monastery.⁹⁴

The prize in this game of historical kitsch must go to the Macedonian government, led by VMRO-DPMNE (2006–16) which stands for Internal Macedonian Revolutionary Organization – Democratic Party for Macedonian National Unity and which, convinced that today's Macedonians are directly descended from the Macedonians of Alexander the Great (who was not born in present-day Macedonia), engaged in a costly project, labelled

'Skopje 2014', to construct amazingly expensive monuments aimed at glorifying Macedonia's 'glorious' past, including a 22-metre statue of Alexander the Great (in whose honour the 'Alexander the Great International Airport' in Skopje was named) and one of Mother Teresa (a native of Skopje), along with monuments celebrating 'heroes' who fought against the Ottoman Empire, of which Macedonia was a part.

This is, of course, what states do: George Washington, Jeanne d'Arc, Nelson, Garibaldi, etc. are all celebrated in public squares. But this is the twenty-first century and Macedonia is one of the poorest countries in Europe, poorer than Peru or Turkmenistan.[95] One cannot help feeling that, given the poverty in Macedonia, which has 22 per cent unemployment, there were better ways of spending public money, but, as usual, nationalism, even kitsch nationalism, prevails over common sense. Common sense appeared to have returned, however, with the victory of the pro-EU social democrats led by Zoran Zaev in May 2017. A compromise was mooted on the name of the state, to indulge the Greek obsession that if the country was called just 'Macedonia' it might imply that it had territorial designs on the Greek region of Macedonia (one might think that the Greeks too had better things to worry about). The country is now known as the 'Republic of North Macedonia', after the new name was massively endorsed by a referendum in 2018. 'North Macedonia' received 94 per cent of the vote, though only 36 per cent bothered to turn out. So now Macedonia is no longer FYROM, 'the former Yugoslav Republic of Macedonia', and the airport is no longer 'Alexander the Great International Airport' but, more simply, the International Airport Skopje. Alexander the Great can rest in peace. Needless to say this disappointed all those who, to coin a phrase, wanted to make Macedonia 'great again'.

The celebration of a pre-communist past, however unsavoury, is an increasingly common feature of post-communist nationalism. In Warsaw an enormous statue was erected to Roman Dmowski, the so-called father of Polish nationalism and a notorious anti-Semite, while a plaque commemorating the birthplace of Rosa Luxemburg in Zamość was removed.[96] As Brecht wrote in his 'Epitaph for Luxemburg' (1948):

Here lies, buried
Rosa Luxemburg
A Jewess from Poland,
Champion of German workers
Killed on the orders of the
German oppressors. Oppressed,
Bury your discord.

In Latvia, veterans of the country's Second World War Waffen SS divisions and their supporters officially parade on 16 March (Remembrance Day in Latvia) through the capital Riga to commemorate their role as allies of Nazi Germany.[97] In March 2019 in Estonia, the far-right party EKRE – defender of Estonian 'ethnicity', anti-European, anti-immigration, homophobic, and anti-Russian minority – won enough seats to be invited into the ruling coalition and granted five out of fifteen ministerial positions.

In (western) Ukraine there has been a proliferation of monuments to Stepan Bandera, a nationalist leader who fought alongside the Nazis during the Second World War. In Hungary there are several statues of Miklós Horthy, an ally of Hitler's. Bálint Hóman, a prominent Hungarian anti-Semite between the wars and a proponent of anti-Jewish laws, was going to get a statue too, on the initiative of Viktor Orbán's government. Israel, a close friend of Orbán, was upset, Barack Obama intervened, and the government backed down.[98] So no statue for Bálint Hóman.

Orbán's government is not even the far right in Hungary. Though Orbán announced in 2014, just before winning a thumping majority, that he wanted to end 'liberal democracy' in Hungary, presumably making the country more like Putin's Russia and Erdoğan's Turkey, and even though he had described asylum seekers as a 'poison', and praised Trump, he is faced by an even more right-wing party, Jobbik, which, forced to reposition itself towards the centre, won a remarkable 20 per cent of the vote in 2014 and in 2018.[99]

Jobbik describes itself as a 'radical', 'patriotic', and 'Christian' party, a champion of Hungarian values and interests. It is pro-capital punishment, an opponent of European integration and of global capitalism (it is convinced that Jews – i.e. George Soros – intend to buy up Hungary, but then so is Orbán). One of Jobbik's fantasies is that Hungarians are descended from the 'Ural-Altaic' race (a category dreamed up in the nineteenth century by assorted nationalists in Finland and Hungary). Jobbik has a paramilitary wing, the Magyar Gárda (Hungarian Guard), founded in 2007 and dissolved by the courts in 2009, widely described as neo-fascist and whose uniform was based on that of the old Hungarian pro-Nazi organisation, the Arrow Cross. The proliferation of right-wing organisations and political parties in Eastern Europe is a part of a widespread disenchantment with the failure of post-communism and liberal democracy.

On 1 May 2004, the European Union welcomed ten new member states, including eight from the old Eastern Bloc. Confident Europeans celebrated. They were soon disappointed: elections held the following month for the European Parliament were a fiasco: in all the new member states, except for Lithuania, the average turnout (42.61 per cent) was inferior to the already poor EU average – in the Czech Republic and in Slovakia the turnout was, respectively, 18 per cent and 13 per cent.

In Russia the mood was equally alarming: a survey conducted in 2017 by the Yuri Levada Analytical Centre confirmed that a majority of Russians regarded Stalin as 'the most outstanding figure' in history, followed by Putin and Pushkin (at the same level!). The previous year, 8 per cent of respondents thought Stalin had 'definitely' played a positive role in the country's history, while 46 per cent thought that his role was 'probably' positive. Only 6 per cent thought it was 'definitely negative' (24 per cent 'probably negative').[100] This is emblematic of what some have called a nostalgia for some aspects of communism such as its welfare state, full employment, and its ability to maintain law and order. A Reuters report in 2009 quoted a thirty-one-year-old Bulgarian woman in the impoverished town of Belene: 'We lived better in the past, we went on holidays to the coast and the mountains, there were plenty of clothes, shoes, food. And now the biggest chunk of our incomes is spent on food. People with university degrees are unemployed and many go abroad.' A 2008 global survey by Gallup ranked

Bulgaria, Serbia, and Romania among the ten most discontented countries in the world.[101]

In the Balkans the situation is so dire that some regret the 'good old days' of communism. Wages are low, unemployment very high, and peace precarious. In Serbia in January 2017, the then president Tomislav Nikolić declared himself ready to send the army into Kosovo if the local Serb population came under threat. In June 2017, in Montenegro, the opposition claimed that the country was on the brink of civil war. In Kosovo, Albin Kurti, the leader of the largest party (Vetëvendosje) and prime minister from February 2020, believed a border dispute with Montenegro was likely to escalate into war. In Macedonia, Albanian minority parties fear the country could be ripped apart, Ukraine-style. Milorad Dodik, the president of Republika Srpska, one of the two 'entities' that make up Bosnia-Herzegovina – is convinced that soon the country will collapse. Albanian Prime Minister Edi Rama, supported by Kosovan president Hashim Thaçi (accused by the Council of Europe of having trafficked in human organs), has threatened to unify Albania and Kosovo, a move which would doubtless lead to war.[102] When in 2017 the EU High Representative Federica Mogherini visited the Montenegrin Parliament, the opposition boycotted her. When she spoke at the Serbian Parliament she was heckled by Eurosceptic nationalists with shouts of 'Serbia, Russia – we don't need the European Union.'[103] Not too long ago, anyone from Brussels was considered a figure to be respected and wooed.[104]

Communism constituted an advance in all Eastern European countries. Before 1940, with the exception of Czechoslovakia, they were all far worse off than most West European countries. Under communism there was economic progress, though they still lagged well behind the capitalist West. Pre-communist Eastern Europe, far from being a bedrock of democracy, was plagued by dictatorial regimes of various hues, and infected with anti-Semitism.

Today's far-right parties do not, at least officially, seek the overthrow of democracy. They compete legally for votes. Few of them have paramilitary organisations. They are quick to denounce the

more outrageous outbursts of some of their less intelligent supporters. They know that Islamophobia is tolerated while anti-Semitism
is not (in fact some of them have an excellent relationship with
Israel – hatred of Muslims makes for some strange bedfellows).
Their objective is that of seizing power legally, through elections. Their main achievement is shifting the agenda to the right.
To succeed one does not need a majority, only sufficient votes to
scare the 'respectable' parties. Thus, in Great Britain, UKIP, a ludicrous party, now moribund (five leaders in eighteen months and
still counting), then led by a popular mountebank, Nigel Farage,
depicted eternally laughing, a pint of beer in hand, (described by
the *Daily Mail* columnist Richard Littlejohn, who fears no ridicule,
as 'beyond doubt ... after Thatcher ... the most influential, most
significant British political figure since Churchill), contributed to
getting Prime Minister David Cameron to call for the fateful referendum on the European Union.

That Islamophobia should also be raging in Israel is hardly surprising, though this does not stop Israel from cosying up with the
Gulf monarchies and Saudi Arabia.[105] In 2016, Israel's Parliament
approved a so-called 'muezzin' bill banning religious leaders from
using loudspeakers to summon worshippers for prayers.[106] The
previous year the leader of a far-right Israeli extremist group, Benzi
Gopstein, had called for the torching of churches. Nothing was done
against the group.[107] Any group in Europe calling for the torching of
synagogues would have been prosecuted, and rightly so. 'Death to
the Arabs' is a common chant at demonstrations. Few are arrested.
In June 2018, outside a courthouse in central Israel, far-right activists chanted slogans cheering the death of an eighteen-month-old
Palestinian as the late toddler's family walked near them following
a hearing. They were not arrested.[108] The Palestinian poet Dareen
Tatour, however, was charged with incitement to violence for a
poem posted on YouTube and sentenced to five months in jail. Here
are extracts from the poem:

> Resist, my people, resist them.
> In Jerusalem, I dressed my wounds and breathed my
> sorrows

And carried the soul in my palm
For an Arab Palestine.
...
They burned blameless children;
As for Hadil, they sniped her in public,
Killed her in broad daylight.
Resist, my people, resist them.
Resist the colonialist's onslaught.
...
Resist, my rebellious people.
Write me as prose on the agarwood;
My remains have you as a response.
Resist, my people, resist them.
Resist, my people, resist them.

Dareen Tatour is one of over 400 Palestinians arrested in 2016–17 for their expressions of resistance to the Israeli occupation.[109] There is resistance also among some young Israelis, sixty-three of whom, in December 2017, sent a letter to the authorities refusing to serve in the army, declaring 'We Won't Take Part in Occupation'. Enlistment rates are sinking and dropout rates run to over 7,000 male and female soldiers annually.[110]

In June 2018, in the northern Israeli city of Afula, a demonstration of Israeli Jews led by the deputy mayor marched through the town's streets to protest against the owners of a house who had decided to sell to Arabs.[111] Imagine a demonstration anywhere in the West against having Jewish neighbours. In most Israeli maternity wards, Jewish and Arab mothers are segregated. Bezalel Smotrich, MP for a far-right religious party, declared that it was only 'natural' that his wife would not 'want to lie next to someone who just gave birth to a baby that might murder her baby in another 20 years'.[112] If you don't want an Arab taxi driver there is even an app for the purpose.[113]

Reflecting this deeply racist mentality, in July 2018 Israel's Parliament seriously discussed introducing a law that would allow a community of people having the same faith and nationality 'to maintain the exclusive character of that community', in other words for Jews to exclude Arabs from their neighbour-hoods.[114] This clause was removed from the final bill, but the new 'nation-state' law officially defined Israel as the national homeland of the Jewish people and asserted that 'the realization of the right to national self-determination in Israel is unique to the Jewish people'. It also asserted that Hebrew was the country's official language, thus demoting Arabic.[115] In the words of Bradley Burston, an edi-torialist for *Haaretz*, it was 'the single most gratuitously hateful legislation in the nation's history'.[116] The celebrated conductor Daniel Barenboim, himself an Israeli, declared that the law the Israeli government had just passed 'replaces the principle of equal-ity and universal values with nationalism and racism'.[117]

Meanwhile in Britain, the MP Margaret Hodge accused Jeremy Corbyn of being a 'fucking anti-Semite' because Labour had not condemned as anti-Semitic the proposition that Israel's existence as a state is racist (the party adopted, eventually, the rather silly 'working definition' of anti-Semitism proposed by the so-called International Holocaust Remembrance Alliance, which conflates anti-Semitism with criticism of Israel). Obviously, according to Hodge, even Barenboim must be an anti-Semite. Hodge is less deli-cate when it comes to UK non-natives, who, she decreed when she was housing minister, should be lower down the list when it comes to allocating housing – a statement for which she was criticised as pandering to the far right and for which she was praised by the latter.[118] Accurately identified in the *Independent* as a 'grandstand-ing narcissist', she described her response to the possibility that the Labour Party would discipline her (as it should have but did not dare to) as feeling almost like being 'a Jew in Germany in the thir-ties', a comparison ridiculed, again by the *Independent*, as deranged hyperbole.[119]

Arab websites throughout the Middle East carry expressions of anti-Semitism. Anti-Jewish sentiments in the Middle East are hardly surprising, since Israel itself conflates 'Jews' and 'Israelis'. The cruelties and injustices, the habitual humiliation and intimida-tion at checkpoints, the detentions, and the constantly increasing number of house demolitions suffered by Palestinians throughout the West Bank have been abundantly documented (including in brave Israeli newspapers such as *Haaretz*), though only the more outrageous outbursts have made it into the European mainstream press, whose members are probably scared of being accused of anti-Semitism.[120] The Jewish settlements in the occupied West Bank were created by confiscating the most fertile Palestinian land and seizing water resources. Jewish settlers now control around 42 per cent of West Bank territory.[121] They are 'protected' by checkpoints, military zones, and the 'Separation Wall', which has created isolated Palestinian enclaves in the occupied West Bank. Cut off from Jerusalem, Palestinians have no freedom of movement. Almost half of Israeli Jews think that Arabs should be expelled from Israel, 46 per cent disagree, and 6 per cent don't know.[122]

There was considerable support in Israel for an army sergeant who shot a Palestinian assailant in the head as he lay wounded on the ground in Hebron in March 2016. The sergeant, Elor Azaria, was eventually charged with manslaughter and sentenced to eighteen months in prison.[123] He served nine months, only one more than the Palestinian teenager Ahed Tamimi, sent to jail for slapping a fully armed soldier.

But there is another 'phobia' in Israel, one directed at Jews by Jews. Zionism was a 'European' project and the Jews of Europe (the Ashkenazim) exhibited towards their fellow 'Oriental Jews' or Sephardim, the same prejudices of Europeans towards non-Europeans. Thus David Ben Gurion, the founding father of Israel and prime minister almost uninterruptedly between 1948 and 1963, described the Sephardi immigrants as being 'without a trace of Jewish or human education', and, in Parliament, called them 'savages'; Abba Eban (deputy PM 1963–66 and foreign minister 1966–74), speaking of the Sephardim, declared that one should 'infuse them with an Occidental spirit, rather than allow them to drag us into an unnatural Orientalism'; while Golda Meir (PM from 1969 to 1974), addressing the Zionist Federation of Great Britain in 1964, wondered whether it was possible 'to elevate these immigrants to a suitable level of civilization'.[124] All three were pillars of the Israeli Labour establishment.

In the West anti-Semitism is barely extant, while Islamophobia is regularly enhanced by alarmist press coverage. *The Times* published an article on 28 August 2017 by its so-called chief investigative reporter, Andrew Norfolk, with the headline 'Christian Child Forced into Muslim Foster Care'. The article claimed that a five-year-old Christian girl (whose mother was reportedly an alcoholic and possibly a drug addict) had been 'forced' into a Muslim foster home where one of the foster carers wore a burqa, derogatory comments were made about European women, no one spoke English, and where the child was banned from eating pork and had her crucifix forcibly removed. A subsequent inquiry proved that these claims were false. The report was of course exploited by far-right activists as well as the *Daily Mail*, which used a picture of a Muslim family, not the actual one, altering the image to cover the woman's face with a veil.[125] *The Times*'s 'chief investigator' should have investigated more, but then he has a track record of peddling unverified and inaccurate stories about Muslims.[126] The *Sunday Telegraph* was no better: in March 2016 it published an article by its 'investigative' reporter Andrew Gilligan (no stranger to defaming Muslims) trying to link Jeremy Corbyn to the 'extremist views' held by Mohammed Kozbar, vice-president of the Muslim Association of Britain and a moderate Muslim in charge of the Finsbury Park mosque in Corbyn's constituency. Kozbar sued and the paper had to pay damages and remove the article from its website.[127] This was all part of creating an atmosphere where the presence of Muslims in Britain was seen as major threat to national identity. Muslims in Britain are significantly less protected than Jews. In 2018 mosques received £375,413 from the government for their protection, while £14 million was granted to the Jewish community.[128] Needless to say Muslims are far more under threat than Jews.

Appeals to nationalism have long been a constant feature of British political life. On 24 September 2007, in his first speech as Labour leader to the party's annual conference, Gordon Brown not only proclaimed his self-deluded vision of a 'Britain leading the global economy' but advocated creating 'British jobs for British workers' – a slogan previously used by the far-right British National Party. Brown's fantasy was particularly alarming when he declared that the UK had 'the skills, the inventiveness, the creativity, and the spirit of enterprise, to make it a British century'.[129] A few years later, during the Brexit referendum campaign, the then Chancellor George Osborne called for a Britain that 'shapes the world – not one shaped by the world'.[130]

The world? The US? China? Europe? Russia? Eight billion people shaped by the United Kingdom? Such delusions can only be entertained by politicians in an old colonial and imperial country which, today, is at best a second-rate power. A country which in 2019 had a slower internet connection than thirty-four other countries, including Madagascar, Poland, and Portugal.[131] A country barely able to keep Scotland a part of it, which no longer has its own automobile industry, whose football teams are owned by Russians (Chelsea), Americans (Arsenal, Liverpool, Manchester United) or Emiratis (Manchester City), whose justly celebrated Newcastle Brown Ale is owned by the Dutch, its noted gin, Beefeater, by the French (who also own famous whiskies such as Chivas Regal and Glenlivet), its Cadbury chocolate by the American Kraft conglomerate, its HP table sauce by the American Heinz, its breakfast cereal Weetabix by a Chinese multinational, and, in a nice reversal of colonial roles, its leading brands of tea, Tetley and Typhoo, by Indian firms. A Malaysian sovereign wealth fund bought Battersea power station (an iconic building soon to be turned into luxury flats), while London's famed black taxi cabs are manufactured (in Coventry) by a Chinese company. To add insult to injury, the contract to produce the new post-Brexit passport was awarded to a Franco-Dutch company. These days, between a third and a half of FTSE 100 companies are led by non-British CEOs and the majority of shares are no longer owned by UK individuals or their pension funds. In fact, more than half the UK stock market is owned by foreigners, which the ever so patriotic *Daily Telegraph* celebrated with the headline 'Good News – Foreigners are Buying up Britain' (26 September 2013). Perhaps one could celebrate instead the age-old cosmopolitanism of England, a country whose patron saint, St George, was (assuming he even existed) a Greek martyred in what is today Palestine, and whose flag was probably borrowed from the Genoese; a country whose founder was the Duke of Normandy (William the Conqueror, also known as Guillaume le Conquérant as well as Guillaume le Bâtard); a country whose royal family is more German than English and whose motto is in French (*Honi soit qui mal y pense*).

A deluded sense of self-importance is one of the most pathetic vestiges of ex-imperial powers. The chief of the British general staff, General Sir Nick Carter, in a blatant and not very clever attempt to secure an increase in defence spending, warned in January 2018 that Russia posed a major threat to the UK. As if there was the slightest chance of the UK having to face Russia alone. NATO as a whole spent $864 billion in 2017 compared to Russia's $46 billion, has 3.1 million troops to Russia's 831,000, and 3,896 combat aircraft to Russia's 1,046.[132] A former chief of the defence staff, General Nick Houghton (now Lord), upped the silliness stakes by complaining, in June 2018, that the government was not spending enough on defence 'at precisely the time when a post-Brexit Britain aspires to rebrand and reassert itself as a global player'.[133] The UK spends proportionately more on defence than any other Western European country, and Boris Johnson wants to spend even more.

Fear of foreigners who are out to get us or about to take our jobs is endemic. Pandering to such fears was not disdained by Gordon Brown's successor at the head of the Labour Party, Ed Miliband, who had the brilliant idea of producing five mugs with election pledges for the 2015 elections (which he lost – the elections not the mugs). One of these was stamped with Labour's promise to institute 'controls on immigration', thereby perpetuating the mistaken belief that immigration to the UK is uncontrolled, excessive, and bad for the economy – the Office for Budget Responsibility, a government body created by the Conservative government in 2010, established that immigration was a key factor fuelling Britain's economic recovery.[134]

Many entrepreneurs are worried by the implications of Brexit. The British Hospitality Association warns that the shortage of British workers in UK hotels and restaurants is so serious that chains such as Pret a Manger would need ten years to replace EU staff if they all left after Brexit. The human resources director of the chain told a parliamentary committee that only one in fifty applicants for jobs at the company were British.[135] The hospitality industry is the UK's fourth-largest employer, providing jobs to 4.7 million people (14 per cent of the workforce), and is the sixth-largest contributor to export earnings. The percentage of EU workers in this sector could be as high as 24 per cent, and, according to a report of March 2017, the industry needs some 62,200 new EU migrants a year.[136]

The building industry, according to the Home Builders Federation, faces similar problems. Its survey revealed that almost 20 per cent of workers on building sites are not from the UK and that 56.3 per cent of workers on London sites are from overseas. Some building skills are dominated by EU workers: more than 70 per cent of carpenters, 61 per cent of general labourers, 54 per cent of decorators, 44 per cent of bricklayers, and nearly 40 per cent of roofers come from other EU countries.[137] Around 39 per cent of academic staff in Britain's leading universities are from overseas,[138] while one-third of doctors working in the NHS were trained abroad – the highest number from India: India's loss, Britain's gain.[139] British Summer Fruits, the body representing soft fruit growers, says they have difficulty recruiting pickers. About 80,000 seasonal workers a year pick and process British fruit and vegetables and most of them are from the EU, mainly Romania and Bulgaria.[140]

Studies demonstrating the benefits of immigration to the wider economy have proliferated. These include the IMF 2016 and 2018 World Economic Outlook reports, which suggest that migration can relieve 'the strain of population aging and contribute to other long-term gains, such as higher growth and productivity'.[141] According to a Home Office report published in 2014, there is little evidence that immigration has displaced UK native workers from the labour market.[142] A study the same year by two University College London economists, Christian Dustmann and Tommaso Frattini, challenged claims that immigrants from Europe exploit the welfare system. They found that immigrants to the UK who had arrived since 2000 (both from within and without the EU) made 'consistently positive fiscal contributions regardless of their area of origin'. They contributed about 12 per cent more than they took out. Even the non-EU immigrants paid into the system about 3 per cent more than they took out. It is the natives, the 'true Brits', who take out more than they pay in.[143]

Lord Kerr of Kinlochard, the diplomat who co-wrote Article 50 of the Lisbon Treaty (to be invoked by countries wishing to leave the EU), speaking at the Institute for Government in November 2016, defended immigration by saying, 'We native Brits are so bloody stupid that we need an injection of intelligent people, young people from outside who come in and wake us up from time to time.' The humourless Eurosceptic Tory MP Peter Lilley (now Lord Lilley) walked out of the event, saying this was 'racially abusive of the British people'.[144] With the consolidation of the Boris Johnson government after its victory in the election of December 2019, a stringent points system has been introduced which will restrict immigration at terrible cost to Britain, particularly to the National Health Service (which is dependent on personnel from abroad and has had to face the coronavirus pandemic), the catering industry, the building industry, and the food industry.

Since Europe's population is ageing, what immigration does is effectively redistribute the world population not just from poor countries to rich countries but from countries with a young population to those with an ageing one. Migration is a remedy against an ageing population. This is not new. In European cities in the eighteenth century, deaths exceeded births. Urban population growth depended entirely on migration. For most of the nineteenth century, population growth in Naples, Odessa, Rome, Prague, and St Petersburg was caused by influx of immigrants mainly from the countryside.[145]

In the hundred years between 1850 and 1950, when the world population doubled, that of the countries which received immigrants (the Americas, North Asia, and South East Asia) grew by over 150 per cent while that of Europe increased by only 67 per cent. The European population looks like being relatively stable for the next thirty years; meanwhile the world population will have increased by another billion.

The movement from the countryside to the city in a single country has now become globalised, continuing the redistribution of the population. Consider Ghana: in 1948, its population was only 4 million; by 2015 it had reached 25 million people – an

increase of 625 per cent. In the same period the population of the
United Kingdom (about 50 million in 1948) increased only by 20
per cent. In 2017 the average age in Ghana was just around twenty;
in Britain it was around forty and that will increase over the next
twenty years. In 2016 in the UK, 18 per cent of the population was
over sixty-five. In thirty years' time it will be 24.7 per cent – almost
one in four. Other European countries are in the same situation.[146]

People who don't like immigration simply brush such arguments
aside, preferring to wallow in their prejudices or pander to the
prejudices of others. And the prejudices are strong enough to sway
many on the left. Thus, in New Zealand – like Australia and the US,
a country of immigrants – Jacinda Ardern, the young leader of the
Labour Party, accepted the idea of restricting immigration, paving
the way for a coalition deal in 2017 with the leader of the nationalist
New Zealand First Party, Winston Peters (who is half Māori, while
his mother is of Scottish descent), a staunch critic of immigration
who had accused Asian migrants of 'imported criminal activity'.[147]
There are serious problems in New Zealand but immigration is
not one of them: UNICEF says 300,000 children in the country
live in poverty, and that a disproportionate number of them are in
Māori families.[148] One wonders how long this unholy party alliance
(or 'coalition of losers' as Richard Prebble, a conservative, dubbed
it) will last.[149] Ardern, however, emerged as remarkable leader
after a right-wing extremist killed fifty people in two mosques in
Christchurch. She offered condolences and went beyond the usual
words of sympathy, saying of immigrants, 'They are us.' She met
and comforted the bereaved – wearing a hijab in solidarity, and
embracing members of the Muslim community with the Arabic
words *as-Salaam-Alaikum* (peace be upon you) – and immediately
proposed stronger firearms regulations. She was widely praised,
particularly when her response was compared to Donald Trump's
pathetic reaction: 'I think it's a small group of people that have
very, very serious problems, I guess,' and his later ranting about
immigrant 'criminals and undesirables'. And Ardern's principled
stand paid off: in 2020 her party won an absolute majority of seats
to global acclaim.

Australia's record on immigration is not impressive. The country accepted refugees from Nazi Germany in the 1930s, but its 'white only' immigration policy had been introduced in 1901 by the country's first prime minister and leader of the Protectionist Party, Edmund ('Toby') Barton, who declared: 'I do not think that the doctrine of the equality of man was really intended to include racial equality. These races are, in comparison with white races … unequal and inferior. The doctrine of the equality of man was never intended to apply to the equality of the Englishman and the Chinaman.'[150] This spirit was maintained until 1973, when the so-called Vietnamese boat people were grudgingly accepted into Australia (which had sent armed forces into Vietnam to help the Americans). In the 1990s a system of 'mandatory detention' was introduced for refugees. It was hoped this would deter them. Of course, refugees continued to arrive from various trouble spots. After 9/11 they were detained outside Australia, in nearby states such as Papua New Guinea and the remote Nauru and Manus islands. The Papua New Guinea supreme court declared the facility used by Australia 'unconstitutional' and it was closed on 31 October 2017, forcing 600 detainees to go elsewhere. The Australian novelist Richard Flanagan (a Man Booker Prize winner) described Manus Island as 'a hell of repression, cruelty, and violence', adding 'the shame of this time will outlive us all'.[151]

Australia had paid such offshore centres to accept the refugees – anything to stop them going on to Australia. The Labour Party, led by Kevin Rudd, having gained power in 2007 with 43 per cent of the vote, adopted a more liberal policy – after all, the number of refugees never amounted to more than a few thousand. This policy failed electorally, and the party lost votes in 2010. By then Julia Gillard, having ousted Rudd as Labour leader, had restricted the entry of refugees. By 2012 the number seeking entry had increased, and Labour reintroduced the punitive offshore policy against which it had campaigned in 2007. In 2013, in what appeared to be an increasingly petty political game, Rudd, having taken his revenge on Gillard by ousting her in turn, kept the essence of her refugee policy intact.

By 2013 Labour had lost power to the centre-right Liberal Party, and the new government led by Tony Abbott escalated the tough anti-refugee policy, which was substantially continued by his successors, Malcolm Turnbull and Scott Morrison. It became, as the former prime minister Malcolm Fraser declared, a race to the bottom.[152] And it was not a cheap race (though it paid off electorally for the Liberal Party when they won again in 2019). Between 2013 and 2016 it cost 9.6 billion Australian dollars (£5.2 billion) to turn back the boats, remove the asylum seekers to remote foreign places, and pay their governments and private security companies to make sure they did not try to get back to Australia. The far right in Europe warmly approved these despicable schemes.[153]

The situation is just as dire in a country largely made up of refugees with a history of persecution: Israel. In 2012, Prime Minister Benjamin Netanyahu warned that refugees and migrant workers from Africa threatened the 'identity' of the 'Jewish' state as well as 'the social fabric of society, our national security and our national identity'. The Israeli police chief struck a more liberal note, declaring that migrants should be permitted to work in order to discourage petty crime since, unable to work legally, they live in overcrowded and impoverished conditions. But the interior minister, Eli Yishai, known for his racist comments, rejected this proposal, using the kind of argument which, if used against Jewish refugees, would be widely (and rightly) regarded as anti-Semitic: 'Why should we provide them with jobs? I'm sick of the bleeding hearts, including politicians. Jobs would settle them here, they'll make babies, and that offer will only result in hundreds of thousands more coming over here.' The crime rate among foreigners, incidentally, is half that among Israelis.[154] In 2012, Miri Regev, later the culture minister, expressed her wish to be rid of African refugees by referring to them as a 'cancer'. As Jonathan Freedland noted, 'She eventually apologised for the comparison – to people living with cancer.'[155] Some rabbis are no better. On 18 March 2018, Yitzhak Yosef, the Sephardic chief rabbi of Israel, called black people 'monkeys', comments properly denounced by the Anti-Defamation League.[156] A couple of months later he blessed Ivanka Trump and her husband Jared Kushner when they were in Jerusalem.[157]

The Prevention of Infiltration Law of 1954 (amended in 2012) mandated the automatic detention of anyone, including asylum seekers, who enters Israel without permission. Many refugees are held in camps in the Negev desert. Amnesty International called this 'an affront to international law'. Israel, 'the only democracy in the Middle East', is a signatory of the UN 1951 Refugee Convention, a document it helped draft and which was inspired by the Holocaust, but this did not prevent it from behaving heartlessly towards the 39,000 or so African refugees escaping war in the Sudan and dictatorship in Eritrea. They were threatened with expulsion or prison.[158] As Michael Brizon wrote in an opinion piece in *Haaretz*, 'the persecuted becomes the persecutor, the refugee becomes the expeller, the uprooted becomes the uprooter, the oppressed becomes the oppressor, the beaten becomes the beater, the trampled becomes the trampler'.[159] Unlike the supine Israeli Labour Party, academics protested vociferously to show they were taking seriously the biblical injunction 'Love the stranger, for you were strangers in the land of Egypt' (Deuteronomy 10:19). Some El Al pilots even refused to fly deported asylum seekers back to Africa.[160]

Anti-immigration parties have blossomed in countries with a reputation for tolerance. Even in 'advanced' Norway, xenophobia has become respectable. Since 2013, the Conservative Party led by Erna Solberg has governed with the help of the 'libertarian' right-wing Progress Party, which seeks a strict immigration policy and a massive reduction in the numbers of asylum seekers, especially if they are 'illiterate' and/or 'poor'. In Denmark the right-wing Danish People's Party became the second biggest party with 21 per cent of the vote in 2015 (though it crumbled to 8.7 per cent in 2019). The government has depended on its support for most years since 2001. 'Forcible integration' has been the policy of a country which, until recently, had been a paragon of social democracy. Now the Danish government aims to force immigrants to put their children into day care for twenty-five hours a week from the age of one, while setting quotas on kindergartens so that they can take no more than 30 per cent of their children from immigrant backgrounds. The children of immigrants are to be brought up with 'Danish values' –whatever that may mean. The aim is to 'eliminate all the ghettos by 2030', ghetto being the now standard term for areas where immigrants cluster. A set of specified crimes will receive longer sentences if the offences are committed within the designated areas.[161] Similar anti-immigration measures are supported by the opposition Social Democrats, still the country's largest party. Their feeble justification is that such measures are necessary to protect the Danish welfare state, though the real reason is to stem the flow of working-class votes to the right. Eventually, after shifting even further towards an anti-immigration platform, the Social Democrats scored a victory in the elections of June 2019, though largely because they were part of a left bloc that included the leftist Socialist People's Party, the Social Liberals, and the Red-Green Alliance. The Social Democrats, under Mette Frederiksen, scored just below their 2015 results.

Meanwhile in Belgium in 2019, the far-right Vlaams Belang party re-emerged as a significant force, and the country's politics is more unstable than ever. In Sweden in 2014, the right-wing anti-immigration Swedish Democrats, founded in 1988 by pro-Nazi sympathisers, received 12.9 per cent of the vote to become the third-largest party. In September 2018 its share of the vote rose to almost 18 per cent. In 2017 in the Netherlands, the far-right Party for Freedom, led by Geert Wilders (who boasts of being a great friend of Israel), became the second-largest party in the House of Representatives with 13 per cent of the vote.

Today's xenophobic, far-right parties are not 'anti-democratic'. They do not challenge democracy as conventionally defined (i.e. elections, parliaments, etc.), in the way Mussolini and Hitler talked about it in the 1920s and 1930s, or the way communist parties in the same period (and some even later) described 'bourgeois' democracy as inferior to the 'dictatorship of the proletariat'. Modern xenophobia in the West rests on some form of democratic legitimacy. Like all major changes and developments, its rise is due to a multiplicity of causes: in particular globalisation and the consequent massive de-industrialisation that has affected the West, more pronounced in some countries (such as the UK) than in others (such as Germany); but also population ageing and the need to spend more on pensions and health and social care, which in turn requires either a high level of taxation or austerity policies, or a combination of both.

3

The Waning of Welfare

The social decline has been accompanied by a decrease in trade union strength, stagnation in wages, and a growth in inequalities. Luxembourg, Ireland, the Netherlands, Belgium, Malta, Cyprus, Jersey, and the Isle of Man enable companies and the very rich to save billions in tax payments, representing 'a massive intergenerational transfer of wealth, which enriches the old and impoverishes the young'.[1]

Xenophobia is clearly not the only problem. If, as Gramsci said, the old is dying, what is the old that is on the way out? And is there something new on the horizon? Identifying the defunct 'old' is relatively easy. The old that has gone is the kind of social democratic and liberal consensus that prevailed in the West in the thirty years after 1945, the so-called *Soziale Marktwirtschaft*, the social market, a German expression used to denote what appeared to be the best of both worlds: a caring capitalism in which sturdy economic growth was accompanied by extended welfare for all and targeted protection for those who did not quite make it. Old people would have secure pensions and the unemployed would be protected. The cost was not huge at a time of full employment, in what were the golden years of capitalism, the *Trente Glorieuses* as the French economist Jean Fourastié labelled them in 1979.[2]

There was free education, not just in schools but also in universities. In the UK the privileged minority going to university in the 1950s and 1960s received, unless their parents were very well off, a maintenance grant, and their fees were paid. Nowadays, universities

are more 'democratic' (almost 50 per cent of the relevant age group
enrol) but also more financialized, and students in England are
forced to borrow huge sums to pay the highest fees in Europe.

The welfare state has turned out to be a costly affair for taxpayers, though of course they are also the main beneficiaries. In
Britain more than two-fifths of national health funding is spent on
the over-sixty-fives, who make up 18 per cent of the population.[3]
Before the Second World War, few families in the UK paid income
tax: only 3.8 million. By 1988–89 there were 21.5 million families in the tax bracket; in 1990–91 there were just over 26 million
individual taxpayers, which had risen by 2017 to over 30 million.[4]
Yet welfare in the UK, contrary to neoliberal propaganda, costs
virtually the same as the OECD average: 21 per cent of GDP (the
OECD includes much poorer countries such as Mexico, Chile, and
Turkey). By comparison, France's is 31.5 per cent and Denmark's
28.7 per cent.[5]

Welfare benefits were not the same everywhere in the West. The
US was backward, but even there one could talk of a welfare state.
Opposition to it, however, was fierce. It took the Great Crash of
1929 to shift the mood. Here is Franklin D. Roosevelt, with words
no recent American president would have dared to use, when he
launched the Social Security Act of 1935:

> We had to struggle with the old enemies of peace – business and
> financial monopoly, speculation, reckless banking, class antago-
> nism, sectionalism, war profiteering. They had begun to consider
> the Government of the United States as a mere appendage to their
> own affairs. We know now that Government by organised money is
> just as dangerous as Government by organised mob. Never before
> in all our history have these forces been so united against one can-
> didate as they stand today. They are unanimous in their hate for
> me – and I welcome their hatred.[6]

Thirty years later, in 1964, Lyndon B. Johnson declared a 'war
on poverty' which led to the Food Stamp programme, Headstart,
Medicare, and Medicaid, as well as the most significant civil

rights legislation in post-war American history. Even Richard Nixon, reviled by the left, extended welfare and health legislation, signing into law in 1970 the Occupational Safety and Health Administration, proposing an Environmental Protection Agency, extending the Food Stamp programme, and increasing Medicare and Medicaid. He even endorsed the Equal Rights Amendment for women, though this failed to be enshrined into the constitution because not enough states ratified it. Last but not least, he successfully defended the Revised Philadelphia Plan, which established affirmative action programmes to integrate (in the race sense) the building and construction trade unions (against opposition from the trade union leader George Meany).[7]

Later presidents were less socially concerned than Nixon, but then times were changing. Jimmy Carter, while running for president in April 1976, supported Senator Ted Kennedy's proposals for a universal national health insurance. But once elected he got cold feet. By the time Ronald Reagan became president, 'monetarism', as advocated by Milton Friedman, was in full swing (and duly dubbed 'Reaganomics', though Reagan never even claimed to understand economics). George Bush senior, having campaigned in 1988 on the slogan 'read my lips: no new taxes', was forced to increase them to reduce the huge deficit brought about by Reaganomics.[8]

Bush's Democrat successor Bill Clinton promised to end welfare 'as we know it', a standard conservative trope. Clinton's Family and Medical Leave Act 1993 granted employees up to twelve weeks leave per year to seek medical treatment or to care for a newborn or other family member, but the leave was unpaid (unlike in most European countries). His Personal Responsibility and Work Opportunity Act 1996 replaced direct federal funding with grants to be administered locally. It was predicted that this was likely to move 2.6 million people, including 1.1 million children, into poverty; 11 million families would lose income, legal immigrants would be denied Supplemental Security Income and food stamps, and, if states decided, Medicaid and welfare as well.[9] Benefits fell by 32.5 per cent.[10]

Clinton also failed miserably to extend health coverage, while capitulating to the forces of neoliberalism by repealing the

Glass-Steagall Act, thus contributing to the global downturn of 2008. This was the culmination, in Joseph Stiglitz's words, of 'a $300 million lobbying effort by the banking and financial-services industries'. The 'investment-bank culture' had won.[11] Clinton, for some reason the darling of liberals everywhere, nevertheless found the money to hire 100,000 new police officers; his Violent Crime Control and Law Enforcement Act 1994 was the largest crime-control bill in US history, costing $30 billion. Supporters declared that this helped bring down violent crimes. Possibly, but the policy of massive incarceration may have done the trick too: by 2017, the federal prison population had more than doubled, from 95,162 in 1994 to the present 214,149. This is the highest prison rate in the world, higher than that of Russia, and five times that of China (whose incarceration rate is lower than that of the UK, if we exclude the detention of the Uighurs).[12] Black Americans are incarcerated at almost five times the rate of non-Hispanic whites, and Hispanics at almost twice the rate of whites (according to US Census data).

The issue of universal health care has remained a constant battle-field in American politics. In 2008 all the main candidates for the Democratic nomination, Barack Obama, Hillary Clinton, and the now mercifully forgotten John Edwards (indicted in 2011 on felony charges for violating campaign contribution laws to cover up an extramarital affair – the charges were later dropped) had enthusi-astically embraced the idea.[13] Once he became president, all Obama could secure after years of struggling against a hostile Congress was the Affordable Care Act ('Obamacare'), which extended provi-sions but failed to meet the goal of universal coverage. His electoral slogan, 'Yes, we can!', sounded good during the electoral campaign. Once he won, he realised that he couldn't. With very different policies, Trump was elected on a similar 'can do' message: we can stop Latinos and Muslims coming into the country, we can build a wall paid for by Mexico, etc. And then he found out he could not. Politicians are often caught out by the impossibility of admitting, during an electoral campaign, that there are real constraints.

During his 2016 campaign, Trump promised to support Medicare and to bring back jobs which had gone overseas. Once elected, he tried to repeal Obamacare in such a way that millions of low-income Americans would have been left without health coverage. He then proceeded to reduce taxes for the rich. They did not need any reduction: in the 1950s the average CEO earned only twenty times as much as the average worker, and the marginal tax rate for the highest earners was 91 per cent. By 2017 the top marginal tax rate was only 39 per cent and the average CEO made 271 times as much as the average worker.[14]

Corporate tax rates were slashed, to the delight of banks such as JPMorgan Chase, which expected its tax rate to fall to 19 per cent from 32 per cent. JPMorgan has a history of being investigated for deceiving investors, abetting the Enron securities fraud, manipulating the energy market, obstructing justice, violating sanctions, etc. While it prospers, there are 40.6 million Americans living in poverty (12.7 per cent of the population) and over 550,000 homeless people in the richest country in the world.[15] This is why the UN Special Rapporteur on extreme poverty and human rights, Philip Alston, visited the United States in December 2017 to examine government efforts to eradicate poverty in the country, and how such efforts comply with US obligations under international human rights law.

The non-partisan Tax Policy Center forecast that Trump's tax package would add more than $1.23 trillion to the federal deficit over the following ten years, even after accounting for the economic growth the bill was projected to generate.[16] Under normal circumstances there wouldn't have been much money left, whether for the promised $1 trillion investment in the nation's crumbling infrastructure, or the six weeks of paid maternity leave for any mother with a newborn child whose employer would not provide the benefit, or for the famous wall on the border with Mexico – particularly since the Democrat-controlled House of Representatives had no intention of releasing the funds (which led to a federal government shutdown). In March 2020, however, an enormous spending package was agreed, once even Trump had accepted that the coronavirus pandemic was not fake news.

The president had also warned of 'consequences' for companies that shipped jobs abroad but, unperturbed, Microsoft continues to shift production to China, General Electric to Canada, IBM to Costa Rica, Egypt, Argentina, and Brazil. A year after Trump's election, the outsourcing of American jobs by *federal* contractors rose to the highest annual level on record, almost triple the number outsourced by contractors in the last year of the Obama administration.[17]

Trump had promised to revive the struggling coal industry, but plants relying on coal continued to close. He promised to protect steel workers but steel imports were almost 20 per cent higher in 2017 than in the previous year.[18] The tariffs on steel and aluminium announced in March 2018 have led to substantial job losses.[19] No one other than the extremely naive thought that the Trump administration would be consistent about anything. The president's trade war on China has been called 'foolish', 'arrogant', and 'ridiculous' by Martin Wolf in the *Financial Times*.[20]

The contrast between the 1960s and '70s and now is telling: back then welfare recipients had 'rights'; now they are stigmatised. Europe has followed a similar pattern: great advances in the period 1945–75; defence or even retrenchment afterwards.

If one wants to know which 'old' it is that is dying, this is it.

The retrenchment was at its most virulent in the UK following the election of Margaret Thatcher as prime minister in 1979. She deregulated the financial markets (the so-called 'Big Bang'), sold off council houses, privatised utilities, curtailed the powers of the trade unions, decreased taxes for high earners, reduced social benefits, introduced a 'quasi-market' in the NHS, while benefits fell behind the growth in wages (reversing the previous trend). Yet public spending on welfare increased because unemployment increased. Of course, the welfare state was not abolished, but it was weakened. Thus the solidarity between the middle classes and the working classes was loosened, even though all continued to benefit from welfare over the course of a lifetime. Countries that adopted neoliberal policies in the 1980s and 1990s saw an increase in health inequalities, particularly in the United Kingdom, the United States, and New Zealand.[21]

Welfare increasingly became 'a matter of "them and us": them being the feckless poor, us being the people who pay for them'.[22]

Obviously there are fraudsters among benefit recipients, and they usually get punished. Middle-class fraudsters get away with it. The UK Financial Conduct Authority prosecuted only eight cases of insider trading between 2013 and 2018 and secured only twelve convictions. In 2015, the UK tax authorities uncovered only thirty or so 'serious and complex' tax frauds, having been criticised for selecting low-value cases to meet its target. By contrast, more than 10,000 benefit 'fraudsters' were prosecuted or penalised in a single year.[23]

After Thatcher was ousted by her own party in 1990 for introducing a poll tax which would particularly hit those on lower incomes, her successor, John Major, introduced the Private Finance Initiative (PFI) to fund infrastructures such as schools and hospitals. A consortium of private firms would own, operate, and lease them back to the government (i.e. the UK taxpayer), for up to forty years. This scheme was dramatically expanded by the Labour government (1997–2010), which rigged the rules so that well-run public alternatives could not compete. Tony Blair's and Gordon Brown's governments were seduced by the wheeze because the debt used to finance the infrastructure was classified as a private sector liability and not government spending, thus 'complying' with Brown's 'golden rule' that public debt could not exceed 40 per cent of national income. It was, in fact, government borrowing in all but name.

The 2010–15 Conservative-Liberal coalition continued the practice with enthusiasm. By 2017, according to the economics editor of the *Financial Times*, the PFI had been 'discredited by cost, complexity and inflexibility'.[24] Margaret Hodge, an early advocate of PFI, admitted 'that we had got it wrong. PFI was a total scandal; we had been seduced by the concept and ripped off by PFI contractors'.[25] The National Audit Office found no evidence that government investment in more than 700 existing PFI projects had delivered any financial benefits.[26]

There is not a word in Gordon Brown's memoirs about PFI having been a failure. Yet there was obviously something seriously wrong with the policy. At the beginning of 2018, Carillion, a major UK construction company heavily involved in PFI schemes, collapsed.

The company employed 43,000 people and used up to 30,000 small sub-contractors, so there were huge job losses. Carillion's former boss, Richard Howson, having stepped down in July 2017, was due to continue receiving his £660,000 salary until October 2018. In 2016 Howson had also 'earned' £1.5 million, including £591,000 in bonuses. The company, which had a huge pension deficit, paid £83 million in dividends in 2016. The former directors of Carillion refused to hand back their bonuses voluntarily. A select committee of MPs branded them 'delusional characters' willing to blame everyone but themselves.[27] 'They were either "negligently ignorant of the rotten culture" or complicit in it. The entire system of checks and balances had failed. The auditors, KPMG, were useless, as was the audit industry's passive regulator.' City advisers to Carillion were obviously asleep and paid while sleeping.[28] To cap it all, the company chairman, Philip Nevill Green, was an adviser to Prime Minister David Cameron on 'corporate responsibility'. This Philip Green is not to be confused with Sir Philip Green, former chairman of Arcadia, and a notorious tax-avoider, also appointed by Cameron to carry out an 'efficiency review' report in 2010.

The PFI system was used particularly in the NHS, which pays an annual charge to the PFI companies for the use and maintenance of the hospitals built under the system. The NHS will also have to pay back the money used for the construction of the hospitals, with interest. As a result, between 2010 and 2015, the NHS and local authorities in England spent more than £10.7 billion on hospitals and other health-care facilities, while the PFI companies made £831 million in pre-tax profit over the same six years, far more than if they had invested the money elsewhere. It was assumed, until the Carillion debacle, that this was a low-risk business, since the loans are guaranteed by the government. And this goes some way towards explaining the massive funding shortfall accumulated by NHS hospitals.[29] According to a report by the left-of-centre Institute for Public Policy Research, hospitals will have to make another £55 billion in payments by the time the last contract ends in 2050, as a direct consequence of PFI.[30]

Unsurprisingly this marketisation of health services was continued by the coalition government led by David Cameron and the

Liberal Democrat Nick Clegg. The Health and Social Care Act 2012 involved a reorganisation which, according to health think-tank the King's Fund, was 'damaging', 'complex and confusing'.[31] By the end of 2017, the NHS was reeling under a massive and unsustainable deficit.[32]

While the self-deluded keep on saying that the British medical system is the best in the world, the sad reality, according to an OECD report, is that Britain has only 2.4 hospital beds per 1,000 population, less than half the EU average (5.2), while France has 6.2 and Germany 8.2. Britain has also fewer doctors per capita than any EU country except for Romania and Poland. British people have also to wait longer than the EU average for routine operations such as cataract and knee and hip replacements.[33] The coronavirus pandemic will inevitably complicate matters further – and not just in the UK. Of course the British welfare state survives, but it has been seriously damaged by the policies of successive Conservative administrations, with Labour doing very little in the way of repair.

In France, by contrast, the welfare state initially fared much better than it did in Britain under Thatcher. Elected president in 1981, and with a massive majority at his command, the socialist François Mitterrand shifted resources towards welfare. Pensions and family allowances were substantially increased, health prescription charges were abolished, immigrants were helped, spending on education more than matched the rate of inflation (as did the minimum wage), the death penalty was finally abolished, the circumstances of single-parent families were improved, and childcare facilities were expanded.

In February 1982 the government nationalised five large industrial corporations and thirty-nine banks; these, however, were simply annexed to an already existing state banking sector which had always behaved as if it were private. Having spent a considerable amount of money, the government did not know what to do with this new instrument, though it satisfied the left-wing aspirations of 'breaking with capitalism'. More modestly and patriotically, some socialists, such as Laurent Fabius, claimed that the nationalisation had saved large French enterprises from a foreign takeover.[34]

In the early 1980s the government also initiated one of the most
vigorous counter-unemployment packages in Western Europe, even
though unemployment in France was at the time less pronounced
than in Britain, Belgium, Italy, or Holland. Public sector employment
was expanded. The working day was reduced on the assumption
that it would reduce unemployment.[35] Yet unemployment increased
from almost 1.7 million in May 1981 to just over 2 million in May
1982.[36] The problem was that the French government was trying to
stimulate the economy while other countries were deflating. The US
and the UK had been in the throes of deflation at least since 1979,
and they were joined by West Germany in 1980. France, though far
more constrained by international factors than Germany, let alone
Japan, tried to be the exception.[37] It gambled and lost. This led to
inflation, which by 1982 was twice that of its main competitor,
Germany.

It was as if France stood alone and pristine, surrounded by the
barbaric hordes of multinational corporations poised to destroy the
uniqueness of her industries and her culture. The further one trav-
elled to the left in the Socialist Party the more one encountered a
peculiar brand of left-wing nationalistic socialism which, elsewhere
in Europe, could only be found in the British Labour Party.

In June 1982 the French government went into reverse. Public
spending was cut and workers' social security contributions were
increased. Devaluation, containment of wages, and a more favourable international situation (a fall in interest rates) provided some
of the supply-side conditions for investment. The belief took hold,
followed later elsewhere, notably by Tony Blair's 'New Labour',
that it was necessary to demonstrate to financial circles that socialists were pursuing economic policies not substantially different
from those of the right – a U-turn widely welcomed as a return to
'realism'. In Britain, Mrs Thatcher proudly declared that 'the Lady's
not for turning'. In France they turned and turned again. The aspi-
ration to 'abolish capitalism' was dropped. France would go for
'modernisation', it was declared. This call sounded appealing, as
it has been for over a hundred years, but here it signalled the end
of ambition, the termination of passion, the beginning of routine.
The Socialist Party became 'a grey party looking for colour', as

the Labour MP Austin Mitchell said of his own party. By 1985 the socialists declared that 'The market has clearly demonstrated that it is one of the roads to freedom ... It is not for the State to produce. This is the task of enterprises.'[38]

With bitter sarcasm the sociologist Alain Touraine wrote: 'If you hear an inflated tribute to profits, enterprise, competition, you can be sure you are listening to a socialist minister ... In a word, France has become Reaganite.'[39] If one wanted to map out the reasons for the rise of the far-right Front National, one could do worse than examine the economic record of successive French socialist governments.

Mitterrand was re-elected president in 1988, when Jean-Marie Le Pen, the Front National candidate, scored an impressive 14.4 per cent, while the Communist candidate obtained less than 7 per cent. The three Mitterrand governments that followed took the path of fiscal prudence, shifting the burden of taxation to indirect taxes, combined with a rigid anti-inflationary policy. Unemployment grew continuously. The rich got richer and the poor poorer.[40] However, by 1991 inflation was under control (as it was elsewhere).[41] A wave of privatisations followed, including many of the firms which had been nationalised just a short time before.

All this was to no avail. In the 1993 election the socialists were wiped out, their percentage dropping from 37.5 in 1988 to 17.6. Pierre Bérégovoy, the prime minister, killed himself. The right-wing parties won 485 seats, the socialists 92. France too was shifting to the right.

Two 'cohabitations' followed. The first began in 1993 with Mitterrand sharing power with the Gaullist prime minister Édouard Balladur. The second, which began in 1995, saw Jacques Chirac as president and the Socialist Lionel Jospin as prime minister. Under Jospin, the major reforms championed by Martine Aubry, the 'ministre de l'Emploi et de la Solidarité', were the extension of health coverage and a reduction in the length of the working week, while Dominique Strauss-Khan, the finance minister, reassured the markets.

By then the left was so fragmented that Jospin did not even make it to the second round in the presidential elections of 2002. Had he secured the support of the entire French left, including Jean-Pierre

Chevènement's centre-left party, communists, assorted Trotskyists, Greens, etc., he would have gained 42.89 per cent to Chirac's 19.88 per cent and perhaps would have won in the second round. But he didn't. He scored a miserable 16.18 per cent in the first round, thus ceding the crucial second place for the final round to Jean-Marie Le Pen (on 16.86 per cent), to the consternation of 80 per cent of the electorate who rallied behind Chirac, *faute de mieux*.

Chirac was succeeded as president by Nicolas Sarkozy (2007–12). The left was not back in power until 2012, when François Hollande became president and the Socialist Party gained a majority for a dismal and unsuccessful five years. Hollande had won by promising significant political and economic changes that would reduce the government's austerity policies, its subservience to finance-led capitalism, and its tax-friendly approach to big business. Hollande assumed the image of *un président normal* in contrast with the 'bling-bling' hyperactivity of his predecessor, Nicolas Sarkozy, who, in 2014, was charged with corruption. However, when it came to policies, the differences were not that significant. During Hollande's presidency, the belt-tightening and fiscal consolidation continued, as did state support for financial markets and big business, while social and economic inequalities widened, and unemployment, especially among the young, soared. Unsurprisingly Hollande's popularity plummeted to unsurpassed depths. His fall opened the way for Emmanuel Macron's 'Third Way', *ni gauche ni droite*.

In Italy, the 1990s saw a complete overhaul of the political system. Following the collapse of communism in the USSR and across Eastern Europe, the Italian Communist Party (PCI), the strongest communist party in the West, changed its name, and in a series of neurotic moves, as if searching for an identity, turned itself into the Partito Democratico della Sinistra (in 1991), then the Democratici di Sinistra (1998), and finally the generic Partito Democratico (2007), a name adopted in imitation of the US party of the same name, a further instance of the growing provincialism of Italian politics. An earlier party, I Democratici, led by the former Christian Democrat Romano Prodi, had as its symbol the donkey, the *asinello*, borrowed from the US Democratic Party, while Walter Veltroni, in awe of all things American, when leader of the Partito Democratico in 2008, even adopted, untranslated, Obama's slogan 'Yes, we can' (Veltroni wrote the preface to the Italian edition of Obama's *The Audacity of Hope*).

Around the same time as the communist states imploded, a series of major corruption scandals, known as Tangentopoli (Bribesville), destroyed the ruling Christian Democrats, in power since 1945, and also pushed the Socialist Party, the third largest, into the abyss. An enterprising group of magistrates known as *mani pulite* (clean hands), failed, of course, to clean up Tangentopoli, as the corruption endemic in the Italian political system became known.

In response to Tangentopoli, Silvio Berlusconi, a popular TV magnate who had originally made his money in real estate, and who had never been elected before, formed a new party in December 1993) – thus preceding Trump by almost 25 years. He called it, patriotically, Forza Italia (Let's Go Italy), the jingoistic cry heard from football terraces. The party won the 1994 election in coalition with the hitherto pariah party Alleanza Nazionale (once widely held to be neo-fascist) and the anti-southern Lega Nord (not yet xenophobic since there were few foreign workers in Italy at the time). The Berlusconi-led coalition was in power for only a year, then in opposition between 1996 and 2001, before returning to power for a full term in 2001–6, and again in 2008–11. The coalition won again in 2018, but the Northern League (now simply La Lega, not so anti-southern but more xenophobic), having done well, deserted Berlusconi in favour of the new Movimento Cinque Stelle (Five Star Movement) and formed a government.

With the rise of Berlusconi, for the first time in European history a governing party had been entirely created and funded by a single entrepreneur who, like Trump, enjoyed little popularity among the elites whether at home or abroad (the *Economist* in particular lost no opportunity to disparage him, usually with good reason). During Berlusconi's entire period in office, no significant reform was promulgated. However, things did not improve under later centre-left governments: GNP, productivity, investment, and wages stagnated or decreased; regional inequalities continued; Italian firms became less and less competitive, while its industrialists, so dynamic in the 1950s, turned out to be increasingly incompetent; universities continued to falter from crisis to crisis; employment remained precarious especially for the young; and, as elsewhere, there was constant deindustrialisation and a loss of foreign markets, while taxes (and tax evasion) remained high and the bureaucracy suffocating.

While the left was as impotent as ever, various electoral cartels and coalitions of the centre emerged, all hoping to contain Berlusconi. Historians will have a problem explaining the proliferation of 'parties' and short-lived coalitions in the decades following 1994: the centrist Lista Dini of Lamberto Dini, the Catholic UDEUR of Clemente Mastella, the Unione Democratica per la Repubblica of former president Francesco Cossiga, the Patto di Rinascita Nazionale of Mariotto Segni (Patto Segni), the Italia dei Valori of Antonio di Pietro (one of the magistrates leading the Tangentopoli investigation), Scelta Civica of the economist Mario Monti (briefly prime minister), the Catholic Unione di Centro of Pier Ferdinando Casini, Futuro e Libertà per l'Italia of the former neo-fascist Gianfranco Fini, and even Libertà di Azione founded by Alessandra Mussolini, the Duce's granddaughter, and its spiritual successor the far-right Fratelli d'Italia (Brothers of Italy, the title of the national anthem), also led by a woman, Giorgia Meloni.

On the centre-left various coalitions emerged, with cute 'botanical' names, as alternatives to Berlusconi – the Ulivo (Olive), the Margherita (Daisy), the Girasole (Sunflower) – but none were able to stabilise the political spectrum. Further on the left there were the Rifondazione Comunista, the Partito dei Comunisti Italiani, Democrazia Proletaria, Alleanza dei Progressisti, Sinistra Arcobaleno, L'Altra Europa con Tsipras, Sinistra Ecologia Libertà, Liberi e Uguali (itself a coalition of tiny parties), etc.

The whole circus was underlined by frenetic debates about electoral and constitutional reforms and lost referendums, such as the one held on 4 December 2016, called by Matteo Renzi, then prime minister, to reform the composition and powers of Parliament, which he lost by a staggering 60 per cent to 40 per cent, a defeat which makes even David Cameron look clever. Renzi resigned, remained party leader, but left the post of prime minister to Paolo Gentiloni (also of the Partito Democratico). Meanwhile the economy performed indifferently, the welfare state stagnated, and the political system continued to implode. The elections of 4 March 2018 signalled a further defeat for the Italian left and for Renzi in particular (who resigned, only to form yet another party, Italia Viva). The Partito Democratico won a miserable 18.7 per cent of the popular vote.

As if Berlusconi and the Northern League were not enough, a new movement had emerged in Italy *né di destra né di sinistra* ('of neither left nor right', like the French Macron): the Movimento Cinque Stelle (M5S). In the European Parliament, however, it knows where to sit: on the right with the Eurosceptic EFDD (Europe of Freedom and Direct Democracy), along with UKIP, the Swedish Democrats, Alternative für Deutschland, and other right-wing groups. The M5S, usually described as 'populist', was founded by the 'charismatic' comedian Beppe Grillo. The movement (it does not want to be called a party) was born in 2009, and by the 2013 elections it had won 25.5 per cent of votes, becoming the second-largest Italian party. By 2016 it had gained the mayoralties of Rome and Turin. Since it rejected alliances with any other party it only contributed to the problem of governing in Italy. By the election of March 2018 it had become the most successful party with almost 32 per cent of the vote. It was then more than ready to make a deal with the xenophobic La Lega to form a government, thus confounding those so naive as to regard it as a leftist force. Its earlier rejection of alliances was a sensible move for a party of this kind. In government it was forced to make choices thus becoming unpopular with its supporters who expect miracles. But its victory in the March 2018 elections has led to a weak, unstable, and xenophobic government. The M5S soon switched sides: threatened by Lega with new elections, it joined forces with the Partito Democratico. No wonder so many Italians are disgusted with politics. They can only despair. And some of them have been despairing for a long time. As Dante wrote in the Sixth Canto of *Purgatory*:

Ahi serva Italia, di dolore ostello,
nave sanza nocchiere in gran tempesta,
non donna di province, ma bordello!

Ah, Italy in servitude, hostel of suffering,
Ship without a helmsman in ferocious tempest,
No longer Lady of the provinces, but of a bordello!

In Germany matters proceeded less dramatically. The Christian Democratic Chancellor Helmut Kohl, elected in 1982 and remaining in office for the next sixteen years, at first extended the welfare state, only to reduce it again in 1989. That was the fateful year in which the Berlin Wall fell, an unexpected stroke of good luck for the increasingly unpopular chancellor. He handled it well, taking the initiative and ignoring the wishes of his liberal coalition partners, whose initial aim was the creation of a special economic zone in the former East Germany. He also ignored the anxieties of Germany's allies in the West, above all those of the British: two months before the fall of the Berlin Wall, Margaret Thatcher had told Gorbachev that she was against the reunification of Germany and that she wanted him to stop it.[42] Mitterrand too was alarmed. A month after the Wall came down, his personal adviser, Jacques Attali, told Vadim Zagladin, a senior Gorbachev aide, that he was 'puzzled' by the apparent Soviet indifference to what was going on: 'France by no means wants German reunification.' Whether Mitterrand was so adamant has been disputed, but he was understandably anxious and perturbed.[43]

Dismissing the objections of the Bundesbank, Kohl imposed a one-to-one exchange rate between marks on both sides of Germany. He triumphed in the election of 1990 and won again, albeit with a reduced majority, in 1994. But reunification had its price: gross domestic product shrank relative to growth in the rest of Western Europe; the unemployment rate doubled; East Germans were dismayed at the welfare cuts and the rising unemployment they had to face (twice the West German rate). Unemployment had been unknown in the DDR and some East Germans harboured a nostalgic longing for the certainties of the past – a phenomenon quickly labelled *Ostalgie*. At the election of 1998 Kohl was defeated, and the SPD candidate, Gerhard Schröder, became Chancellor as head of an SPD-Green coalition. The situation did not improve. With some glee, the *Economist* labelled Germany 'the sick man of the euro'.[44]

Re-elected in 2002, and in synchrony with Tony Blair's New Labour, Schröder, having promised during the election campaign not to cut welfare, announced in March 2003 the so-called Agenda 2010. This aimed to cut taxes and, consequently, make cuts in health services, pensions, and unemployment benefits. It was the German turn towards neoliberalism. Agenda 2010 was supported by the centre-right parties and opposed by social democrats within Schröder's own party as well as by the much weakened trade unions. Yet he received a confidence vote not only from the SPD but also from his coalition partners, the Greens. At first unemployment rose to over 5 million, but by 2007 it was lower than in 2002. All to no avail. The SPD, increasingly unpopular, lost its majority at the 2005 election. A grand CDU/SPD coalition was eventually formed. The Christian Democrat Angela Merkel began her long rule as Chancellor. Schröder retired from politics and went on to make real money when he joined the board of the Russian energy giant Rosneft. (Making a fortune after leaving high office has become almost commonplace. Few, however, seem to have bettered Tony Blair, who is 'estimated to have earned between £50 million and £100 million since quitting as prime minister, largely through his consultancy businesses', according to the *Telegraph*. The same newspaper has reported that Tony Blair Associates 'earned millions of pounds over at least six years advising the Kazakhstan government and its autocratic president Nursultan Nazarbayev'. Blair praised the despot for having displayed 'the toughness necessary to take the decisions to put the country on the right path'.[45]

Even though by 2015 Germany was, once again, Europe's economic locomotive, with the second-largest export industry in the world, poverty and inequality were on the rise. Wages barely increased. Some 12.5 million Germans were classified as poor. Both the recovery as well as the rise in poverty were attributed to Agenda 2010, hence the continuing unpopularity of the SPD.[46]

Even Sweden moved to the right. The basis and the strength of the Swedish welfare state was its generous universalism, which is why it had enjoyed considerable middle-class support in spite of the high taxes necessary to fund it. The long rule of social democracy came to an end in 1976, when the so-called 'bourgeois' parties achieved power. They had spent much energy during the electoral campaign denying any intention to destroy the welfare state. Their victory was a temporary blip, however, and the Social Democratic Party (SAP) won again in 1982, 1985, and 1988. In the last of these elections, the SAP gained more seats than the combined vote of the bourgeois parties, the communists achieved their best results in twenty years (nearly 6 per cent), and the new Green party won 5.5 per cent. But voters had acquired a taste for electoral mobility.

By 1989, as the economic situation in Sweden deteriorated, the popularity of the Social Democrats declined. By 1991 their share of the vote had plummeted below 40 per cent for the first time since the 1930s, though they were returned to power, once again, in 1994. Swedish manufacturing began to lose its dominant position. Its textiles could no longer compete. Its shipbuilding industry had to face formidable competition from the Koreans and Japanese.[47] Scandinavian capitalism was unable to achieve growth rates compatible with a high level of public expenditure and the willingness of taxpayers to tolerate a high tax burden. Sweden's dependency on the vicissitudes of the international economy had increased remarkably throughout the 1980s. The Social Democrats – like neoliberals elsewhere – dismantled the system of foreign exchange controls, which had become far less effective in a world dominated by multinational firms and international capital markets.

Rapidly deteriorating public finances led to cuts in unemployment benefits, higher health-care charges and much stricter sick-leave rules. A major shift in the organisation of the Swedish national health service occurred, away from the centralised rational planning model and towards an internal market.[48] By 1993, in preparation for the following year's election, the Social Democrats had given up the possibility of a return to full employment unless Sweden became a member of the European Union, which it did the following year.

Sweden was now the home of a battered model of social democracy. The paragon of full employment had an unemployment figure of 13 per cent.[49] The Social Democrats remained out of power from 2006 to 2014. They returned in 2014, forced into a coalition (with the Greens) for the first time in decades. What's more, it was a coalition without a majority. The SAP had obtained just over 30 per cent of the vote, its worst result ever. Their Green partners had taken less than 7 per cent. Since the SAP had turned down the possibility of a coalition with the Left Party (which won 5.7 per cent), its government was so weak that it needed support from the right just to pass the budget. The next general election in 2018 resulted in another hung parliament and another Red–Green coalition with no majority, again with Stefan Löfven as prime minister. For over fifty years (between 1932 and 1988), the SAP had always received over 40 per cent of the vote in every election. Those days were over.

What does all this tell us? It tells us that, as it became increasingly difficult to keep taxes low and welfare spending high, traditional social democracy has had to occupy, at least in part, the terrain which had once been the prerogative of the right. It has had to become 'modern', i.e. more neoliberal. The era of nationalisation, of the 'paternalistic' state trying to run the economy rather than leaving it to the entrepreneurial class, was over. It was necessary to allow the market to let rip and, with the cash generated, help the poor.

This is what countries lucky enough to have important raw materials, such as oil, have done and still do. Qatar, Chávez's Venezuela, and Putin's Russia had this in common: after the entrepreneurs had taken their cut, the oil bonanza could be spent on the masses in exchange for popularity. There was no need for reforms, new economic models, strategies, or policies that changed anything. The rich could get richer while the poor would be less poor. And everyone will be happy – as long as the oil bonanza lasts, which of course it never does.

Not everyone has the luck to have ample reserves of raw materials. Still, one must move with the times and, by the twenty-first century, this meant moving right. In Britain this strategic response was developed by Tony Blair when he became Labour prime minister in 1997, after eighteen years of Conservative rule. He called his political stance the 'Third Way', meaning he would take what was useful from both right and left – another way of saying neither right nor left. His victory was particularly popular with social democrats throughout Europe. In the US this move took the name of 'triangulation', a term adopted by Bill Clinton when he was re-elected in 1996. In his State of the Union Address that year, Clinton came up with the soundbite 'The era of big government is over', while conceding that 'we cannot go back to the time when our citizens were left to fend for themselves'.[50] In the words of his political adviser Dick Morris, this meant that the president would take the 'best' of Democrat and Republican policies and blend them so that the resulting cocktail would be a new 'third force'.

Twenty years later, in 2017, the successful candidate for the French presidency, Emmanuel Macron, did exactly the same thing, calling his move, less elegantly, *ni gauche ni droite*, and acting as if he had just invented a theme that pervaded the twentieth century – as the Israeli historian Zeev Sternhell explained in his justly celebrated book on inter-war fascism in France, *Ni droite ni gauche: L'idéologie fasciste en France* (1983). In 1931 the essayist Émile Chartier (writing under the pseudonym Alain) wrote that, when asked whether the division between left and right still has any meaning, 'the first thought which comes to my mind is that the person who asks the question is not on the Left'.[51]

The slogan was revived by the Front National in 1995, with the addition of one word: *Ni droite, ni gauche: Français!* Macron won the 2017 presidential election having repeatedly used his favourite expressions (for which he was widely mocked) *en même temps* and *mais aussi* ('at the same time' and 'but also') in order to disguise any apparent contradiction. He was in favour of a military intervention in Syria and 'at the same time' reluctant to insist that Bashar al-Assad should go; in favour of investing in the future and 'at the same time' being strict with spending; believed in reinforcing national borders and 'at the same time' observing one's duty towards refugees. In October 2016, he reminded his audience of France's crimes against humanity in Algeria '*mais aussi*' that France had '*éléments de civilisation'* mixed with *'éléments de barbarie'*.[52] Walter Veltroni, the 'Third Way' leader of the Italian Partito Democratico, had the same habit, ten years before Macron, of saying *ma anche* (but also), and was consequently satirised by a comedian: 'We are open to immigrants but also to the Ku Klux Klan.' For some this *en même temps* epitomised Macron's moderation and his ability to see both sides of the argument; for his opponents it was yet more evidence of his confused and confusing approach to politics.

In fact, once the hype is discounted, Macron is a run-of-the mill pro-business centrist, whose aim is to loosen labour laws in favour of enterprises, water down France's taxes on wealth (not that they are particularly significant), and cut housing benefits. This, he thinks, is how to deal with the country's high unemployment rate: at 9.6 per cent before the pandemic, double that of the UK and Germany.

Having won an easy victory against Marine Le Pen in 2017, Macron's party (and its allies) secured in the first round of the subsequent parliamentary elections one-third of the votes cast, on an exceptionally low turnout (48.7 per cent). In the second round Macron's party reached 49.11 per cent, which ensured 60 per cent of the seats, while the Socialist Party received only 5.6 per cent. The turnout in the second round was even more appalling: 42.64 per cent. In other words Macron gained an absolute majority in the National Assembly with just over 15 per cent of the electorate.

He had been lucky. His opponents in the presidential elections were particularly hopeless. The conservative candidate François Fillon spent much of the campaign denouncing corruption. It turned out he had employed most of his family in pseudo-government jobs. The outgoing president, François Hollande, did not even stand, his unpopularity compounded by his lack of dignity, his use of security personnel to bring croissants in the morning to him and to his mistress. He knew he didn't stand a chance. He offered barely any support to the official socialist candidate, Benoît Hamon, who was trounced at the election. The leftist candidate, Jean-Luc Mélenchon, was too left-wing; Marine Le Pen too right-wing.

Since his election, Macron's popularity has slumped continuously, and he is seen as *le président des riches*.[53] An opinion poll published in *Le Monde* in July 2018 revealed that only 34 per cent of the French trusted him (it had been 44 per cent the previous year), but then only 10 per cent trusted political parties, 26 per cent members of Parliament, and 30 per cent the media.[54] Macron's initial tax reform replaced the solidarity tax on wealth with a tax on real estate. This favoured the rich at the expense of the middle classes.[55] Taking a leaf from Marine Le Pen's book, he announced in December 2017 that he would get tough on immigration. *Le Monde* decried this with the headline 'En France, une politique migratoire d'une dureté sans précédent' (An Immigration Policy of Unprecedented Harshness).[56] By March 2018 public sector workers were mobilising against Macron's neoliberal reforms aimed at cutting drastically the state sector. He was still wedded to the utterly discredited 'trickle down' theory beloved of the rich since it justifies their increased wealth on the grounds that the richer they are the more they can spend. Macron, a former banker, should read his Keynes. He seems to be more *droite* than *gauche*. Indeed his government is full of people from business or from previous right-wing governments. By November 2018 a new movement had emerged, the Gilets Jaunes, with no clear position except that of being opposed to the president (initially over his decision to increase fuel taxes). Macron was clearly unaware of the pent-up anger among the bottom half of the country, who had seen their incomes decrease since the 2008 global downturn.[57]

Macron's older opponents have even bigger problems. The Socialist Party is in a total shambles, the Front National is licking its wounds, and the traditional right is, in the words of *Le Monde*, à terre, affaiblie, déboussolée et fracturée (prostrate, weakened, disoriented and fractured).[58]

In the UK, it was Iraq, not the economy, that seriously undermined Tony Blair's popularity. By 2017 one-third of the British public (and 31 per cent of Labour supporters) thought he should be tried for war crimes.[59] For a long time he was given credit for winning the 1997 election, though after eighteen years of Tory rule one might have expected almost any Labour candidate to have won, if not with such a stunning majority. With the Conservatives in disarray and displaying a succession of unimpressive leaders – from William Hague (1997–2001), who boasted that when a teenager he could drink fourteen pints of beer a day, to Iain Duncan Smith (2001–3), whose lack of charisma became legendary, to Michael Howard (2003–5) the son of immigrants who ran the electoral campaign on a strong anti-immigration platform – Blair won again in 2001 (on an exceptionally low turnout, and losing 3 million votes) and then again in 2005. In this third successive victory, unprecedented in Labour history, the party won with the smallest share of the vote ever. In England Labour had fewer votes than the Tories. It won thanks to Scotland and Wales. These figures would soon look ominous. They did not mean New Labour was popular, only that it was less unpopular than the Conservatives. In the short term that was all that mattered.

Nevertheless Labour was in power with comfortable parliamentary majorities for thirteen years, the longest period in its history. What were its achievements? The list, trotted out by Labour supporters with tedious regularity, is long, but it all amounts to spending money on public services, the 'Sure Start' scheme aimed at improving childcare, and the introduction of a national minimum wage which helped to decrease poverty.[60] These were not insignificant achievements, but they cannot match the major social reforms of the Attlee governments of 1945–51 (above all the creation of the National Health Service and the nationalisation of major utilities) or the civil rights legislation of the Wilson governments (1964–70) when the Race Relations Act and Equal Pay Act were introduced, capital punishment was abolished, homosexuality was decriminalised, abortion was legalised, divorce was made easier and censorship less suffocating, and corporal punishment in prisons was ended.

Decreasing poverty is not a reform. It consists in spending public money (or compelling employers to increase wages) without tackling the causes of poverty. In fact much of this achievement of New Labour was later undone. According to the Institute for Fiscal Studies, by 2022 over 35 per cent of children will be in relative poverty, thus eliminating the progress of the previous decades.[61] The Child Poverty Action Group estimated there were already 3.9 million children (28 per cent) living in poverty in 2014–15,[62] while according to a 2017 report by the Joseph Rowntree Foundation, 14 million people live in poverty in the UK, 20 per cent of the population, including 8 million working-age adults, 4 million children, and 1.9 million pensioners.[63]

New Labour continued the deregulation policies of the Conservatives, pandering to big business to an extent unequalled in the rest of Europe. In the mid-1980s, Thatcher's government deregulated fire safety standards in homes, abandoning enforceable requirements for guidelines, which the building industry could choose to follow or not. The Blair government did not reverse this policy (partly responsible for the tragedy of the Grenfell Tower fire in 2017, which caused the deaths of eighty people), insisting that a fire inspector should simply 'inform and educate' rather than enforce – as Chris Williamson, the shadow minister for fire and emergency services admitted in 2017.[64]

In 2006, Gordon Brown, having been Chancellor of the Exchequer for almost ten years (the longest in British history), and a year before the unleashing of the global downturn, congratulated the City of London for its achievements and for showing 'that Britain can succeed in an open global economy, a progressive globalisation, a Britain that is made for globalisation and a globalisation that is made for Britain'.[65] His glowing verdict on the City had changed dramatically ten years later (well after the financial crisis, which the bankers had not seen coming) when he published his self-serving memoirs in which he lamented that fraudulent and risk-taking bankers had not been jailed, 'banned from future practice', and had their 'assets confiscated' – a state of affairs which will simply give the 'green light' for similar behaviour in the future, increasing the risk of another crisis. If only he had not been so afraid to appear anti-business when he was Chancellor.[66]

This was not something which perturbed Boris Johnson, who, as foreign secretary, when asked about the worries expressed by the business world over the coming exit of the UK from the EU, declared, with characteristic bluntness: 'Fuck business'.[67] Had Jeremy Corbyn said that, when he was Labour leader, he would have been abused; but not Boris, who went as far as declaring, during the European referendum campaign, that the EU had the same goal as Adolf Hitler.[68] The media loves clowns, and clown Boris eventually became prime minister in yet another morbid symptom of our times. Johnson's incompetence was particularly evident during the coronavirus pandemic. His initial reaction was terrible. According to former government advisers, had he imposed the lockdown earlier the number of fatalities in Britain would have been halved.[69]

In Northern Ireland too, the 'old' was on the way out: by November 2003 the (Catholic) SDLP and the (Protestant) Ulster Unionist Party – the true champions of the Good Friday Agreement – had been replaced by Sinn Féin (closely associated with the terrorist IRA) and by Ian Paisley's Democratic Unionist Party. Paisley, a fundamentalist Christian who had opposed homosexuality (in 1977 he had launched the 'Save Ulster from Sodomy' campaign), civil rights, and the Good Friday Agreement ('Never! Never! Never!' he shouted), became First Minister of Northern Ireland. Sinn Féin's Martin McGuinness, a former IRA member, became Paisley's deputy. While the two unlikely bedfellows got to know and like each other, the SDLP and the Ulster Unionist Party, who represented the Northern Irish establishment, were relegated to the increasingly capacious dustbin of history.

The winds of change could also be felt in the Republic of Ireland. In the February 2020 election, Sinn Féin won 24.5 per cent of the vote, finishing ahead of the two parties that had ruled over Irish politics for nearly a century: Fianna Fáil, on 22.2 per cent, and Fine Gael with 20.9. The election was dominated by welfare issues such as housing and pensions, and not by Irish unity or Brexit and the border with Northern Ireland.

As the welfare state dwindled throughout the rich West, those the Victorians had called the 'undeserving poor' were increasingly grudgingly kept alive on state benefits; hence the mounting number of mendicants and homeless and the widespread use of food banks, even in rich countries such as the US (where they started), Germany, France, Belgium, Italy, and the UK.[70] For all the propaganda about the benefits of the free market, one thing is certain: markets do not provide social protection and cannot ensure that globalisation will work for all or even most citizens.[71]

The welfare state was supposed to create a national community which, though its members were still unequal in income, wealth, and educational level, was sufficiently cohesive to make living under advanced capitalism better than living under any other kind of social system. This almost generalised unity began to break up in the 1980s and 1990s, but only in the last twenty years or so has it begun to affect the post-war party system by weakening the traditional centre-left and centre-right. The social crisis has turned into a political crisis: morbid symptoms galore.

4

The Collapse of Established Parties

The Crisis of Traditional Social Democracy

By 2020 it had become obvious, even to those on the left for whom optimism is a necessary position, that reformist social democracy had been comprehensively defeated throughout Europe. Will it survive in some form or other? Perhaps in Sweden, where it is still in power, but it is in deep trouble even there.

If the once celebrated Swedish model now makes a sad spectacle for social democrats, the rest of Scandinavia can only be described as an iceberg of tears. Under the Social Democrat prime minister Helle Thorning-Schmidt, an exponent of the so-called 'Third Way', Denmark participated in NATO bombing missions in Libya, cut taxes for the rich as well as welfare payments, and in 2014 sold shares in DONG Energy (a state company) to Goldman Sachs and others (who made a 150 per cent profit when they sold up three and a half years later).[1] The sale wrecked the government and, a year later, Thorning-Schmidt was out of power, paving the way for a weak centre-right coalition supported by the far-right Danish People's Party. Soon there was a new shift to the left with the victory of the Social Democrat Mette Frederiksen, as prime minister in a coalition government which includes various left and centre-left parties.

In Norway, the Labour Party was for a long time regarded as the natural party of government, having been in power continuously from 1945 to 1963, and then for some twenty-five years between

1971 and 2013. In the 2001 election it obtained its worst result ever (24.3 per cent). In 2017 it did a little better: 27.4 per cent. In government it became more and more enamoured of the market economy, privatised public assets, cut the health service, and helped the rich to get richer. It has been in opposition since 2013.

In 2016 in Iceland, one of the countries hardest hit by the 2008 financial crisis, the Social Democrats, who had over 30 per cent of the vote as recently as 2003, were reduced to 5.7 per cent at the 2016 elections, their worst result ever, gaining only a miserable three parliamentary seats. They regrouped at the election of 28 October 2017, with 12 per cent of the vote and seven seats, but they were now the third party. The first was the conservative and Eurosceptic Independence Party, though it lost support after sex and tax scandals involving the outgoing prime minister. The second party was the Left-Green Movement, Eurosceptic, environmentalist, and anti-NATO. Complicated negotiations followed, leading to a government under the Left-Green Movement leader, Katrín Jakobsdóttir, in coalition with the Independence Party and the centre-right Progressive Party. It is a heterogeneous and precarious alliance.

In Finland too, in 2015, the Social Democrats obtained their worst results with 16.5 per cent, becoming the fourth party, and muddling through in opposition. The Centre Party led by Juha Sipilä was in power in coalition with the Eurosceptic right-wing Finns Party, the second largest in the parliament, though it split in July 2017, with only members of the new formation remaining in the coalition. At the April 2019 elections the Social Democrats slightly recouped, becoming, by a whisker, the first party with 17.7 per cent; the Finns Party had 17.5 per cent and the centre-right National Coalition 17 per cent, while the Centre Party of outgoing PM Juha Sipilä lost a third of its vote (down to 13.8 per cent). The Social Democrat leader Sanna Marin formed a five-party coalition leaving as the only opposition the Finns Party.

When we move away from what used to be regarded as the stronghold of European social democracy, matters are even worse for the traditional left. Sometimes it loses to the far right, sometimes to the far left. In Portugal in the late 1990s, the Socialist Party was in power, continuing with alacrity the privatisation policies of its predecessors. It was eventually able to meet the criteria for membership of the eurozone with the kind of creative accounting that prevailed in Greece and Italy. At first, under António Guterres (now UN secretary-general), there was substantial economic growth, but this had abated by 2002. Then the Socialists were out of office and the conservatives (the Partido Social Democrata), under José Manuel Barroso (once a Maoist, later president of the European Commission, and now non-executive chairman of Goldman Sachs), formed a coalition. This achieved almost nothing and made way for the Socialists' landslide victory in 2005. The economy slumped even further, wages barely increased (and remained well below those of the rest of Western Europe), while unemployment shot up. The global downturn of 2007–8 made matters even worse. The Socialists almost lost the 2009 election. At the 2011 elections they were comprehensively trounced: down to 28 per cent from 45 per cent of the vote in 2005. In 2015, on 32.3 per cent, they were able to form a government only because the Eurosceptic 'Left Bloc' (on 10.2 per cent) and the equally Eurosceptic Unitary Democratic Coalition of Communists and Greens (8.3 per cent) agreed to support them.

In spite of widespread scepticism about the stability of this 'left' coalition Portugal has done relatively well, with a reasonably high growth rate in 2017–18. The government engineered an economic recovery, halved unemployment (though it is still high), and eliminated the budget deficit in 2018 for the first time in over forty years.[2] The Socialists consolidated their position in the 2019 election, while the conservatives had the worst result in their history. The situation remains extremely unstable, not only because Portugal is poor and its economy in difficulty but because voter turnout has shrunk spectacularly: from over 90 per cent when democracy was established in 1975 to under 56 per cent in 2015 and only 48.6 per cent in 2019.

In 2013, in Austria, the Social Democratic party (SPÖ) was still the first party, but with only 26.8 per cent of the vote, just ahead of its Christian Democratic opponents (the ÖVP, now called,

Blair-like, the 'New' ÖVP). The right-wing FPÖ (Freedom Party) obtained 20.5 per cent, its best result ever, while the Greens reached a respectable 12.4. The way was open for yet another coalition between the Social Democrats and the ÖVP. These two parties had dominated Austrian politics since 1945, usually ruling together and sharing various posts, including civil service appointments. However, they were becoming less and less popular. The SPÖ-ÖVP coalition had already tried to placate xenophobia by restricting immigration, closing the border to refugees coming via the Balkan route, and introducing a 'burqa ban'. Such opportunistic policies did not help. Quite the contrary. Ominous changes were ahead. At the presidential elections of May 2016 the candidates of the two governing parties scored miserably, coming in fourth and fifth place. Third place went to Irmgard Griss, an independent, and former president of the Supreme Court. This was the first time since 1945 that the candidates of the two main parties had failed to make it to the final ballot. The two remaining contestants were the far-right candidate Norbert Hofer and the Green Party's Alexander Van der Bellen, who won by a few votes. But this was only a momentary respite (besides, the Austrian president is just a figurehead). At the October 2017 election, Sebastian Kurz of the Austrian People's Party (ÖVP), who was just over thirty, shifted his party to the right (as did the SPÖ) in a desperate bid to stem support for the far-right FPÖ, led by Heinz-Christian Strache, who as a twenty-year-old had been arrested for taking part in a march organised by a banned neo-Nazi movement modelled on the Hitler Youth. Kurz won the elections but with only 30 per cent of the vote. He formed a coalition with Strache's Freedom Party, which obtained key cabinet posts including the foreign, home, and defence ministries. The SPÖ managed, with 26.9 per cent, to come just ahead of the FPÖ (26 per cent) – a dismal performance for a party almost uninterruptedly in power since 1945, and which in 1975 had just over half the votes. Faced with the prospect of the anti-Semitic Freedom Party in government, the Jewish community in Austria expressed its concern in strong terms, later announcing they would boycott the Holocaust memorial day if Freedom Party politicians attended. However, the prime minister of the 'Jewish

state', Benjamin Netanyahu, lost no time in phoning Kurz to congratulate him.[3]

In April 2016, Strache had already done his bit to recycle himself
as a pro-Semite and 'make himself kosher' by going to Israel and
paying his respects at Yad Vashem, the Holocaust remembrance
centre (he had been invited by Netanyahu).[4] The recycling was
limited however. In May 2019 a video revealed that he had promised to help a woman posing as the niece of a Russian oligarch to
acquire business contracts in exchange for providing his campaign
with support from an Austrian tabloid – thus proving that he was
both corrupt and idiotic. He resigned, regretting having reacted as
a strutting teenager before a good-looking woman. The Austrian
government crumbled. At the September 2019 election, the far right
crumbled too, as did the SPÖ, while the Greens surged ahead and
Kurz increased his percentage. The future of Austrian politics is as
uncertain as ever. In November 2019 the Greens entered into formal
talks with Kurz's ÖVP; by the end of the year they had formed a
coalition. So much for those who thought the Greens had principles.

Politics has become a circus in which everyone turns to whoever
is available, following Bismarck's cynical dictum (in a letter to his
wife): 'One clings to principles only for as long as they are not put
to the test; when that happens one throws them away as the peasant
does his slippers.'[5]

The Dutch election results in March 2017 were catastrophic
for the left: three left parties, the Labour Party, the Socialists, and
the Greens, secured in total a smaller percentage of votes (23.9
per cent) than the Labour Party had on its own in 2012 (24.8 per
cent). The Labour Party had the worst result in its history, with
fewer votes than the other two left parties. To keep Geert Wilders'
far-right PVV out, the four centre-right parties formed an unstable
coalition under Mark Rutte, leader of the pro-business VVD party.
The coalition had a majority of just one in the fragmented thirteen-
party system, a system destined to become even more fragmented
as a new far-right party emerges to challenge Wilders: the Forum
for Democracy launched in 2016 by Thierry Baudet, who made
remarkable gains in 2019.

In 1997, social democratic and labour parties had been in power in eleven out of the fifteen states that were then EU members. Just over twenty years later, these parties were barely in power in only a handful of countries.

In Italy the Partito Democratico (PD) remained in power until the elections of March 2018. The PD was part of the social democratic 'family', and heir to the Communist Party. But it was soon completely 'de-communised'. The unrepentant communists survived in formations such as Rifondazione Comunista, but to secure parliamentary representation Rifondazione has had to forge alliances with other even smaller entities. The PD itself is hardly a 'real' social democratic party, whatever that may mean, since it is a melange of ex-communists and various groups, parties, and remnants of parties, including progressive liberals and Catholics who have no roots in anything resembling a socialist tradition.

Between 2011 and 2018, when Silvio Berlusconi lost power to the PD, there were four Italian prime ministers. The first, Mario Monti was an independent liberal economist supported by a grand coalition which included the Partito Democratico. He ruled for less than eighteen months, pursuing austerity policies. His successor, after the election of 2013, was Enrico Letta, who lasted less than a year. Then it was the turn of the PD leader Matteo Renzi, prime minister for twenty months at the head of a coalition which included a dissident faction of Berlusconi's party. Finally, in 2016, Paolo Gentiloni became prime minister as head of the same coalition. None of these four prime ministers in an apparently 'centre-left' coalition had ever been communist, socialist, or even left-wing: Monti was a liberal, Letta and Renzi had been Christian Democrats, and Gentiloni, though on the far left as a student, was the founder of a now defunct 'left' Christian formation called La Margherita (the Daisy). Before 2011, the leader of the left-of-centre L'Ulivo, Romano Prodi, prime minister in 1996–8 and 2006–8, had been a Christian Democrat. Only Massimo D'Alema (in power 1998–2000), of all prime ministers in the post-Tangentopoli era, had a clearly left past (as a former communist). So, for a long time, no Italian 'left' government has been led by anyone belonging to the socialist tradition.

Elsewhere the situation for traditional social democracy is even worse. In Britain between 2010 and 2019, the Labour Party lost four elections in a row. It obtained a creditable result in 2017 when led by Jeremy Corbyn – reviled and pilloried by virtually all his parliamentary colleagues and much of the liberal press – but in 2019 Corbyn lost decisively (see below).

In France, at the presidential election of April 2017, the official Socialist candidate, Benoît Hamon, only managed to obtain 6.3 per cent of the vote, and was out in the first round, coming fifth, after the 'neither left nor right' candidate Emmanuel Macron, the far-right Marine Le Pen, the moderate-right François Fillon, and even the far-left Jean-Luc Mélenchon. Two months later, in the first round of the legislative election, the Socialist Party (along with its allies) achieved 9.5 per cent, less than the Front National (13.2 per cent) and less than Mélenchon's 'La France Insoumise' (11 per cent). This was the most disastrous result for the Socialist Party in the entire history of the Fifth Republic, with the exception of Gaston Defferre who got only 5 per cent in the presidential elections of 1969.

In Germany it was no better. The SPD, whose leaders had been Chancellor in 1969–74 (Willy Brandt), 1974–82 (Helmut Schmidt), and 1998–2005 (Gerhard Schröder), was either a junior partner in a Christian Democrat-led coalition under Angela Merkel (2005–9 and 2013–17) or in opposition, as in 2009–13. At the general elections of 2017 the SPD mustered a miserable 20.5 per cent of the vote – its worst result ever, half what it had in 1979. The party leader, Martin Schulz, acclaimed as a 'safe pair of hands' who would revive the SPD and who, unlike Corbyn, was regarded as electable, wasn't. He eventually resigned and was succeeded by Andrea Nahles, the first woman to lead the SPD in its history. The true winners were the far-right AfD, who became the third party, though the FDP (the liberal Free Democratic Party) did well too, re-entering the Bundestag after four years out of it. The anti-establishment vote was particularly pronounced in the former East Germany, where the far-left party Die Linke did better than the SPD, while the AfD did better than the CDU.

Merkel's CDU too had its worst results since 1949 (246 seats, sixty-five fewer than in 2013) and found it difficult to form a government with liberals and Greens once the SPD (with 153 seats, forty fewer than in 2013) decided it would not be part of a new coalition. Then the SPD changed its mind. After over five months of painful negotiations, a new CDU-SPD 'grand coalition', or GroKo, finally emerged. The prospects were bleak. The CDU's Bavaria-based 'sister' party, the CSU (Christlich-Soziale Union), started to behave in a most unsisterly way. This did not pay off, electorally speaking: at the local elections in October 2018 the CSU dropped to below 40 per cent for the first time ever, while the Greens did very well (17.5 per cent); the SPD saw its vote halved, and AfD obtained 10 per cent. A similar result occurred the same month in Hesse, when the two main parties lost more than 10 per cent each, to the advantage of the Greens (which nearly replaced the SPD as the second party) and the AfD which secured 13 per cent. By the end of 2019 Merkel's government was in peril as a left-wing duo, Norbert Walter-Borjans and Saskia Esken, took charge of the SPD – a party desperate for a new role after years of subordination and incompetence.

In the countries of the former Soviet bloc the reaction against communism appears to have been extended to newly constituted social democratic parties, often born out of the ashes of communism.

Hungary was the most 'liberal' of the communist countries. It had a large and thriving private sector. In September 1989, the reformist communist leadership opened the border with Austria, allowing thousands of East Germans to flee to West Germany. The Berlin Wall had lost its purpose. It was the end of communism. The heir to the Communist Party was the Hungarian Socialist Party (MSZP). After a faltering start, it became the leading party in the new system. In 2006 it could still muster 43 per cent and form a government. In 2010 it crumbled to 19 per cent, improving slightly in 2014 (25 per cent). In April 2018, however, as Viktor Orbán confirmed his supremacy, the Hungarian Socialists could only muster a miserable 12 per cent.

In Slovenia the Social Democrats were in power until 2014, but only as a very junior partner in a centrist government: at the election of July 2014 they obtained less than 6 per cent of the vote, after a respectable 30 per cent in 2008. As in other former communist countries, politics in Slovenia is extremely volatile. A party calling itself 'Positive Slovenia' was the leading party in 2011; three years later it had disappeared. By 2014 the main party was the Modern Centre Party, which had just been formed and won over 34 per cent of the vote in that year's election. Previously it had been called the Party of Miro Cerar, led unsurprisingly by Miro Cerar. Cerar was one of the few liberal leaders in Eastern Europe: he faced impeachment over his support for a Syrian asylum seeker (Ahmad Shamieh) threatened with deportation, and who, though only recently arrived, had learnt Slovenian and integrated successfully. Opposition to Cerar continued without respite. He resigned in March 2018. Elections held two months later saw the anti-immigrant Slovenian Democratic Party (SDS) in first place with 25 per cent of the vote. Its leader, Janez Janša, had spent six months in prison in 2014 after being convicted on bribery charges (the conviction was later overturned by the Constitutional Court). Cerar's party finished fourth with only ten seats. Instability continued as a new centre-left party, the List of Marjan Šarec (LMS), emerged in second place with only 12.6 per cent of the vote. In September 2018, Šarec, who happens to be a comedian, was asked to form a minority government. This did not last long. In February 2020 Janša became prime minister at the head of a four-party coalition. The situation is as unstable as ever. Life is difficult for liberals in Eastern Europe.

In the Czech Republic the rise of Andrej Babiš also meant the end of the line for the traditional parties. The Social Democrats were the largest party at the elections of 2013 and formed a government, but since they had only 20 per cent of the vote, they were forced into a coalition with the small centrist Christian Democrats and ANO, another party which claims to be 'neither left nor right'. Its acronym stands for Action of Dissatisfied Citizens (Akce nespoko-jených občanů), and it is led by Andrej Babiš, who has little reason to be a dissatisfied since he is a billionaire. Founded in 2011, ANO was already the second party by 2013, with nearly 19 per cent of the vote. By 2017 it had polled almost 30 per cent.[6] The Social Democrats were pulverised (down to just over 7 per cent, their worst result ever, even behind the Communists), as were the Christian Democrats, though the economy was doing better than in most other EU countries. Even the so-called Pirate Party, champion of direct democracy, polled better than the Social Democrats (10.6 per cent).

Babiš, often referred to as the Czech Trump, had been a member of the Communist Party under communism and became a billionaire under capitalism with a strong financial stake in the chemical and food-processing industry, the profits of which he used to purchase media outlets. He was finance minister from 2014 to 2017, until being dismissed because of alleged improper financial dealings and tax evasion. He was formally charged on 9 October 2017 (a fortnight before the election). ANO, of course, is strongly against corruption and tax evasion. Babiš enjoys the protection of the Czech president, Miloš Zeman, re-elected in January 2018. A report by the EU anti-fraud unit concluded that Babiš had broken numerous laws to obtain European subsidies and, as a direct consequence, a vote of no-confidence in him was passed and he resigned. He resurfaced a few months later, in July 2018, when he was able to form a minority government with the Social Democrats and the support of the fifteen Communist MPs who, however, were to remain outside the government: a weird (and unstable) alliance of unprincipled politicians. The charges against Babiš were eventually dropped, but the Czechs did not remain quiet: June and November 2019 saw the biggest political protests since the fall of communism as an estimated 120,000 people gathered in Prague to demand Babiš's resignation. As I write he is still prime minister.

Babiš has rejected the EU refugee quotas and made pejorative remarks about the Romani, but there is worse than Babiš in the Czech Republic. The far-right Freedom and Direct Democracy Party was established in 2015. It is led by Tomio Okamura, a part-Japanese entrepreneur, born in Tokyo, who is rabidly anti-immigrant, wants to leave the EU, and who urged Czechs to walk pigs near mosques and stop eating kebabs. Okamura's party won just under 10.7 per cent of the vote in 2017.[7]

The situation is no better in the country which used to be the other half of Czechoslovakia, and where the left was still in power in 2017: Slovakia. This is an odd 'left'. The prime minister, Robert Fico (in office since 2012, having already been in power in 2006–10), is the leader of Direction – Social Democracy Party, a breakaway from the mainstream social democratic party (which has since disappeared), and began to rule the country in coalition with the far-right anti-Roma and anti-Hungarian Slovak National Party (SNP). In 2016, weeks before taking over the presidency of the EU, Fico declared that 'Islam has no place' in Slovakia.[8] His party was expelled from the Party of European Socialists (PES) in 2006 for its alliance with the SNP, but was readmitted in 2008 and is still a member even though it formed another coalition with the SNP in 2016. With remarkable hypocrisy, the PES declared, on 19 November 2015, that 'We firmly reject any form of racial hatred, xenophobia, anti-Semitism, Islamophobia, and all forms of intolerance and extremism.'[9] But Fico is still welcome in their ranks.

After the murder of an investigative journalist who had linked Fico to the Italian Mafia, Ján Kuciak, and his fiancée, and following huge demonstrations, Fico resigned and was succeeded by his deputy, Peter Pellegrini. All liberal hopes were not lost: the presidential elections of March 2019 saw the victory of the anti-corruption and environmentalist candidate, Zuzana Čaputová, but she has little political experience and the powers of the president are fairly limited. Besides, the neo-Nazi Marian Kotleba surged into fourth place with 10 per cent of the vote

At the February 2020 general election, Igor Matovič, the million aire leader of the conservative OLaNO party (short for 'Ordinary People and Independent Personalities' – Obyčajní Ľudia in Slovak) obtained 25 per cent of the vote and fifty-three seats in the 150-member Parliament. His party might well be against corruption but it is also homophobic and anti-abortionist. OLaNO also opposes the idea of distributing refugees around the EU according to a formula drawn up in Brussels, thus joining forces with Hungary, Poland, and the Czech Republic. This anti-immigrant stance is virtually the norm in Eastern Europe, with one analyst, writing in 2016, noting that in this matter, the left–right distinction has 'proved almost irrelevant … Hardly any mainstream party in the region dared challenge the prevailing attitude of rejecting

refugees.'[10] In terms of percentage of immigrants in the total population, Hungary, Lithuania, the Czech Republic, Slovakia, Bulgaria,
Romania, and Poland are at the bottom of the league table.[11]

Unlike its counterparts elsewhere in Europe, the Social Democratic
Party of Romania (SDP) is by far the largest party, notching almost
46 per cent of the vote in 2016 (admittedly on the lowest turnout
in the EU – less than 40 per cent), although this was not enough
to govern on its own. The level of corruption in the party (which
is in fact a centre-right party) and its allies has been high even by
Eastern European standards: since 2006 the former prime minister
Liviu Dragnea has been convicted and twenty current and former
ministers, fifty-three deputies, and nineteen senators have been
indicted. Dragnea was found guilty in April 2016 of vote-rigging
and received a two-year suspended sentence, but his party enthu-
siastically re-elected him as leader. Shortly afterwards the ruling
coalition produced a decree to pardon those in jail for corruption as
long as the sum involved did not exceed 200,000 lei (44,000 euro).
In other words, if you steal, don't steal too much. This sparked
massive protests in February 2017 and the decree was withdrawn.
In June 2018, Dragnea was sentenced to three and a half years in
prison for incitement to abuse of office, pending appeal. By October
2019 the SDP-led government fell on a vote of no confidence. A
month later the centrist president, Klaus Iohannis, was easily re-
elected (63 per cent) while the Social Democrats obtained their
worst ever result.

In Romania illiberalism is rife. The SDP has appointed itself the
champion of the peasantry and even tried to organise a referendum to restrict the constitutional definition of family, which would
effectively rule out the possibility of legalising same-sex marriage.
Same-sex marriage is legal in most of Western Europe but not
in most Eastern European countries. Poland, Slovakia, Bulgaria,
Lithuania, and Latvia do not offer *any* legal recognition for same-
sex relationships. For gays, the advent of post-communism has not
been much of a liberation.

In Spain, the PSOE (Partido Socialista Obrero Español – Socialist
Workers' Party), which had ruled uninterruptedly from 1982 to

1996 with an absolute majority of seats, lost in 1996, then ruled again between 2004 and 2011, led by José Zapatero. In 2011 disaster struck when the party suffered its worst defeat since the return of democracy in 1977. At the 2015 election the PSOE only managed to get 20 per cent, and a little more in 2016. In April 2019 it celebrated as a 'victory' the 28.7 per cent it obtained in the fourth election since 2011. Yet in 1982 the party had 48 per cent of the vote, one of the highest percentages ever gained by a social democratic party in post-war Europe. Popular discontent with the socialists as well as the conservative Christian-democratic Partido Popular (People's Party, PP) manifested itself with the surge of two new parties. The first, the leftist Podemos, obtained about 20–21 per cent in 2015 and 2016. The second, the liberal Ciudadanos (Citizens), reached just over 15 per cent in 2019. This led to the collapse of the two-party system.

To add to the complications facing Spain's traditional political parties, there was also a surge in Catalonian nationalism, leading to the crisis of 2017, while in May 2018 Spain's highest criminal court found that the governing Partido Popular was implicated in an illegal kickbacks-for-contracts scheme. On 1 June 2018 its leader, Mariano Rajoy, resigned. The socialist leader Pedro Sánchez was sworn in as prime minister, though his party had only eighty-four seats in the 350-seat Parliament. And though Sánchez behaved with remarkable generosity in welcoming refugees in peril turned away by the Italian interior minister Matteo Salvini (who also declared that the Romani should be expelled), uncertainty reigns more than ever, even after the progress achieved by the PSOE in 2019. More worrying was the rise of yet another party in 2019: Vox, a far-right party which obtained just over 10 per cent, a further sign that even Spain was not being spared the morbid symptoms of our time. In fact, in the second elections of 2019 Vox became the third party with 15 per cent, while Ciudadanos crumbled, the PP advanced, and the PSOE remained around the 28 per cent mark. After four elections in four years the result was a weak coalition between the PSOE and Podemos.

The economy played a major part in the crisis of the established political parties in Spain. In the twenty years prior to the global downturn of 2007, Spain grew more rapidly than the EU average. The opposite happened after 2007: growth plummeted, unemployment massively increased, there were more poor people, and the distribution of income was even more unequal, while private debt skyrocketed. Austerity policies simply made things worse.[12]

Matters evolved even more disastrously for social democracy in Greece, where the economy performed far more poorly than in Spain. As in Spain, the social democrats of PASOK (Panhellenic Socialist Movement) had dominated politics for much of the 1980s and 1990s. In the elections of 1981 PASOK won a landslide victory with 48 per cent of the vote, under the charismatic leader Andreas Papandreou. A period of substantial reforms followed, including the introduction of a national health service and civil rights. The party won again in June 1985 (with 46 per cent). It felt obliged to adopt austerity policies and as a result, though it still gained 40 per cent, PASOK lost the June 1989 election to the conservative opposition, New Democracy, on 44 per cent. This was not however sufficient for anyone to form a government without PASOK. Weak governments and further elections followed. PASOK was not yet dead and at the October 1993 elections it won another landslide victory (47 per cent) and Papandreou was prime minister once again. He was succeeded by the less charismatic Kostas Simitis, who was in turn succeeded by the even less charismatic George Papandreou, son of Andreas. So, between 1981 and 2011, PASOK was in power for some twenty-three years.

With the help of Goldman Sachs – later one of the beneficiaries of the 2007 subprime mortgage crisis which led to Greece's woes – statistics were modified to meet the European Union's requirements and hence to allow Greece to join the eurozone.[13] But accountants cannot resolve real problems forever and, during the global downturn, Greek GDP dropped by almost 7 per cent, and with it also PASOK's popularity. By 2015 the party was down to 5 per cent (in 2009 it had almost 44 per cent) and soon disappeared from the political scene. Into this vacuum stepped the far-left Syriza, founded in 2004 as a coalition of left parties, led by Alexis Tsipras. Syriza obtained 36 per cent of the vote – leaving it just one parliamentary seat short of an absolute majority and forcing it into an unholy alliance with the Independent Greeks, a nationalist, conservative, and anti-EU party. Ominously, the neo-Nazi Golden Dawn Party achieved 7 per cent, though it failed to reach the minimum 3 per cent in the election of July 2019. Greek Solution, a new party roughly on the same waveband – led by Kyriakos Velopoulos who claims to have received the blessing of the Holy Spirit – obtained close to 4 per cent and ten seats in Parliament. Most of its leaders are now in jail, convicted of criminal activities, including attempted murder.

In Turkey, of course, where the left was never strong, the situation was not much better. The People's Democratic Party (HDP), a coalition of assorted leftist forces (almost half from Kurdish regions), managed to secure 13 per cent in the 2015 elections, which was the highest ever vote for the left in Turkey. The following year there was an attempted coup by the supporters of the US-based Islamic cleric Fethullah Gülen. This was followed by repression which went well beyond Gülen's followers, involving other parties and, above all, the media. In this climate there is very little chance of the HDP emerging as a significant force. It will be lucky to survive.[14] To strengthen his authoritarian rule President Erdoğan held a referendum in April 2017 to change the constitution, dramatically increasing his powers. He won, albeit narrowly. The elections held on 24 June 2018 confirmed Erdoğan's power, though he lost control of Ankara, the capital, and of the largest city, Istanbul, in the municipal elections of March 2019.

Further afield, in India the long rule of the left-leaning Indian National Congress Party had given way to that of the Hindu nationalist Bharatiya Janata Party (BJP, Indian People's Party) led by Narendra Modi, back in power after the 2014 elections and handsomely re-elected in May 2019 even though he failed to deliver on his main promises: he had committed to create 20 million jobs, yet the unemployment rate was as high as ever; to erect 'smart cities' with skyscrapers and fast trains but they were nowhere to be seen; he had vowed to purify the Ganga, yet it is as filthy as ever.[15] Soon after the 2019 election victory Modi ratcheted up his anti-Muslim stance by abolishing the autonomous status of Jammu and Kashmir, where Muslims are a majority. He then enacted a new Islamophobic law, the Citizenship Amendment Act, which grants undocumented migrants from neighbouring countries Indian citizenship *unless they are Muslim*. This led to widespread protests, not just from Muslims but also from Hindus still committed to the idea of India as a secular nation. As for the defeated Congress Party, it tried to adopt a form of Indian nationalism, 'Like some ageing amnesiac chameleon, … attempting to relearn how to change colour, from the safe camouflage of Nehruvian secularism to a provocative Hindutva saffron', in the words of the Pakistani columnist F. S. Aijazuddin.[16]

Japan seems to have avoided the crisis of the established parties, since the ruling conservative Liberal Democratic Party won the October 2017 election with 48 per cent of the vote, and Shinzō Abe will go down as one of the longest serving in post-war Japanese history. This, however, does not mean there are no novelties in Japan. The second-largest party, the so-called Party of Hope (Kibō no Tō), also a conservative party, was formed just before the 2017 election on an anti-nuclear power platform, and obtained 20 per cent. Another new party, the Constitutional Democratic Party, which emerged from a split from the Liberal Democratic Party, notched up 8.7 per cent. In other words, two new conservative parties managed to obtain almost 30 per cent. As for the left, the situation is catastrophic: while the Communist Party drummed up 9 per cent but only one seat, the Social Democratic Party, which had been at 33 per cent in 1958 and was still receiving a respectable 24 per cent in 1990, barely registered with a derisory 1 per cent.

Meanwhile Japan, whose economy has been stagnant for over twenty years, suffers from an exceptionally low birth rate which will bring its population down from about 127 million in 2015 to 107 million in 2050. By then, 42.5 per cent of the population will be sixty-five or older. Some might claim this is all the fault of women, who do not have enough children (Japan has one of the lowest birth rates in the world) and tend not to go out to work (as compared to similar economies). But opinion polls suggest that women would be willing to have more babies if their husbands helped with child-rearing and housework (only 1.7 per cent of husbands took advantage of paternity leave in 2009). Besides, when women get pregnant they are often 'encouraged' to quit their jobs. Finally there are hardly any immigrants in Japan.[17] No immigrants, no babies, plenty of pensioners. The future looks bleak, though disaster for Japan has often been predicted and failed to materialise.

The future looks even bleaker for the left in Latin America. Around 2005 it was in power in Argentina, Bolivia, Brazil, Chile, Ecuador, Nicaragua, Paraguay, Uruguay, and Venezuela. In Venezuela many saw Hugo Chávez's victory in 1998 as a new revolutionary advance. By 2013, when Chávez died, the Venezuelan economy was in ruins, devastated by inflation and serious mismanagement by Chávez's successor, Nicolás Maduro. Millions of people left the country. Maduro's main rival, Juan Guaidó, though backed by fifty countries (including the US), has turned out to be a disappointment even to his supporters. Meanwhile Maduro's own political sagacity became ever more problematic as he advised women to have six children 'for the good of the country', even though 13 per cent of Venezuelan children were malnourished, according to UNICEF.[18]

In Brazil, the Workers' Party – in power for fourteen years after 2002, led by Luiz Inácio Lula da Silva (known as Lula), and later by Dilma Rousseff – was ousted in 2018 by the far-right candidate, Jair Bolsonaro, who became president. In Chile the Socialist Michelle Bachelet ruled from 2006 to 2010 and from 2014 to 2018. Her successor as president was Sebastián Piñera of the conservative National Renewal Party. In Peru, the last five presidents – none of whom were leftist, and who between them ruled the country for a total of thirty-three consecutive years – have either served time in jail for corruption or have been under investigation for it.[19] In Bolivia, Evo Morales, a socialist who became president in 2006 (and was the longest serving president so far and the only one with an indigenous background), introduced massive economic reforms, but by the end of 2019 he was facing major social unrest and was forced to resign. The following year, however, the left, having won the election, was back in power.

In Argentina, in 2015, former centre-left president (2007–15) Cristina Kirchner was indicted for fraud. However, by 2019 she had become vice-president under President Alberto Fernández, her former chief of staff. In Nicaragua, still one of the poorest countries in Latin America, Daniel Ortega, once the darling of the left, has turned out to be responsible for a repression of major proportions, thirty-nine years after the victory of the so-called Sandinista Revolution (though the Sandinistas were in opposition between 1990 and 2006).[20] The election in Mexico in 2018 of the anti-corruption candidate for the presidency, Andrés Manuel López Obrador, provides some hope for the future, but it is early days.

Traditional social democracy, then, has been comprehensively defeated not only in Europe but almost everywhere. None of this should be particularly surprising. It is always risky for a political party of the left to accept so much of the agenda of the right. Most social democratic parties sooner or later embraced a policy of austerity, allowed wages to stagnate and inequalities to increase, and privatised public services to an extent unimaginable thirty years ago. They allowed inequalities to increase and did not dare to tax the prosperous beneficiaries. And yet as Joseph Stiglitz has written, 'The theory that tax cuts and deregulation would ... lead to a new era of high growth has been thoroughly discredited.'

'Austerity', he adds, 'has never worked.'[21]

Even the IMF, once a stronghold of neoliberalism, has begun to doubt the wisdom of the past. Its most recent reports acknowledge that decreasing taxes for the rich has been counter-productive and has increased inequality, and that it was not true that giving the rich more money would increase investments, jobs, and growth. In other words, even the IMF thinks that, after all, 'trickle-down' economics is bunk. The 'trickle-down' was used by President Ronald Reagan to justify his income tax cuts, and given a (very) thin veneer of pseudo-academic respectability by Arthur Laffer and his totally discredited Laffer Curve which claimed that lower taxes may increase tax revenue. A report written by IMF economists in 2016 stated that 'Aspects of the neoliberal agenda ... have not delivered as expected'; that benefits from neoliberal policies 'seem fairly difficult to establish when looking at a broad group of countries'; and that 'the costs in terms of increased inequality are prominent'. It concluded with the following understatement: 'the benefits of some policies that are an important part of the neoliberal agenda appear to have been somewhat overplayed'.[22] No wonder some commentators suggested that the IMF had turned 'Corbynista'.[23]

The very rich of the 2020s may be even richer than the rich of yesterday, the much disparaged tycoons of the American Gilded Age at the turn of the twentieth century – families such as the Carnegies, the Rockefellers, and the Vanderbilts. The five richest people of our time – Jeff Bezos, Bill Gates, Warren Buffett, Amancio Ortega (the Spanish owner of Inditex, the world's largest clothing retailer, which includes Zara), and Facebook's Mark Zuckerberg – hold $425 billion of assets between them, equivalent to one-sixth of the UK's gross domestic product. None of them are manufacturers – in fact there are only thirteen industrialists in Bloomberg's list of the 100 richest people.[24] Today's capitalism, more than ever, is either up 'in the clouds' or in the retail trade.

Wealth inequality has even hit places that were once regarded as havens of capitalist decency, such as Sweden, where 'income inequality rose more rapidly than in any other OECD country since the 1990s, albeit from a very low level.'[25] In the US inequalities have grown even more dramatically, as the accompanying chart shows.

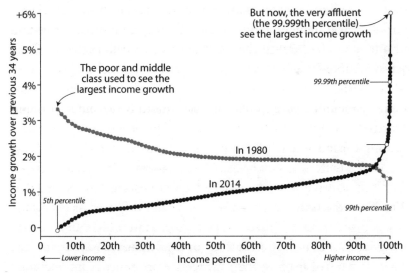

Figure 2 Income inequality in America, 1946–80 and 1980–2014

Note: Inflation-adjusted annual average growth using income after taxes, transfers, and non-cash benefits.

Source: David Leonhardt, 'Our Broken Economy, in One Simple Chart', *New York Times*, 7 August 2017.

However, according to the *World Inequality Report 2018* (whose editors include the French economist Thomas Piketty), income inequality, defined as the share of national income owned by the top 10 per cent, has grown since 1980 far less in Europe than in the Middle East (which is the highest, followed by India and Brazil). The bottom 50 per cent has nevertheless benefited from growth rates thanks to high growth in China, but, since 1980, the top 1 per cent of the richest individuals in the world has captured twice as much growth as the bottom 50 per cent.[26] The rise in wealth inequality has also been pronounced in the United States, where the share of wealth of the top 1 per cent rose from 22 per cent in 1980 to 39 per cent in 2014. Most of that increase was due to the rise of the top 0.1 per cent, i.e., the super-rich. In the UK relatively few households receive an income well above the average GDP per person.[27] The top 0.1 per cent number only 50,000 people in a population of 65.5 million. Since no one can win an election by favouring the top 0.1 per cent, let alone the top 10 per cent, even conservatives are worried. In fact the UK is much more unequal (in terms of the ratio of the top 1 per cent to median income) than Germany, France, Italy, or Spain.[28] Growing income inequality is 'one of the major economic events of our time'. Its level in the most unequal of affluent countries is 'unsustainable'.[29]

The struggle against inequalities could have been an obvious social democratic card to play. Instead these parties opted for what they thought was caution: pandering to the dominant pro-market ideology. And so they lost the game.

The Nasty Parties

In 2002, after two election defeats for the British Conservative Party, Theresa May, still more than thirteen years away from becoming prime minister, warned her party at its annual conference: 'let's not kid ourselves. There's a way to go before we can return to government … Our base is too narrow and so, occasionally, are our sympathies. You know what some people call us: the nasty party.'

Sometimes politicians tell the truth. She went on, pitilessly: 'At the last general election 38 new Tory MPs were elected. Of that total only one was a woman and none was from an ethnic minority. Is that fair? Is one half of the population entitled to only one place out of 38?'[30]

And yet, when May was home secretary (2010–16), new rules came into force requiring migrants from the Caribbean (in the country at Britain's invitation) to prove they had lived in Britain for decades or face deportation (it later emerged that the Home Office had destroyed landing cards that could prove when they came to UK). Even the anti-immigration *Daily Mail* was outraged at the 'horrendous' treatment of these migrants.[31] Some found themselves in a state of deep anxiety when, after decades of working and paying taxes, they lost their jobs and their homes, and even had cancer treatment withheld.

The outcry was such that May, by then prime minister, and Amber Rudd, her home secretary, were forced in April 2018 into a grovelling apology, dishonestly blaming civil servants who, after all, were just obeying orders. This was no 'mistake'. In 2012 David Cameron had set up the 'Hostile Environment Working Group' to deal with immigrants who might be in the UK without adequate documentation – the outrageous term 'hostile environment' was first used under a New Labour home secretary, Alan Johnson. Later, in a March 2013 speech on immigration, Cameron – supported by the leader of the Liberal Democrat Party Nick Clegg and by the home secretary Theresa May – declared that 'we're going to radically toughen up the way we deal with illegal migrants working in this country. Frankly, right now, today it is too easy to be an illegal migrant in Britain.'[32] To make clear how nasty she was going to be, May encouraged illegal migrants to leave voluntarily by having vans carrying the threatening message 'In the UK illegally? Go home or face arrest' drive around aimlessly for one month in 2013. One result of the 'hostile environment' policy was that thousands of foreign students, legally in the UK, were ordered to leave on the basis of dubious and questionable evidence.[33] The 2014 and 2016 Immigration Acts, promulgated by the Home Office, also mandated that landlords, employers, banks, and NHS services should run immigration status checks, thus turning them into de facto police snoopers and encouraging them to discriminate and humiliate anyone who did not seem to be 'really' British. The country itself was becoming increasingly nasty.

Conservatives, in Britain and elsewhere, were not always the 'nasty' parties. Western Europe was once characterised by a kind of compassionate conservatism which did not celebrate capitalism but accepted it within certain constraints. This is why, in nineteenth-century Germany, Bismarck was a pioneer of the welfare state, as was the British Liberal Party, and why even the Tories promoted social reforms. In France, under the Third Republic, pro-monarchist Catholics were 'reactionary' in every sense, but on social questions they were not as regressive as politicians of the centre, the so-called Radicals. Towards the end of the 1950s, French conservatism, under the banner of Charles de Gaulle, was 'compassionate' in many ways, above all in adopting social reforms and using a planning system to mellow the untrammelled development of market forces. This allowed de Gaulle to refuse to be characterised as either left or right (well before Macron used this ancient formula as if he had invented it).[34] In Austria, the Christian Democrats, usually in alliance with socialists, were in charge of the country with the largest public sector in Western Europe. In Germany, Christian Democrats proclaimed a 'social market' economy in which the 'social' was as important as the 'market'.

In Britain, the Tories, in power throughout the 1950s and until 1964, refrained from dismantling the welfare state and built more public housing than Labour had done previously.[35] In Italy the Christian Democratic Party, in power uninterruptedly from 1945 to the 1990s, tried, often successfully, to stem the advance of socialism by introducing welfare reforms and aimed at a kind of 'historic compromise' between capitalism and socialism. They even had their own trade unions and dramatically expanded a public sector that had been created by Mussolini to protect the Italian banking system threatened by the crash of 1929. When the Christian Democrat Party collapsed in 1993, crushed by the weight of the Tangentopoli scandals, it reverted to its original name, Partito Popolare, but no one, not even political parties, can be virgins twice. In order to survive, the more progressive elements of Italian social Catholicism merged eventually with the left-of-centre Partito Democratico (heirs to the communists).

But eventually, European conservatives turned 'nasty', above all in Britain, where Margaret Thatcher reconstituted the Conservative Party as a clearly defined neoliberal party with a fig-leaf of nationalism. The poor became scroungers and single mothers became 'feckless'; traditional Conservatives who opposed this 'nastiness' were dubbed 'wets'.

At the 1992 Conservative Party conference, Peter Lilley, then secretary of state for social security, produced a very nasty parody of Gilbert and Sullivan's *The Mikado*. It was one of the most disgusting speeches in modern British politics, the well-heeled making fun of the poor before a well-heeled audience. Lilley declared he was, in his best odious mode, 'closing down the something-for-nothing society' ('something for nothing' became a well-established trope in right-wing anti-welfare circles – it sounds good and means nothing). He then intoned:

> I've got a little list
> Of benefit offenders who I'll soon be rooting out
> And who never would be missed
> There's young ladies who get pregnant just to jump the housing
>   queue
> And dads who won't support the kids
>   of ladies they have ... kissed
> And I haven't even mentioned all those sponging socialists
> I've got them on my list
> And there's none of them be missed
> There's none of them be missed.[36]

In spite of Lilley's promises, the 'scroungers' have yet to be rooted out: over twenty years later the government was still at it, while the likes of Richard Branson, the boss of Virgin, was a 'tax exile' and his company preserved its offshore status to minimise the taxes it paid to the UK. Did anyone put him on the list? Not even when, with amazing chutzpah in the middle of the coronavirus crisis, he not only asked for state aid but requested his staff at Virgin Atlantic to take weeks of unpaid leave.[37]

Meanwhile Lilley himself, a convinced Brexiteer, received over $400,000 in share options (legally) as non-executive director of Tethys Petroleum, a Cayman Islands-based oil company, while still a 'full-time' member of the House of Commons. He was one of three MPs to vote against the Climate Change Act 2008 (overwhelmingly supported by both government and opposition) – a brave stand which must have been warmly applauded by his employers at Tethys Petroleum. He was elevated to the peerage in 2018.

With the Conservatives back in power in 2010, the Chancellor of the Exchequer George Osborne embarked on a massive austerity programme while cutting taxes for the rich, i.e. those earning more than £150,000 a year. In 2010, the former Tory leader Iain Duncan Smith, now works and pension secretary and one of the least likeable exponents of the recently formed Conservative-Liberal coalition, introduced the idea of 'universal credit', aimed at simplifying the welfare system. The plan was to bring a number of benefits into a single monthly payment devised to get people 'back to work'. One of the many problems was that people would have had to wait six weeks before getting any benefits, and for many, six weeks was far too long: bills have to be paid, rents cannot wait, and children have to be fed every day. Recipients who called a 'help' line were charged 55p a minute. The outcry was such that the government was shamed into withdrawing the phone charges and cutting the waiting time – but only from six to five weeks. Some unemployed people would have to spend thirty-five hours a week looking for work under supervision, thus 'simulating the working day' and thus ending Britain's supposed 'something-for-nothing culture'.[38] In 2014 the very same Iain Duncan Smith restricted benefits to the first two children in families receiving tax credit. Only the well-off, it seemed, should be allowed to have more than two children. Duncan Smith described the measure as a 'brilliant idea'. Even the *Daily Mail* was critical.[39] On 18 March 2016, Duncan Smith, to general amazement, resigned from the government claiming he was unable to accept its planned cuts to disability benefits and attacking its austerity programme as divisive and unfair. The previous year he had told disabled people to work their way out of poverty. A year later he had found a conscience, presumably his own.

For some families, universal credit meant being worse off by £2,800 a year, according to the think-tank The Resolution Foundation, whose executive chairman is the former Conservative minister David Willetts.[40] The UK National Audit Office, having analysed the universal credit system, concluded in a damning report that it cost more than the benefit system it replaced and does not help anyone. In other words the whole scheme was an unmitigated disaster.

Austerity continued after the Conservative victory at the 2015 election. They now had a small but working majority and no longer needed the Liberal Democrats, who had been punished severely for having participated in straightforward austerity policies. So jejune were the Lib Dems of the basic strategic principles of coalition politics, that, when in coalition, they did not seek or obtain any of the major offices of state: the chancellorship of the Exchequer, the Home Office or the Foreign Office. Their leader, the ineffectual Nick Clegg, was content to become the deputy prime minister, a powerless position whose powerlessness was amply demonstrated by the fact that his predecessor in that post under Labour had been John Prescott, a second-rate politician full of himself.

Though the Liberals had been ineffectual and incompetent, they constituted a weak barrier against nastiness. Now there was no barrier. George Osborne launched, with obvious relish, a crack down on benefits claimants. His Welfare Reform and Work Bill (piloted in July 2015 by Duncan Smith) included forcing 200,000 long-term unemployed people either to undertake 'community work' or attend a job centre every day. Failing to find work was obviously their fault. The Parliamentary Labour Party, more than ever in disarray having lost yet another election, and in the middle of electing a leader, decided to abstain on the welfare bill instead of voting against it (as oppositions are supposed to do), terrified that voters might think they were soft on scroungers. Labour's acting leader, Harriet Harman, explained that 'We cannot simply say to the public you were wrong at the election' – an absurd non-sequitur, equivalent to saying that those who voted Labour were wrong.[41]

This was reminiscent of 1997 when Labour, pandering to Tories and fearful of not being sufficiently pro-business, decided to stick with Tory spending plans for the following two years in an attempt to show they could be trusted with the economy; as a consequence the Labour government, with Harriet Harman as secretary of state for social security, decided to cut benefits to all new lone parents (mainly women) of children under five.

Back in 1997 the Labour dissidents amounted to forty-seven MPs; in 2015 forty-eight voted against the welfare bill. They were joined by the Scottish National Party, the Liberal Democrats, Plaid Cymru, the one Green MP, and even by the Democratic Unionist Party of Northern Ireland. Of the four candidates for the leadership of the Labour Party, only Jeremy Corbyn voted against it. He soon became party leader. London mayoral candidates Diane Abbott, Sadiq Khan, and David Lammy also defied the whip. Sadiq Khan was soon elected mayor, despite the predictions (such as those of Peter Kellner's YouGov) that Tessa Jowell, a Blairite who toed the party line, was best positioned to win the mayoralty.[42] Labour politics was unravelling, to the surprise of the 'commentariat'.

The Conservatives have been the 'nasty' party for a long time, particularly the activists and even more so the faithful who turn up at the party's annual conference, often pejoratively described by some Tory leaders (and not just them) as the 'flog 'em and hang 'em' brigade. In the old days, before Thatcher, the party leadership was confident that, along with having normal reactionary views, activists were also imbued with an old-fashioned sense of deference and were content, sheep-like, to leave actual policies to the grandees who dominated the party. But 'flog 'em and hang 'em' had become a fairly accurate description of rank-and-file Tories. According to a study by Queen Mary University of London, Conservatives are 'a breed apart' from members of the other main political parties, with strong tendencies towards illiberal and authoritarian attitudes: more of them are homophobic, support the death penalty, favour controlling the media to uphold conventional morality, and are overwhelmingly pro-austerity (according to the study, 98 per cent of Labour supporters, 93 per cent SNP supporters, and 75 per cent of Lib Dems were opposed to austerity).[43]

For decades the Conservative rank and file had been held at bay by the party leadership and their own sense of deference. Then Thatcher arrived and she spoke the language of the rank and file. She let the nasty genie out of the bottle; activists could finally say what they were thinking. But after the crushing victories of the Thatcher era (in 1979, 1983, and 1987) and John Major's narrow victory in 1990, the Tories lost three elections in succession (1997, 2001, and 2005), were unable to achieve a majority in 2010 (hence the coalition with the Liberal Democrats), before winning with a small majority in 2015 which they promptly lost in 2017. In other words, between 1987 and 2019 there had not been a satisfactory win for the Tories. Finally, in 2019, the buffoonish and arguably still nasty Boris Johnson led his party to an overwhelming victory.

The Conservatives had been in opposition for thirteen years in spite of having more campaign money than Labour, most of the press on their side, and the help of the Australian Lynton Crosby, a political strategist some called the 'Wizard of Oz', who was clearly very good at convincing people he could win elections but not that good at actually winning them. He had managed the Conservative campaign in 2005, which the Tories lost in spite of the racist slogans he advised them to use. He advised them again in 2015, when they just scraped a win. He also advised them in the 2016 election for the London mayoralty – another defeat, though Crosby was awarded a knighthood. His despicable attempt to link the Labour candidate Sadiq Khan to terrorism backfired, and Khan trounced the photogenic but not very intelligent Conservative candidate Zac Goldsmith (one of the few Conservatives to lose his seat in the 2019 elections, only to be given a peerage by Boris Johnson). Finally, Crosby was also Theresa May's election strategist in the 2017 general election, in which, though she was widely expected to win by a landslide, she lost her parliamentary majority.

Crosby's strategy consisted in running opinion polls and then telling people what they want to hear. He was paid millions (four millions according to the *Daily Telegraph*) for such a clever insight.[44] Tim Bell, the advertising and PR man who advised Margaret Thatcher during her election victories in the 1970s and 1980s, said

of Lynton Crosby in 2017 'The campaign was entirely negative ...
That's Lynton Crosby's style. He's a one-trick pony.'[45] It was Crosby
who devised Theresa May's slogan for the campaign: 'Strong and
Stable Leadership' – the butt of jokes ever since. Apparently, she got
fed up with hearing herself say 'strong and stable'. 'You're making
me sound stupid,' she complained in vain to Sir Lynton Crosby.[46]
Crosby, meanwhile, went on doing what he is good at, namely,
getting paid for lobbying on behalf of the Saudi government, fossil
fuel producers, tobacco and sugary drinks producers and, allegedly,
even anti-cycling campaigners.[47]

In 2009 the Tories formally aligned themselves with the nasti-
est parties in Europe when David Cameron, in order to appease
his party's Eurosceptic wing, withdrew his MEPs from the
centre-right European People's Party (EPP-ED) in the European
Parliament to form the Alliance of Conservatives and Reformists
in Europe alongside clearly right-wing and far-right anti-EU
parties including the Belgian New Flemish Alliance, the Czech
Civic Democratic Party, the Finns Party, the Greek Solution, the
far-right Swedish Democrats, the almost-fascist Fratelli d'Italia (to
the right of Salvini's Lega), the Polish Law and Justice Party, and,
more recently, the Croatian Conservative Party, and the Spanish
far-right Vox.

Elsewhere where nastiness in some form or other prevailed,
the ones who really suffered were, as usual, the poorer members
of society. In France, during the five years of Nicolas Sarkozy's
presidency (2007–11), more than half of the tax cuts went to the
better-off households. Another chunk was handed over to enterprises. The cuts were embedded in a law described with the acronym
TEPA: Travail (work), Emploi (employment), and Pouvoir d'achat
(purchasing power).[48] France became less competitive and unemployment increased.[49]

Of course, there are far nastier parties in power in Europe than
the British Tories or Sarkozy's Les Républicains. In Poland there is
the Law and Justice Party (PiS, Prawo i Sprawiedliwość), founded in
2001 by the twin brothers Jarosław and Lech Kaczyński (Lech died
in a plane crash in 2010). After the party won the 2005 election,
Lech Kaczyński became president and Jarosław prime minister. The

PiS lost the 2007 and 2011 elections to conservative parties, before returning to power in 2015, a victory confirmed in 2019 with an improved majority.

Polish politics has veered to the right. The left died in 2015 when the United Left, a political alliance of various left groups, failed to reach the 8 per cent threshold for a coalition and ended up with no parliamentary representation. The main conservative party (to the 'left' of the Law and Justice Party) is Civic Platform, an unabashedly neoliberal outfit, which in 2015 achieved just under 25 per cent. To add to the surrealism of Polish politics, the third party in 2015 was 'Kukiz'15', a right-wing party named after its leader, the punk rock musician Paweł Kukiz. The Law and Justice Party, though winning only 37.5 per cent of the votes achieved, thanks to the electoral system, secured an absolute majority in Parliament. Though pro-welfare, it favours a strong authoritarian state and defends Poland's 'traditional moral values', i.e. those of the Roman Catholic Church. It seeks to control the judiciary and the civil service, restrict abortion, and make life difficult for homosexuals. Oral contraceptives are difficult to obtain, while the 'morning after' contraceptive pill requires a prescription, in defiance of human rights groups and European Medicines Agency guidelines.[50]

The stripping away of women's rights had started much earlier, in March 1993, under 'normal' conservative governments, including one led by a woman, Hanna Suchocka. This produced some of the most restrictive abortion legislation in Europe: abortion is allowed only when the pregnancy threatens the life or the health of the mother, or if the foetus is seriously damaged, or if the woman has been raped.[51]

In December 2017 the Polish Parliament approved proposals which in effect granted the Law and Justice Party control of judicial appointments, a move strongly criticised not only by the European Union but also by the president of the European Council, Donald Tusk, himself a former conservative Polish prime minister, and the former Polish president and founder of Solidarność, Lech Wałęsa. The European Commission has formally warned Poland that 'fundamental values' are at risk if the country continues with its plans to control the judiciary and the media.

The PiS is strongly Islamophobic in a country where (see above) there are virtually no Muslims.[52] The party wallows in fake self-pitying memories, supported by the 'other Poland – rural, pious, the silent losers by reckless neoliberal "transformation" and the collapse of state industry'.[53] In November 2017, tens of thousands of nationalist demonstrators marched through Warsaw to mark Poland's independence day. Some were carrying or shouting slogans in favour of 'white' Europe; others chanted 'Pure Poland, white Poland!', 'Refugees out!', and 'Pray for an Islamic Holocaust!' One demonstrator interviewed by state television, which described the event as 'a great march of patriots', declared he was marching to 'remove Jewry from power'. The interior minister, Mariusz Błaszczak, praised the marchers.[54]

Poland is not a nice place for liberals, Jews, Muslims, gays, social-ists, or women who might need an abortion. When the prime minister, Beata Szydło, resigned in December 2017, her successor Mateusz Morawiecki (the real boss remained Jarosław Kaczyński) immedi-ately declared that his 'dream' was to 're-Christianize the EU'.[55] As elections for the European Parliament were approaching, Kaczyński called 'LGBT ideology' a 'threat to Polish identity, to our nation, to its existence and thus to the Polish state', while almost 100 munic-ipalities across a third of Poland have declared themselves to be 'LGBT-ideology-free', thus creating a hostile space for anyone who is not heterosexual or committed to the so-called 'natural family'.[56] In Poland as in Hungary, feminism is seen by those in power as a foreign project working against the national interest.[57]

These morbid symptoms have a multiplicity of causes. The Polish 'shock therapy', attributed, perhaps unfairly, to the econ-omist Jeffrey Sachs (not a neoliberal), led to massive emigration (more than 2 million since Poland's accession to the EU in 2004) and contributed to the conviction of many of those who remained that the country had been betrayed by pro-Western cosmopolitan elites (even though much of what improved was due to EU funds, of which Poland is a major recipient along with Hungary).

In Hungary too, the prime minister Viktor Orbán invokes 'Christian values', while building razor-wire fencing and putting water cannons on the country's borders to keep refugees out. The European Commission decided to take both Hungary and Poland to the European Court of Justice (ECJ) for refusing to take in refugees as part of the EU's quota system. Along with 'political correctness' and the independent media, Orbán lambasts the alleged immorality of the West and its 'liberal elites' as well as 'greedy bankers'; declares wars on NGOs (to the alarm of the United Nations and of Amnesty International), whom he accuses of interfering in Hungary's internal affairs; and has tried to close down the Central European University funded by George Soros, his bête noire.[58] While the Socialists, once enamoured with Blairism, remain strong in Budapest (where the opposition candidate won the 2019 mayoral race), Orbán's party, Fidesz (Hungarian Civic Alliance), once the party of progressive urban youth and of the intelligentsia, is now the party of Hungary's rural backwaters, of nationalist Catholicism, of xenophobia, Euroscepticism, family values, and, last but not least, of oligarchs.[59]

Orbán became prime minister in 1998, when his party obtained only 26 per cent of the vote. It soon had to give way to a Socialist administration and remained out of power until 2010, when Orbán romped back in with a staggering 52 per cent and two-thirds of the parliamentary seats. Re-elected in 2014, he used his majority to take control of the judiciary as well as public radio and television, closing down the leading opposition paper, *Népszabadság*. *Népszabadság* was then bought, along with other papers, by Lőrinc Mészáros, one of his closest friends, who had become a wealthy oligarch only after Orbán became prime minister. Orbán routinely attacks the 'weak, sclerotic, out-of-touch leadership of the EU'. He was quick to congratulate Recep Tayyip Erdoğan after the successful referendum of April 2017 which granted the Turkish leader more powers. And, of course, he is a supporter and admirer of Vladimir Putin as well as of Donald Trump. There is virtually no left opposition of any significance in Hungary.

On 22 July 2017, in a speech at the 28th Summer Open University in Bálványos (part of Romania with a significant Hungarian minority), Orbán described the worldwide struggle between a 'transnational elite' and patriotic national leaders like himself and

Donald Trump ('we were forerunners of this approach, the new patriotic Western politics'). He then attacked the 'alliance' forged in Brussels against Hungary:

> The members of this alliance are the Brussels bureaucrats and their political elite, and the system that may be described as the Soros Empire.... there is a Soros plan [to bring Muslim immigrants into Europe] ... both the Brussels bureaucrats and George Soros have a vested interest in weakening Central Europe ... we'll have to stand our ground against Soros's mafia network and the Brussels bureaucrats, and the media operated by them.[60]

The anti-Soros hysteria knows no limits in Hungary. A large poster depicting George Soros was glued to the floor of the number 49 tram in Budapest so that passengers would walk all over his face.[61] During the 2018 election campaign, mired in scandals and unremitting anti-immigration and Islamophobic rhetoric, Orbán compared the struggle against 'Uncle George' to the struggle of the Hungarians against the Ottomans, the Habsburgs, and the Soviets.[62] It obviously paid off: he was returned with an increased majority (on an increased turnout), thus confirming his two-thirds majority in Parliament (with just under 50 per cent of the vote).

On 9 October 2017, András Aradszki, the secretary of state for energy, declared that what he called the 'Soros Plan' was 'inspired by Satan' and that it was the duty of Christians to fight against it.[63] György Schöpflin – who lived in the UK from 1950 to 2004, eventually becoming an undistinguished professor at the School of Slavonic and East European Studies, before becoming an MEP – disgraced his former profession but secured his fifteen minutes of fame when he advocated putting pigs' heads on Hungary's borders to repel Muslim refugees, tweeting that a 'pig's head would deter more effectively'.[64] Both Aradszki and Schöpflin are members of the Hungarian Christian Democratic People's Party, which would be unable to pass the election threshold without the help of Fidesz.

Israel too has ditched any pretence of liberalism. This was a country founded by 'socialist' Zionists and long ruled by a Labour Party, which, under the name 'Zionist Union', was unable to master more than 18.6 per cent in the 2015 elections. Israel has been ruled for many years by Benjamin Netanyahu (five times prime minister), an outspoken advocate of the 'free market'. He has liberalised banking, privatised what was a huge state sector, introduced a welfare-to-work programme, cut pensions, and massively subsidised the 600,000 settlers in the illegally occupied West Bank – to the alarm of progressive Jews.[65]

Netanyahu has hysterically tried to scare the Israeli press into submission, and has regularly attacked the judiciary and the police, who have recommended that he be indicted on corruption, bribery, and fraud.[66] He would not be the first major Israeli politician involved in crimes (Wikipedia even has an entry titled 'List of Israeli public officials convicted of crimes'). Avraham Hirschson, a former minister of finance, was convicted in 2009 of stealing millions of shekels from the National Workers Labor Federation while he was its chairman. He was sentenced to five years and five months, serving three years and four months. Ehud Olmert, a former prime minister (2006–9) and for ten years mayor of Jerusalem, was convicted of corruption and tax evasion and given twenty-seven months (he served sixteen). Even more seriously Moshe Katsav, president of the State of Israel 2000–7, was convicted of two counts of rape, jailed, and then released in 2016 having served only five years.

Netanyahu is a foreign-policy hawk who would love to obliterate Iran, has no intention of withdrawing from the illegally occupied West Bank or making life easier for its Palestinian inhabitants, all this while pretending to be seeking peace, a ploy which only convinces useful idiots and those in bad faith. In October 2017 even the Israeli president, Reuven Rivlin (a member of Netanyahu's party), lost patience and, in a speech to the Knesset criticised Netanyahu's anti-democratic behaviour.[67]

In the US many Jews are torn; the majority still support the Zionist dream while voting for the Democrats, but are perturbed by the growing influence of right-wing Zionists and their pandering to American nationalism. Israel is rapidly losing its hold on young American Jews, who realise that the 'Jewish state' is antithetical to their liberal values.[68] They are right to be worried: in 2017 the Zionist Organization of America invited the Islamophobic 'alt-right' activist Steve Bannon to its annual gala, alongside a number of hawkish Zionists, including the prominent lawyer Alan Dershowitz and Joe Lieberman (Democratic candidate for vice-president in 2000).

Netanyahu boasts of his friendship with all those on the right: Matteo Salvini, Viktor Orbán, Narendra Modi, Sebastian Kurz, Jair Bolsonaro, and, of course, Donald Trump. Candidates for the nationalist Alternative for Germany (AfD) overwhelmingly profess to be pro-Israeli.[69] Netanyahu is even on good terms with Saudi Arabia and the Gulf monarchies, all keen to face the 'threat' from Iran.[70]

Obama is not a friend of Netanyahu: at the G20 meeting in 2011, microphones accidentally left switched on picked up Obama telling Sarkozy, who had just told him that Netanyahu was a 'liar': 'You're fed up with him? I have to deal with him every day!'[71] This did not stop Obama from signing, in 2016, an agreement to give Israel $38 billion in military assistance over the following decade, the largest such aid package given to any country in American history.[72] Matters improved further for Netanyahu with Trump's election, and even more with the US recognition of Jerusalem as Israel's capital – a widely criticised new low in American foreign policy. Only seven states (in addition to Israel and the US) immediately supported the American recognition in a vote at the UN. And what states! They were Guatemala (run by Jimmy Morales, a right-wing evangelical Christian and TV comedian who boasts an honorary degree from the Hebrew University), Honduras (an authoritarian regime with one of the highest murder rates in the world), Togo (a particularly bloodthirsty dictatorship), Nauru (a de facto Australian dependency known, incidentally, for topping the world obesity league), and Micronesia, Palau, and the Marshall Islands – all members of the US-dominated COFA (Compact of Free Association). Eventually, in November 2019, Trump even recognised the illegally occupied territories of the West Bank and its Jewish settlements.

Israel had already reciprocated Trump's gesture in advance by being the only country to vote against a United Nations resolution in November 2017, condemning America's economic embargo against Cuba (the resolution was approved by 191 to 2). Trump had threatened to cut off aid to states which supported the resolution (which would have included some of the main recipients of American aid in the Middle East). This scared no one and led the former CIA Director, John O. Brennan, to tweet that the White House's threat 'is beyond outrageous. This shows that Trump expects blind loyalty and subservience from everyone – qualities usually found in narcissistic, vengeful autocrats.'[73]

The love affair between Israel and Trump continued in March 2019 when Trump recognised the Israeli claim to the Golan Heights, an annexation which is almost universally regarded as in contravention of the Fourth Geneva Convention, which makes it illegal for an occupying power to allow its civilians to settle in occupied territory.

Trump may be a friend of Israel, but is he a friend of the Jews? He has praised pastor Robert Jeffress of the First Baptist Dallas Church, who once said Jews can't be saved.[74] Jews, though, are in good company, since the lunatic pastor also said the same about Mormons, Muslims, and Hindus. None of this stopped him from being invited to contribute to the service at the opening of the new US embassy in Jerusalem.[75]

Netanyahu is actually the 'soft' face of the Israeli government. The 'hard' one is that of Avigdor Lieberman, a Moldova-born immigrant and leader of the nationalist Yisrael Beiteinu Party who enjoys the support of the million or so Jews who left the former USSR. Zeev Sternhell, the renowned Israeli historian, called him 'perhaps the most dangerous man in Israel'.[76] Lieberman regards Iran as 'the biggest threat facing the Jewish people since the Second World War'.[77] He has called for the execution of Israeli Arab MPs who meet with Hamas.[78] He said in 2002: 'if it were up to me I would notify the Palestinian Authority that tomorrow at ten in the morning we would bomb all their places of business in Ramallah', adding: 'Destroy the foundation of all the authority's military infrastructure, all of the police buildings, the arsenals, all the posts of the security forces ... not leave one stone on another. Destroy everything.' After 250 Palestinian prisoners were granted an amnesty in 2003, he declared: 'It would be better to drown these prisoners in the Dead Sea ... since that's the lowest point in the world.'[79] Almost as hard as Lieberman is Netanyahu's fellow Likud member Tzipi Hotovely, Israel's deputy foreign minister (Netanyahu holds the foreign ministry portfolio himself), who would be regarded almost anywhere else as a religious fanatic and is now ambassador to the UK. As Netanyahu was pretending to be willing to negotiate a settlement, Hotovely announced, referring to the occupied territories, 'We need to return to the basic truth of our rights to this country. This land is ours. All of it is ours.'[80] A strong majority of Israeli Jews, 61 per cent, actually believe that Israel was given to the Jews by God.[81]

Hotovely and other Israeli religious politicians do not seem to be aware that, if we go by the biblical account, God 'gave' the Jews *all land* from the Euphrates to the River of Egypt. According to Genesis 15:18–21, God told Abraham: 'To your descendants I give this land, from the river of Egypt to the great river, the Euphrates – the land of the Kenites, Kenizzites, Kadmonites, Hittites, etc.' Since the Euphrates flows from Turkey to the Persian Gulf (having joined the Tigris) – and assuming that the 'river of Egypt' is the Nile and not the half-dried stream Wadi el-Arish just south of Gaza – a claim could be made, on the basis of Genesis, that God promised the Jews not only present-day Israel and the occupied territories but also Lebanon, Syria, Jordan, Iraq, Kuwait, most of Turkey, and perhaps even Saudi Arabia, the Emirates, and bits of Egypt. You can go a long way towards folly with the Bible in one hand and the sword in the other.

This divine promise might have been at the back of the mind of the orthodox rabbi Eli Ben-Dahan, of the Jewish Home Party, who also declared that Palestinians are 'animals, not human' (*Times of Israel*, 11 May 2005). At the time he was deputy minister for religious services. There is worse: Dov Lior, when Rabbi of Kiryat Arba (a settlement in the occupied West Bank), 'ruled' that Baruch Goldstein (who massacred twenty-nine Arabs at the Cave of the Patriarchs in 1994) was 'holier than all the martyrs of the Holocaust'.[82] He has also justified the killing of non-Jews, said that Jews should not rent to Arabs, and that the terrorist attacks in at the Bataclan theatre in Paris in November 2015 (in which 170 people were killed) were punishment for what Europeans did to Jews in the Holocaust.[83] He now lives peacefully in East Jerusalem. In any other country he would be regarded as a psychopath.

On the Israeli 'left', i.e. the Israeli Labour Party, matters are better but not much better. Its new leader, Avi Gabbay – who until 2013 was the boss of a telecommunications company, then a minister in one of the Netanyahu governments, and who joined the Israeli Labour Party only in 2016 – has pushed the party further to the right by declaring that the settlements were 'the beautiful and devoted face of Zionism' and that Israel must retain control of the Jordan Valley in any peace deal with the Palestinians.[84] In November 2017 he backed Netanyahu's plan to expel African migrant workers, adding, just like Tzipi Hotovely, that 'the whole Land of Israel is ours, because it was promised to our patriarch Abraham by God'.[85] On 1 January 2019 he ended the party's alliance with Tzipi Livni (a former foreign minister and leader of the small liberal Hatnua Party), declaring, not too elegantly, 'I was constantly eating shit because of Livni. She didn't have a good word to say about me' (*Jerusalem Post*, 1 January 2019).

And that is the Israeli mainstream left, so-called. It was trounced at the 2019 and the 2020 elections, and deservedly so. The party which once ruled Israel was down to only six seats in the Knesset, its worst results ever. The only threat to Netanyahu came from the 'centrist' Blue and White Alliance led by Benny Gantz, a political novice and a former chief of staff of the Israel Defense Forces, who presided over the 2014 'Operation Protection Edge' in Gaza, in which 2,251 Palestinians were killed.[86] Gantz had little to say except that he was not 'Bibi'. Yet in 2019 he managed to end up neck and neck with Netanyahu (each on around 26 per cent), who yet again had to form a right-wing government with the 'nasty' parties that tend to proliferate in Israel, such as the ultra-orthodox Shas and United Torah Judaism, parties which make American evangelical Christians seem like permissive liberals. Trying to form a coalition with religious fanatics as well as far-right secularists such as

Avigdor Lieberman turned out not to be easy. Only seven weeks after the election, 'Bibi', unable to form a new government, was forced to call for new elections in 2020, when he was again unable to secure a majority. The only silver lining in the Israeli cloud is the positive result of the 'Joint List', which became the third party with over 12 per cent of the vote. Joint List is an (unstable) coalition of Israeli-Arab groups and parties, but it seeks and obtains the support of some progressive Jews.[87] They would be willing to support Gantz as long as he refrained from favouring the annexation of parts of the occupied territories of the West Bank. Gantz, however, may remain firm in his 'principled' racist refusal to countenance an alliance with a non-Jewish party.[88]

Europe today is awash with nasty parties, far nastier than run-of-the-mill conservatives: in Switzerland there is the Swiss People's Party (with almost 30 per cent in 2015); in Belgium the New Flemish Alliance (31 per cent in Flanders in 2014, but to its right there is the even nastier Vlaams Blok, dissolved in 2004 but re-emerging in 2019 as Vlaams Belang); in Bulgaria the National Front for the Salvation of Bulgaria (only 7 per cent); in Latvia the National Alliance (official name; the National Alliance 'All For Latvia!' – 'For Fatherland and Freedom'), with 16 per cent in 2014 and part of the ruling coalition; and the already mentioned Progress Party in Norway, the Order and Justice Party in Lithuania, the Northern League in Italy, the Front National in France, the Swedish Democrats, the Finns Party (previously known as the True Finns), the Freedom Party in Austria, Jobbik in Hungary, the Party of Freedom in the Netherlands, Golden Dawn in Greece, etc.

The rise of the right has been accompanied by a deterioration of political language. Donald Trump, via a series of tweets and tirades, to the despair of some and the amusement of others, has used the kind of language and voiced the kind of thoughts associated with angry bar-room banter or raucous racist male aggression, and/or with vicious teenagers affected by insecure narcissism. 'Send them home' he tweeted hysterically about four congresswomen of colour, three of whom had been born in the US: 'Why don't they go back and help fix the totally broken and crime infested places from which they came.'[89]

Not for nothing has Senator Bob Corker remarked that 'the White House has become an adult day care center', while James Comey, former head of the FBI, sacked by Trump, wrote in the epilogue to his book *A Higher Loyalty: Truth, Lies, and Leadership*, 'This president is unethical, and untethered to the truth and institutional values', and compared him to a mafia boss. Working with Trump had given him 'flashbacks to my earlier career as a prosecutor against the Mob. The silent circle of assent. The boss in complete control. The loyalty oaths. The us-versus-them worldview. The lying about all things, large and small, in service to some code of loyalty that put the organization above morality and above the truth.' Michael Wolff, author of *Fire and Fury: Inside the Trump White House*, wrote an article for the *Hollywood Reporter* (January 2018) entitled '"You Can't Make This S--- Up": My Year Inside Trump's Insane White House'.[90]

The turnover in this 'insane day care centre' is remarkable: Michael Flynn, Trump's former national security adviser, was in the job for one month; Reince Priebus, chief of staff, for six; Katie Walsh, White House deputy chief of staff, for two; George Papadopoulos, foreign policy adviser, for ten; Sean Spicer, the press secretary, lasted six months; Steve Bannon, White House 'chief strategist', seven months; the health secretary, Tom Price, eight months (after revelations that he used huge sums of public money travelling on private chartered planes). Secretary of state Rex Tillerson lasted just over a year. He was sacked by Trump in March 2018 in favour of Mike Pompeo, who was head of the CIA (a job he owed to Trump), but before that was a mere Kansas congressman and Tea Party stalwart. He loves Israel, dislikes Muslims and gays, is anti-abortion, and is a climate change sceptic. His successor as head of the CIA was his deputy, Gina Haspel, the first woman to run the agency, and who, according to the *New York Times*, had a leading role in torture.[91]

In March 2018, Gary Cohn, Trump's chief economic adviser (and formerly president of Goldman Sachs) announced his resignation. His worthy successor was Larry Kudlow, an exponent of trickle-down pseudo-economic theories, TV and radio pundit, and a former cocaine addict (for which he was fired from Bear Stearns in 1995), who, just months before the global downturn of 2007, predicted the economy would rebound.[92]

There was also the ridiculous Anthony Scaramucci, the director of communications who lasted less than two weeks. His successor, Hope Hicks, lasted longer: almost seven months. In October 2018, Nikki Haley, the US ambassador to the UN, announced she was quitting before the end of the year amid rumours that she had accepted gifts when she was governor of South Carolina. A month later Trump sacked his Attorney General, Jeff Sessions, who had been reluctant to intervene in the Mueller investigation into Russia's links with Trump. Lower down the ranks the offences get more serious: Robert Roger Porter, the White House staff secretary, had to resign in February 2018, after no fewer than two ex-wives accused him of domestic abuse. Trump's reaction was, 'He did a very good job' (as staff secretary, not as a husband). In October 2017, Trump's campaign manager Paul Manafort was charged with laundering millions of dollars 'earned' from lobbying work on behalf of Ukraine's former pro-Russian president Viktor Yanukovych.[93] In March 2018, H. R. McMaster was sacked as national security adviser and replaced by arch-hawk and warmonger John Bolton, a relic of the Bush era who, like Donald Trump and Bush Jr, had avoided being sent to Vietnam during the conflict. Bolton was sacked by Trump in September 2019. In July 2018, Scott Pruitt, the climate change-denying administrator of the Environmental Protection Agency, faced with investigations and scandals, was forced to resign. In 2019, Kirstjen Nielsen, secretary of state for homeland security, was asked to leave, as was Randolph Alles, director of the Secret Service (who, however, denied he was pushed). Last but not least – though at the time of writing the saga continues – in July 2019 the labor secretary Alex Acosta resigned over the Epstein sex trafficking case which, as the BBC noted, 'is a perfect storm of scandal and outrage. It mixes allegations of sex crimes with abuse of power and influence reaching into the highest corridors of US political and financial power.'[94]

To be fair, Bill Clinton's White House was almost as dysfunctional as Trump's. Mark Gearan, deputy chief of staff and then communications director, said that the staff at the White House 'was too often like a soccer league of ten-year-olds'.[95] Still, a step up on Trump's adult day care centre. A step down might have been Theresa May's 10 Downing Street, described by 'sources close to the cabinet' as being 'run by lunatics' during the Great Brexit Debacle of 2016–19 (but the show will run and run).[96]

As Machiavelli put it: *E la prima coniettura che si fa di un signore e del cervel suo, è vedere gli uomini che lui ha d'intorno* ('The first opinion one forms of a prince and of his intelligence is by observing the men he has around him').[97] Significantly, there are no economists in the White House. Ignorance reigns: at a Senate Judiciary Committee hearing in January 2018, Kirstjen Nielsen, secretary of state for homeland security, was asked whether Norway (a country from which Trump would welcome immigrants, unlike 'shithole' countries such as Haiti) is predominantly white. She replied, disarmingly, 'I don't know sir, but I imagine that is the case.' With a name like Kirstjen Nielsen how could she possibly know anything about Norway or any other Scandinavian country? Perhaps she was trying to protect the president. The right answer, of course, should have been: why should Norwegians move to a country with no parental leave, expensive universities, no statutory paid vacations, and no gun controls. Trump forced Nielsen to resign a year later, accusing her of having failed to stem the 'tide' of illegal immigrants.

Trump won the 2016 presidential election but not the popular vote. All sorts of 'theories' were advanced to explain his victory, suggesting that he had been able to mobilise the 'left behind', in other words the losers. The truth is that Hillary Clinton obtained 2,868,691 *more* votes than Trump, and that Trump won because 77,744 voters in three key states – Pennsylvania, Michigan, and Wisconsin – were decisive in giving him a majority in the electoral college. The electoral college is an institution originally devised by founding fathers James Madison and Alexander Hamilton who, not trusting ordinary voters, preferred that the final choice should be made by those of a higher intellect, i.e. an elite. They must be turning in their graves. We are far from a true landslide victory such as that of Ronald Reagan against Walter Mondale in 1984, when Reagan obtained 58.8 per cent of the popular vote.

Then there is the 'theory' that the Russians enabled Trump to win. This is rather absurd: if the Russians were so sophisticated as to be able to target key voters in three states, they would be ruling the world. Russian 'interference' seems to have amounted to sending emails and secret meetings between some of Trump's advisers – such as Michael Flynn, Trump's son Donald Jr, and perhaps his son-in-law Jared Kushner – and Russian officials who might have had some 'dirt' on Clinton. As of March 2018, thirteen Russian citizens were indicted for planting ideas on social media, presumably with the Russian government's support, to damage Clinton and boost Trump. The whole issue got amazing coverage in the Western media, as if it had made the slightest difference to the presidential election result. In fact the issue is totally politicised: in April 2018 the US House Intelligence Committee released its lengthy report (over 300 pages) on alleged Russian interference and came up with the verdict that there was no evidence of collusion between the Trump campaign and Russia. The problem is that those who voted in favour of this report were all Republicans (the majority) and those who voted against were all Democrats.[98] Even the *New York Times*, in a generally anti-Putin comment, admitted that there is no hard evidence of Russian interference.[99] There was plenty of evidence, on the other hand, that Trump asked Ukraine (and even China) to interfere in the next US presidential election by providing some dirt on rival presidential candidate Joe Biden. The House impeached Trump, but the Senate, or, more precisely, its Republican majority, made sure that no witnesses were called and that Trump was 'cleared' in what had obviously become a farce.

Meanwhile, in another farce, Alexander Nix, the CEO of an obscure outfit called Cambridge Analytica (which has since gone bust), managed to convince journalists who wanted to be convinced (in liberal papers such as the *Guardian* and the *New York Times*) that Cambridge Analytica had persuaded 77,000 voters in three key states to switch their votes from Clinton to Trump. The only thing hard to believe is that so many people were taken in by such puerile bragging, or what the *Financial Times* described as 'an adman bigging up his data-science firm'.[100] But then it is equally hard to believe that Nix was so dim-witted and naive as to be taken in by a 'sting' orchestrated by reporters working for Channel 4 News in which he offered 'beautiful Ukrainian girls' to discredit politicians.

In March 2019 even the official inquiry led by Robert Mueller, for twelve years (2001–13) director of the FBI (and a Republican), in its 400-page report, admitted that there was no evidence that members of the Trump campaign conspired with the Russians – something that should have been obvious. The report was examined and re-examined, interpreted and reinterpreted. One would have thought it not excessive to ask of a report that it should have a clear conclusion.

It is of course quite possible that a few Russians tried to damage Hillary Clinton (a foreign-policy hawk), but she still got far more votes than Trump. Besides, the US has 'interfered' for decades all over the world as a matter of routine. There is an entire database aimed at tracking the long history of American meddling in foreign elections, quite apart from sponsoring military takeovers if the meddling does not do the trick.[101] America has intervened in Italian elections since 1948 (this is amply documented), as well as in elections in Germany, Japan, Israel, the Congo, etc. In the 1980s and the early 1990s the US gave financial and military backing to the Contra rebels against the Sandinista leader Daniel Ortega, who had been elected in 1984. In 1990 it provided aid and money to Václav Havel in Czechoslovakia (as it then was), in Israel to Shimon Peres, and later to Ehud Barak against Netanyahu, to Vojislav Koštunica against Slobodan Milošević in Serbia, and to whoever happens to be the anti-Russian candidate in Ukraine. It has, of course, systematically interfered in Latin America, including sponsoring coups against democratically elected governments. During the Brexit referendum in the UK, Barack Obama (presumably prompted by David Cameron) openly intervened, warning Britain that if the country left the EU it would have to join 'the back of the queue' when it came to trade deals.[102] In April 2019 Nancy Pelosi, the Speaker of the House of Representatives, while visiting the border between Northern and Southern Ireland, declared that if the UK left the EU in a way which damaged the Good Friday Agreement then the British could forget about a US–UK trade deal.[103]

Earlier, in defiance of diplomatic protocols, the new Trump-appointed ambassador to Germany, Richard Grenell, in office for four weeks, declared in an interview he gave to the ultra-right website Breitbart that he wants to strengthen other conservative (i.e. far-right) leaders in Europe.[104] Trump, on the eve of a visit to Britain in July 2018, gave an interview to the *Sun* in which he broke with the most elementary principles of diplomacy (a word he does not seem to have mastered), reprimanding Theresa May for not following his advice on the Brexit proposals and expressing his admiration for Boris Johnson, who, he said, would make 'a great prime minister'.[105] After May's resignation Trump confirmed his endorsement of Johnson in the race for the leadership of the Conservative Party, just as he was about to embark on an official visit to the UK on the occasion of the anniversary of D-Day.

The foreign leader who 'interferes' the most in US politics (and much more overtly) is Israel's 'Bibi' Netanyahu, whose chief backers, such as the billionaire casino magnate Sheldon Adelson, also backed Trump's campaign to the tune of $25 million and who long cherished the goal of having the US move its embassy from Tel Aviv to Jerusalem.[106] On this one Trump complied. The $25 million was well spent.

As for the Russians hacking into Hillary Clinton's emails ... In 2010 Barack Obama was told that the National Security Agency had been monitoring the German Chancellor Angela Merkel's mobile phone (even before she became Chancellor). He allowed this to continue as he allowed the continuation of a global network of eighty eavesdropping centres, including nineteen European listening posts (not sparing allies: Paris, Berlin, Rome, and Madrid).[107]

Many of the 'explanations' for Trump's 2016 victory are based on a reading of the speeches of the main candidates, a few interviews with voters to select those that fit the 'theory', and on the unwarranted assumption that voters must have been in agreement with this or that aspect of the candidates' programmes. Surveys conducted as close as possible to the elections are a better, though far from perfect, indication of who voted for whom. We thus know that a majority of whites (including a majority of white women) voted for Trump, and that the overwhelming majority of black voters (88 per cent) and two-thirds of Hispanics supported Clinton. The view that Trump was supported by angry working-class men is not backed by the exit polls, which show that Clinton had the majority of voters on lower incomes (below $50,000 a year) compared with 41 per cent voting for Trump. Clinton's support among those on incomes below $30,000, though down on Obama's in 2012, was far greater than that of Trump. Trump won the rural vote by 62 per cent to 34 per cent and the suburban vote by 50 per cent to 45 per cent, while Clinton won the urban vote by 59 per cent to 35 per cent. Trump had a clear majority among those aged forty-five and over, while Clinton was more popular with younger voters. It was not the 'working class' that voted for Trump, it was a majority of the *white* working class, people who benefit from welfare programmes such as food stamps and Medicaid. So why did they vote for people, like Trump, who favour the rich and prosperous? Is it because they are both ignorant and prejudiced?

The vast majority of traditional Republicans voted for Trump, while the vast majority of traditional Democrats voted for Hillary Clinton. Trump's support from evangelical Christians was almost 80 per cent, even though, unlike previous presidents, he hardly ever mentions God (and has had, so far, three wives and countless affairs).[108]

This is not to deny that behind the Trump vote (as also the Brexit vote) there was a 'left' element: opposition to neoliberalism and to freedom for capital to move around, a rejection of Wall Street barons (who supported Hillary Clinton), Washington corruption, etc. But those who capitalised on this were people of the right, from Donald Trump to Nigel Farage in the UK. As Anthony Barnett has noted, 'The Left has truly lost when it does not even understand that it has lost.'[109]

The message of both Trump and Farage was 'no global', a theme which had previously been a distinctive 'left' sub-text. Similarly, the idea that the United States is run by a few millionaires in Wall Street or by a powerful Washington establishment is a well-established populist trope of both left and right, enshrined in many a Hollywood film in which the 'little man' confronts the system, from Frank Capra's *Mr. Smith Goes to Washington* (1939) to Oliver Stone's *Wall Street* (1987), with its famous 'Greed Is Good' speech, and Steven Soderbergh's *Erin Brockovich* (2000), in which Julia Roberts fights (and wins) against a large energy corporation. Clinton's famous 'It's the economy, stupid' sounded good but was stupid itself, since it assumed that the economy always determines elections and that 'the economy' is not a matter of interpretation.

This populism is not at all part of the traditional ideological make-up of Republican elites. They are for big business, and are certainly not 'no global'. The gap between these elites and rank-and-file Republicans has existed for a long time, but had not previously been so easily discernible. Now it is. Senior Republicans, including George W. Bush, John McCain (candidate for the presidency in 2008), and Senator Bob Corker have expressed their dismay at Trump while, so far, the rank and file remains aligned behind 'their Trump'.[110] At the time of writing, it remains to be seen whether 'Donald Trump's extraordinary ascension to the presidency in 2016 was a fluke of idiosyncratic celebrity and circumstance' or a harbinger of a huge transformation in the US party system.[111]

Did Trump's supporters vote 'rationally'? Bryan Caplan, in his *The Myth of the Rational Voter: Why Democracies Choose Bad Policies* (2007), thinks that voters are economically irrational. Of course they are, since it is difficult to calculate what is in one's economic interest (I for one can't) and which policies are likely to benefit a particular individual. In fact it is almost impossible to establish what would be a 'rational' reason to vote for anyone, or even to vote at all. It is difficult enough to be 'rational' when shopping for food or clothes.

The reactionary nineteenth-century thinker Gustave Le Bon, in his *La Psychologie des foules* (1895), argued, well before contemporary political scientists, that 'the crowd' would always be swayed by sentimental and irrational thought. While he complained that educational progress was utopian – since free schooling created an army of discontented youth, unwilling to return to peaceable rural life – he was also pleased that crowds, being submissive, would always be ready to follow a superior leader, someone able to seduce the masses, pretend to have sympathy for their plight, and make exaggerated promises.[112] This sounds like Trump, but how many would regard him as a 'superior' leader?

Voters often do not need to be duped: in 2003 seven in ten Americans continued to believe that Iraq's Saddam Hussein played a role in the 11 September 2001 attacks, even though the Bush administration and congressional investigators always maintained that there was no evidence.[113] Ordinary Americans simply chose to give a rational reason for what was obviously totally irrational (invading Iraq).

This is the context within which Trump's victory over Clinton should be seen. Yes, he got fewer votes but he still managed to have on his side nearly half of the electorate and had clearly won the Republican primaries against sixteen other candidates. But what candidates! Some of these even managed to make Trump look like a serious politician, people like senators Ted Cruz and Rand Paul (both staunch supporters of the Tea Party, a conservative lobby in chronic decline), or like Jeb Bush (brother of Bush Jr, and son of Bush senior), the governor of Florida known mainly for an expensive and ineffectual campaign. Then there was Ben Carson, a creationist neurosurgeon who happens to be black, who declared that Obamacare was the worst thing 'since slavery'; Rick Santorum of Pennsylvania (who is anti-abortion and anti-gay); Mike Huckabee, former governor of Arkansas and a Southern Baptist minister; and Senator Marco Rubio of Florida, who accused Barack Obama of trying to make America 'more like the rest of the world', while he (Rubio) will make 'America the greatest country in the world' … etc. Republican candidates for the presidency seem to have one thing in common: dismal mediocrity.

The American 'liberal' press and networks such as CNN did not believe that Trump could win the primaries, let alone the top job. Thomas Frank, author of the angry and clever *Listen, Liberal!*, warned that 'To defeat Trump, the media must face their own flaws', listing some of what he called:

> the many monstrous journalistic failures of the last few decades: the dotcom bubble, which was actively cheered on by the business press; the Iraq War, which was abetted by journalism's greatest

sages; the almost complete failure to notice the epidemic of professional misconduct that made possible the 2008 financial crisis.
Everything they do, they do as a herd – even when it's running
headlong over a cliff.[114]

But Trump, the arch-vulgarian, trumped them all, deploying a
simple, repetitive, and often vulgar language, a hallmark of our
morbid age. It is difficult to imagine Franklin Roosevelt or Charles
de Gaulle, Konrad Adenauer, Harold Wilson or Willy Brandt,
sinking to anything remotely comparable to contemporary vulgarity – though in private de Gaulle did resort to foul language.[115] One
cannot imagine any of them boasting about the size of their penis,
as Trump did in a television debate on 3 March 2016 with a rival
candidate (and, once president, that his nuclear button was 'bigger'
than that of Kim Jong-un, with whom he eventually got on better
than with his European allies, declaring that Kim is 'a very smart
guy, he's a great negotiator and I think we understand each other');
or calling women he does not like fat pigs, dogs, slobs, and disgusting animals; or (but not publicly and in a distant 2005) explaining
what one might call his 'seduction technique' with women: 'And
when you're a star. You can do anything. Grab them by the pussy';
or his campaign promise in 2015 to 'bomb the shit out of ISIS'; or
the comments, following the violence in Charlottesville, Virginia, on
12 August 2017 (where a civil rights campaigner was killed by a car
driven by a white supremacist), putting anti-racist non-violent demonstrators on a par with violent racists.[116] Or when, in November
2017, he re-tweeted tweets from a tiny neo-Nazi British group
(Britain First), one of whose supporters was the murderer of the
British MP Jo Cox, thus providing Britain First with an enormously
enhanced platform (he was duly thanked by one of the leaders with
a 'God Bless Donald Trump'). Earlier that year, in public, he called
(black) American footballers who knelt instead of standing for the
national anthem 'sons of bitches'. In January 2018 at the White
House, discussing immigration from Haiti, El Salvador, and some
African countries with members of Congress, he asked rhetorically,
'Why are we having all these people from shithole countries come
here?'[117] Trump denied having said that, but no one believed him.

And he cannot deny having said, repeatedly, during his presidential campaign, that immigrants from Mexico are rapists and that Muslims are terrorists.

According to *Washington Post* fact-checkers, in his first 347 days in office Trump made 1,950 misleading or outright false claims.[118] As of May 2019, he had used Twitter to insult 598 people and institutions: calling Joe Scarborough (NBC Host, 'Morning Joe') 'crazy', 'psycho'; Don Lemon (CNN anchor) a 'joke', 'dumb as a rock'; Tom Steyer (philanthropist and environmentalist) 'totally unhinged'; and Kim Jong-un 'short and fat'. Hillary Clinton has been the most insulted, usually as 'crooked' but also as 'a Wall Street puppet', 'the most corrupt person to ever run for the presidency', 'should be in jail', 'very dumb', 'pandering to the worst instincts in our society', and 'totally flawed candidate'. As for Obama, he fares a little better: 'insane', 'a disaster', 'weak', 'terrible', 'horrible', 'incompetent', 'trying to destroy Israel', 'the worst president in US history'.[119]

Trump speaks in what one might call 'demotic', i.e. the way ordinary people speak. As John McWhorter, a linguistics specialist at Columbia University, has noted, 'Mr. Trump's come-as-you-are-speaking style' is part of his appeal; he 'talks the way any number of people would over drinks, and many of us might be surprised to see elements of that style in our own downtime speech if transcribed'.[120] Trump is certainly an extreme case of public vulgarity and lack of decorum, but not the only one.

In February 1988, the then French president, Jacques Chirac, was caught on a microphone during difficult European negotiations with Margaret Thatcher, muttering, 'Mais qu'est-ce qu'elle me veut de plus cette ménagère? Mes couilles sur un plateau?' (What more does this housewife want from me? My balls on a plate?)[121] In 1991 Edith Cresson, a socialist politician and the first female French prime minister, declared that the Japanese were like laborious 'yellow' ants and that homosexuality was an 'Anglo-Saxon' problem.[122]

Boris Johnson, who, to the amusement of some and the amazement of many, became foreign secretary of the United Kingdom in

June 2016, had previously developed his diplomatic skills by likening Hillary Clinton to 'a sadistic nurse in a mental hospital' with 'dyed blonde hair and pouty lips' (*Daily Telegraph*, 1 November 2007), by commenting that the Queen loves the Commonwealth partly because it supplies her with regular cheering crowds of 'flag-waving piccaninnies ... with watermelon smiles' (*Daily Telegraph*, 10 January 2002), and by penning a poem in which the Turkish prime minister Recep Tayyip Erdoğan has sex with a goat, for which he won the *Spectator*'s 'President Erdogan Offensive Poetry' competition:

> There was a young fellow from Ankara
> Who was a terrific wankerer
> Till he sowed his wild oats
> With the help of a goat
> But he didn't even stop to thankera.

In 2015, when mayor of London, Boris Johnson, responding to Trump's claim that areas of London have become so radicalised that police fear for their lives, declared: 'The only reason I wouldn't visit some parts of New York is the real risk of meeting Donald Trump' (*Daily Telegraph*, 8 December 2015). But in politics principles are ditched as times change and, by 2018, Foreign Secretary Boris Johnson was pandering to Trump like the rest of the conservative establishment.

French president Nicolas Sarkozy, while visiting the Salon de l'Agriculture in February 2008, told someone who refused to shake his hand 'Casse-toi, pauv' con!' (Fuck off, you miserable cunt!).[123] Italy's Silvio Berlusconi has entire websites dedicated to his gaffes and vulgarity, all the more noteworthy since Italian politicians prior to the 1990s were often criticised for using excessively complex and refined language. At the European Parliament at the start of Italy's EU presidency (July 2003) Berlusconi, then prime minister, told Martin Schulz, the leader of the SPD delegation, that he would be 'perfect' in the role of a Kapo (a collaborator) in a film on Nazi concentration camps.[124] In April 2009 Berlusconi advised the homeless survivors of an earthquake forced to sleep in the mountainous

Abruzzi region in wintry weather to regard it as a camping holiday. In the same year he attempted to persuade bankers in New York to invest in Italy with a line he obviously thought was funny: 'Another reason to invest in Italy is that we have beautiful secretaries ... superb girls.'[125]

Berlusconi was eventually convicted of tax fraud in October 2012, and sentenced to four years in prison, reduced to one year of 'community service'. In March 2013 he was sentenced to one year in jail for arranging a police wiretap of a member of the opposition. In June the same year, he was convicted of paying for sex with an under-age prostitute (when he was prime minister). He is not serving any time in prison because of the numerous appeals and, given the unbelievable delays in Italian courts, the chances that he will ever see the inside of a jail are slim. Many cases, including one of bribery, expired under the statute of limitations or were waived because of parliamentary immunity. All together there have been over thirty court cases.

In Italy the champion of vulgar language was Umberto Bossi, leader of the anti-southern and later xenophobic and Islamophobic Lega Nord. In public speeches to assembled crowds Bossi would scream 'Noi della Lega, ce l'abbiamo duro' (roughly translated as 'We of the League, we have got it hard'); or 'When I see the *tricolore* [the Italian flag] I am pissed off. I use the tricolore to wipe my arse ... '.[126] He added to his notorious racism a pronounced homophobia: 'How many democratic parties have in key positions avowed homosexuals, that is to say, pansies [*donnicciole*]'?[127]

In Poland, the Eurosceptic demagogue Andrzej Lepper, who became deputy prime minister in 2006 (when Jarosław Kaczyński was prime minister and his twin brother Lech was president), said in 2002, 'When they are in the European Union, the Poles will be slaves. They will wipe the buttocks of German women or else sweep the streets.'[128] Lepper, having faced charges for slander, was accused of sexual harassment in 2010 and found guilty. This did not prevent him from being awarded an honorary doctorate from a private Ukrainian 'university', the Interregional Academy of Personnel Management in Kiev, which actively promotes anti-Semitism and blames the Jews for the devastating famine of 1932–33 (the KKK leader David Duke also obtained a fake PhD in history there). Lepper committed suicide in 2011.

Rodrigo Duterte, president of the Philippines, called Barack Obama an *hijo de puta* ('son of a whore') in 2016. He used the same epithet for Philip Goldberg, the US ambassador to the Philippines, and for Pope Francis, whose visit in 2015 had caused a traffic jam in Manila.[129] Having toned down his war on drugs to satisfy 'bleeding hearts' in the West (after thousands were killed by police and unknown assailants), he lashed out at Western powers: 'You sons of bitches … You are interfering in our affairs because we are poor. You bullshit. We are past the colonisation stage. Don't fuck with us.' In February 2018, speaking to soldiers, Duterte told them to shoot female rebels 'in the vaginas', because, without vaginas, 'women are useless'.[130] Unsurprisingly, the UN high commissioner for human rights declared that Duterte 'needs to submit himself to some sort of psychiatric examination'.[131] Equally unsurprisingly Duterte has withdrawn his country from the International Criminal Court.

In Asia there are rivals to Duterte though no one is as crude. In Pakistan, for instance, in his regular column in the English-language daily *Dawn*, Fakir S. Aijazuddin, one of the country's most brilliant columnists, wrote in despair:

> Islamabad is gradually degenerating from drollery to slapstick, and now into farce … Centre stage is a puppet prime minister [Shahid Khaqan Abbasi] who periodically has to visit his marionettist – an ousted prime minister [Nawaz Sharif] – to have his strings tightened … Off-centre is a finance minister [Ishaq Dar] under indictment for financial turpitude. Yet he sits unconcerned in Cabinet meetings, leaving his soiled reputation at the cloakroom outside.[132]

At least Islamic cleric Khadim Hussain Rizvi, president of the newly founded Tehreek-e-Labbaik, declared he will not put up with 'bad language'. By that he means ridiculing the Prophet Mohammad, a criminal offence in Pakistan, punishable by death.

In 1999 Vladimir Putin explained his anti-terrorism feelings in terms of chasing terrorists down lavatories: 'We will chase terrorists everywhere. If in an airport, then in the airport. So if we find them, excuse me, we'll piss them off in the toilet. That will bring the matter to a close.' Discussing with the then Israeli prime minister Ehud Olmert the case of the Israeli president Moshe Katsav (subsequently convicted of two counts of rape), Putin exclaimed, 'He turned out to be a strong man, raped ten women. I never would have expected it of him. He has surprised us all, we all envy him!'[133] Putin's main rival, Alexei Navalny, an ethnic Russian nationalist, later praised in the West for being anti-Putin, was expelled from the liberal Yabloko Party in 2007 for xenophobia, and during the conflict with Georgia in 2008 described Georgians as 'rodents'.[134]

Elsewhere the behaviour is simply loutish: Sir Michael Fallon, then British defence secretary, told his colleague Andrea Leadsom, who was complaining about having cold hands, 'I know where you can put them to warm them up.'[135] In June 2019, Mark Field, a Foreign Office minister, forcibly expelled a female Greenpeace activist who disrupted the chancellor's Mansion House speech. Wearing the statutory black tie, foaming at the mouth, he grabbed her neck, pushed her against a pillar and then out of the room. No one tried to intervene to stop his loutish behaviour.

In 2002, the British Conservative MP Ann Winterton was sacked from the shadow cabinet for telling, in public, a racist 'joke' about Pakistanis. Two years later she had the Conservative whip withdrawn for telling another tasteless and racist joke alluding to the recent death of twenty-three Chinese cockle-pickers in Morecambe Bay. In 2005 she declared herself thankful that the UK was 'a predominantly white, Christian country'. She and her husband, also an MP, were later found to have fiddled her parliamentary expenses. Thankfully, following that scandal, she is no longer in Parliament.[136]

At a campaign event during the primaries, Joe Biden, presumably trying to keep up with Trump, told a Detroit construction worker who had disagreed with him over gun control that 'he was full of shit'. [137]

These vulgarities are perfectly in tune with our morbid times. Once perfumes were called, in an understated way, No. 5 (Chanel, 1921) or 'Gentleman' (Givenchy, 1969). By September 2017 a unisex fragrance had been launched by the American fashion designer (and film director) Tom Ford with the catchy name of

'Fucking Fabulous'. The scent cost $310 for 50ml and the name obviously attracted far more publicity than if it had been called 'Ford No. 6'.

Election slogans, however, have almost always been inane. In 1952 the slogan for Dwight Eisenhower was 'I Like Ike'; in 1964, Barry Goldwater, the right-wing Republican candidate, came up with 'In Your Heart You Know He's Right', copied by Michael Howard in the 2005 British elections with the creepy 'Are You Thinking What We Are Thinking?' (sub-text: there are too many immigrants); then there were the unimaginative 'Nixon's the One' in the 1968 US presidential election; 'Putting People First' (Bill Clinton, 1992); 'Yes, America Can!' (George W. Bush, 2004), and the similar but better known 'Yes, We Can!' (Obama, 2008). Mitterrand, in 1981, had the meaningless 'La force tranquille', Sarkozy in 2007 opted for a socialist-sounding 'Ensemble tout devient possible' (Together everything becomes possible). Berlusconi regularly dished out the appealing 'Meno tasse per tutti' (Fewer taxes for all), before coming up with, in 2013, 'Un Presidente operaio per cambiare l'Italia' (A working-class president to change Italy) which, coming from one of the richest men in Italy, should have won the chutzpah prize of the year. In Spain in 2015 the conservative People's Party produced the puzzling 'España en serio' (Spain seriously), while the leftist Podemos proposed the unoriginal 'Un país contigo' (A country with you) as well as *Sí se puede* (Yes, we can) borrowed from Obama (Podemos also means 'we can').

All this makes Trump's 'Make America Great Again' sound almost Shakespearian. Such political slogans, inspired by modern advertising, treat voters with contempt while pretending to be pandering to the people. Those who despair of politics have a point.

The 'Far' Left

The advance of the right has not been matched by the advance of the 'far' left. Even the expression 'far left' has today been stretched to include positions which, in the thirty years after 1945, were part of mainstream social democracy. Though it acts as if it was new, much of the language of this new left is old. It makes the populist claim to speak on behalf of the overwhelming majority, the 99 per cent against the despicable 1 per cent, as if the 99 per cent were not themselves divided by class, gender, politics, religion, education, location, and age. The 1 per cent stands for what used to be called the 'ruling class', the 'upper classes', the 'rich', the 'elite', 'the system', 'the establishment', or, in Italy and Spain, *la casta*.[138]

At one time, communists and assorted leftists sought to unite everyone against an ill-defined 'monopoly capitalism'. In the 1930s, in France, the Popular Front parties – radicals, socialists, and communists – urged everyone to join forces against the *deux cents familles* who, they claimed, ruled and owned the country. Populism may be today's buzzword to describe the far right and, occasionally, the far left, but populism is hardly new, even if we discount the 'classic' populism of the Russian Narodniks or of the American People's Party of the last decades of the nineteenth century. Fifty years ago, two distinguished political theorists, Ghiță Ionescu and Ernest Gellner, had already announced that 'a spectre is haunting the world – populism'.[139]

The so-called far left (formerly known, more simply, as 'the left') – which would include Syriza in Greece, Bernie Sanders in the US, Podemos in Spain, the Bloco de Esquerda in Portugal, Jean-Luc Mélenchon's La France Insoumise, and Jeremy Corbyn in the UK – has enjoyed relative successes in the last ten years, but it won power, and not for long, only in Greece, which was a special case. In Spain and Portugal the far left had to be content to play a supporting role to the social democrats.

In Portugal, the Bloco de Esquerda under Catarina Martins, an actress with a PhD turned politician, obtained 10.2 per cent of the vote in 2015, while the Communists got 8.3 per cent. In other words, almost one in five Portuguese electors voted for the 'far' left. The Socialists formed a government with the three leftist parties, thus going against the grain of traditional social democracy. The initial moves have been more than symbolic: a rise in the minimum wage, the elimination of some health charges, the reversal of the privatisation of the country's main airline, greater access to social benefits, an increase in state employees' salaries, a reduction in income tax for those on low incomes, a return to the thirty-five-hour working week for public servants, and the approval of adoption by gay couples.[140] By October 2019, new elections proved the resilience of the Portuguese Socialists, who improved their percentage slightly (on the lowest-ever turnout for parliamentary elections in Portugal, at 54 per cent). The conservatives suffered a serious defeat while some smaller parties, left and right, improved their position. With nine parties represented in Parliament, ruling the country will not be easy.

In Spain Podemos (the full name is Unidos Podemos – *United We Can*) received 21.2 per cent in 2016, while the established PSOE obtained 22.63 per cent. PSOE and Podemos together might have gained far more seats than the victorious right-of-centre People's Party (PP), which received 33 per cent. Podemos owes its success to its oppositional stance, partly originating in the *indignados*, an anti-austerity movement which arose around 2011, but also to very high unemployment, corruption scandals, and the realisation that something has gone wrong with Spain's integration in the wider globalised economy. The Podemos leader, Pablo Iglesias, was quite certain that it was the debacle of the eurozone which provided the opportunity for his party to emerge.[141]

The key factor in the emergence of Podemos, as in that of other similar movements, was that it had the advantage of being new and untainted, and was therefore able to denounce the corruption scandals that had tarnished the traditional parties, while unemployment increased at a faster rate than anywhere else in Western Europe, and while the governing parties pursued an unpopular policy of austerity. What Podemos stands for is unclear – which, in these circumstances, is an advantage. In June 2016, just before the elections, Pablo Iglesias, speaking to an audience of entrepreneurs in Madrid at the opulent Ritz Hotel (alongside the communist Alberto Garzón), announced that Podemos is 'la nueva socialdemocracia', praised Marx and Engels, but then added, 'If there is a word that defines our candidacy it is "patriotic".'[142] As is often the case, self-contradiction is unavoidable, particularly in opposition 'movement' parties.

ഇ

Podemos, Syriza, the Bloco de Esquerda, but also movements on the right in Eastern Europe and elsewhere, such as the Italian Movimento Cinque Stelle (M5S), could all be labelled anti-austerity and anti-establishment 'movement parties'.[143] In fact this period might be regarded as the era of the rise of the political comedian. There are those who could be regarded as mere buffoons if they did not wield power, people such as Donald Trump, Silvio Berlusconi, and Boris Johnson. All three owe part of their fame to television. Trump was the show host of *The Apprentice* for fourteen seasons. Boris Johnson appeared several times on the satirical quiz show *Have I Got News For You*. Berlusconi, having been a crooner on cruise ships before building a real estate empire, ended up with a large stake in Italian private television. But there are also those who are professional comedians, such as the Ukrainian Volodymyr Zelensky who, in the 2019 presidential election, soundly defeated (with 73 per cent of the vote!) the incumbent Petro Poroshenko (a chocolate manufacturer whose silly nationalist message 'Army, Language, and Faith' failed to impress). A few months later, on 21 July 2019, Zelensky's new party (the 'Servant of the People' Party, after the name of his television sitcom) gained an absolute majority in Parliament; the first time in Ukraine's post-Soviet history that a single party had done so.

Zelensky is far from being the first comedian to make it big in politics: in Italy there is Beppe Grillo, the founder of the M5S; in Slovenia, Marjan Šarec, who became prime minister in 2018 but who started his career with the stage persona of 'Ivan Serpentinšek', a rural simpleton. Guatemala can boast, since 2016, having as its president Jimmy Morales, a right-wing TV evangelist; in Uganda, the leading opposition to the long-ruling Yoweri Museveni is the pop star Bobi Wine (real name Robert Kyagulanyi). As mentioned earlier, in Poland in the 2015 elections, the third party (with 21 per cent of the vote) was 'Kukiz'15', led by the punk rock musician Paweł Kukiz. In Croatia, the anti-establishment folk musician Miroslav Škoro forced the president, Kolinda Grabar-Kitarović, to shift to the right. She was hoping to be re-elected as president in January 2020 (she failed and Zoran Milanović, a social democrat and a former prime minister, won). The previous month the former

Croatian prime minister Ivo Sanader, within whose government Grabar-Kitarović was a minister, was sentenced to six years in jail for having taken a large bribe from an oil company in exchange for a major stake in a newly privatised energy company.

Of course, in the US, Ronald Reagan had been an actor and, like Arnold Schwarzenegger after him, also governor of California. This seems to confirm the situationist Guy Debord's famous thesis in *The Society of the Spectacle*, which opens with a paraphrase of Marx's first line in *Capital*: 'In societies where modern conditions of production prevail, all of life presents itself as an immense accumulation of spectacles.'[144]

But it doesn't require a new party, let alone a funny guy or a pop singer or an actor, to challenge the establishment. Jeremy Corbyn and Bernie Sanders (like Donald Trump) had to work within existing parties, largely because the strongly entrenched party systems of the UK and US, buttressed by particular electoral systems, make it difficult for a third force to emerge. Sanders, originally an independent senator from Vermont who described himself as a democratic socialist (in a country where socialism is a dirty word), sought the nomination for president in the 2016 Democratic primaries, a party he had only recently joined. He did very well, gaining among registered Democrats 43 per cent to Hillary Clinton's 55 per cent, a sign of the resentment against Clinton, widely regarded as the establishment candidate. Sanders campaigned on a programme which, underneath the inevitable populist rhetoric ('down with the rich'), had fairly moderate social democratic aims (a minimum wage, a national health service, etc.). He was back in the race in 2020, against the former vice-president Joe Biden, having defeated a crowded field of aspirant presidents, and, for a while, did remarkably well in the primaries.

In France, in the first round of the 2017 presidential election, the 'far left' Jean-Luc Mélenchon received 19.58 per cent, routing the official Socialist candidate Benoît Hamon, who got only 6.3 per cent. Had even half of Hamon's votes gone to Mélenchon, then Mélenchon would have obtained more votes than Marine Le Pen (who obtained 21.3 per cent), and the second round in the presidential would have been between him and Emmanuel Macron. It is unlikely that in these circumstances Macron would have won so clearly as he did against Marine Le Pen.

The Jeremy Corbyn case in Britain is rather special, since Corbyn was fighting almost as much against his own party establishment as against the Conservatives. It's worth telling the story in some detail. In 2015, as the general election approached, it was generally but mistakenly assumed that the Conservatives would fail, once again, to obtain a clear parliamentary majority and would have to rely on the Liberal Democrats as they had done since 2010. But the Tories succeeded in obtaining a working majority. However, the election also saw the clear defeat of the Labour Party led by Ed Miliband, who immediately resigned. The collapse of the Labour vote must be attributed not so much to losses in England but to the loss of almost all its Scottish seats to the Scottish National Party, which obtained fifty-six seats out of the fifty-nine available. The Labour Party was reduced to being largely an English and Welsh party. Without Scottish seats it will be difficult for Labour to win another election.

The battle was open for Ed Miliband's successor. There were four candidates, one of which was Jeremy Corbyn, an eternal dissident, by then in his late sixties, with no great personal ambition. The other three were fairly nondescript. Andy Burnham tried to position himself slightly on the left – though in 2010 he was still approving of 'the original decision' to intervene in Iraq since 'it gave 20 or so million people in Iraq hope of a better life and you just cannot walk away from that truth'.[145] Then there was Yvette Cooper, the best of the three, but whose leadership manifesto unoriginally ticked the right boxes – increase low wages, protect the climate, create more jobs, build more houses, help refugees, etc. Finally there was Liz Kendall, who claimed to be the 'modernising' candidate but was widely regarded as a 'Blairite' (the kiss of death in many quarters, hence her repeated mantra of 'I am not a Blairite').

These three candidates had only one message: Labour needed an *electable* leader (obviously Ed Miliband had lacked such quality in 2015, as had Gordon Brown in 2010, Neil Kinnock in 1987 and 1992, Michael Foot in 1983, Jim Callaghan in 1979, Harold

Wilson in 1970, Hugh Gaitskell in 1959, and Clem Attlee in 1951
and 1955). There was hardly a smidgen of insight into what had
actually gone wrong with Labour's opposition to Cameron's Tories
over the preceding five years, or as to whether Kendall, Cooper,
or Burnham was actually electable. For many party members they
were dull and tired; nobody thought they could win. They came
out with the usual pro-business rhetoric, did not challenge austerity, and abstained on the Welfare Reform Act (unlike Corbyn who
voted against it), which seemed a betrayal too far.

Corbyn was obviously the anti-establishment candidate, the only
one of the four who had never held office either in government
or in the shadow cabinet. He had a long history of ignoring party
discipline, of being anti-war, and of being against the so-called
'independent' British nuclear weapons. He was even a republican
in an overwhelmingly monarchist country.

It was not clear at the time that Corbyn's lack of ambition would
turn out to be one of his great selling points. He was the man at the
margin: a headbanger for most and a man of principles for a few. In
fact he was barely able to secure the thirty-five nominations from
fellow Labour MPs that he needed to get on the ballot. Some of
those who nominated him, such as the former Labour foreign secretary Margaret Beckett, did so out of pity and to stop the left from
whinging. She later regretted it, saying she had been a 'moron'.[146]
So out of touch were the majority of Labour MPs, and most commentators, that they never thought Corbyn would actually get
anywhere. But he did, trouncing his three rivals in the first round
by obtaining more votes than all of them combined: 59.5 per cent.
Even without the so-called '£3 registered supporters' he would have
won, since he had the support of 49.6 per cent of full members.
No party leader had previously obtained so many votes from the
membership. And no party leader had so little support in the parliamentary party – or from the media: an academic study undertaken
by the LSE's Media and Communications Department found that
during his first two months in office as leader of the opposition
most of the press either ignored or misreported his views.[147]

Corbyn was unfairly represented, often denied his own voice, and
systematically treated with scorn and ridicule. He was repeatedly

associated with terrorist organisations such as the IRA, Hamas, and Hezbollah (particularly in the *Sun* and *Daily Express*), and repeatedly labelled as an anti-Semite or at least as unwilling to confront the anti-Semitism which allegedly pervaded the party (an absurd proposition diffused without scruples by all his opponents, including the *Guardian*, assorted rabbis, the *Jewish Chronicle*, and, of course, the Board of Deputies of British Jews – an organisation taken by all and sundry as representing *all* Jews, as if the 'Jewish community' was a monolithic bloc, itself a common anti-Semitic trope). Of course, the discovery that Corbyn was a 'rabid anti-Semite' was made only after he became leader of the Labour Party; before that he was just an ordinary anti-racist socialist.[148] Most of the people expelled or suspended from Labour for anti-Semitism, or the anodyne accusation of bringing the party into disrepute, were Corbyn supporters, including many Jews. A thorough debunking of the anti-Semitism claim was regularly produced by Jewish Voice for Labour as well as in books such as Jamie Stern-Weiner's *Antisemitism and the Labour Party* – not that much of this output found its way into the media, including the BBC and the *Guardian*.[149]

Not untypical was the portrait of Corbyn in the 'respectable' *Daily Telegraph* by the right-wing columnist and shoddy journalist Allison Pearson, who, only a few days after his election, wrote that he was 'a rather dreary bearded fellow who takes pictures of manhole covers as a hobby, doesn't drink alcohol or eat meat, and wears shorts teamed with long dark socks exposing an expanse of pale, hairy English shin'.[150] The novelist Martin Amis – in the pathetic category of personalities who feel a desperate need to keep themselves in the limelight by trotting out outrageous pronouncements, often revealing a paranoid obsession with Islam – pontificated: 'He is undereducated ... He is humourless ... the humourless man is a joke – and a joke he will never get ... everything Corbyn says, without exception, is pallidly third-hand ... He is without the slightest grasp of the national character – an abysmal deficit for any politician, let alone a torchbearer.'[151] The prize for the most ludicrous exposé, however, must go to the *Sunday Express*, whose article, headlined 'REVEALED: The Evil Monster Haunting Jeremy Corbyn's Past', revealed that, over 150 years ago, Corbyn's great,

great, grandfather was the master of a workhouse in Victorian England.[152]

As the leadership election got under way, Tony Blair resurfaced from making money advising dictators, to advise Labour supporters 'If your heart's with Jeremy Corbyn, get a transplant' (*Guardian*, 22 July 2015); Peter Mandelson, with an assurance that past blunders had not dented, explained that 'the Labour Party is in mortal danger' (*Financial Times*, 27 August 2015); while the unelectable Gordon Brown urged Labour 'not to be a party of protest by choosing Jeremy Corbyn' (*Guardian*, 17 August 2015).[153] The venom against Corbyn was particularly pronounced in the *Guardian*. Jonathan Freedland was disconsolate: 'The Corbyn tribe cares about identity, not power'; Suzanne Moore was mocking: 'Corbyn's Labour is a party without a point, led by a rebel with a cause'; Anne Perkins was worried: 'Labour party members, please think before you vote for Jeremy Corbyn'; Andrew Rawnsley warned that Corbyn was the Conservatives' 'dream candidate', adding a week later, 'Labour downs a deadly cocktail of fatalism, fury and fantasy'.[154] Then, defiantly, 'Labour should go right ahead, make David Cameron's day, choose Jeremy Corbyn and field him as its leader at the next election, so that the thesis that Labour loses because it isn't left wing enough is finally tested to the destruction that it so richly deserves.' What was destroyed was Rawnsley's credibility as a perceptive commentator (he still comments). Martin Kettle, another 'shrewd' *Guardian* columnist, declared 'Jeremy Corbyn's nomination has helped Burnham because it means he can't be so easily cast as the leftie in the race' (thus assuming that lefties can't win) and that Liz Kendall 'has proved that there is a sizable level of support' for a Blairite candidate.[155] Kendall's 'sizeable level of support' amounted to 4.5 per cent.

Caroline Wheeler, then political editor of the *Sunday Express*, not noted for her political acumen or the accuracy of her predictions, produced a front-page headline: 'As Corbyn Becomes Leader it is ... BYE BYE LABOUR' (13 September 2015). In the *Daily Telegraph* (30 September 2015), Allister Heath (a future editor of the *Telegraph*), who was born in France and came to England at the age of seventeen, proclaimed 'One Thing Is Clear – Jeremy Corbyn Has No Understanding of the British People'.

In fact no one 'understands' the British people, since it should be obvious even to a *Daily Telegraph* columnist that the 'British people' are not a monolithic bloc (one of the many reasons why we have elections). Poor David Cameron thought he did 'understand' them, hence the referendum on Europe, which he lost. Theresa May also thought she 'understood', which is why she called an election in June 2017 on the badly mistaken assumption she would be returned with a massive majority. No one 'understands' the 'British people'. Commentators simply rely on polling agencies which often, though not always, get it wrong.

On 23 June 2016, just under 52 per cent of referendum voters voted to leave the EU (on a 72 per cent turnout; so the 'British people', i.e. the 'leavers', were 37.48 per cent). The Labour Party had campaigned in favour of remaining, but it had a low profile, except for those Labour MPs, such as Kate Hoey, who were strongly in favour of Brexit. Predictably, Corbyn was criticised for being half-hearted about staying in the EU, even though in speeches in the run-up to the referendum he declared that 'We, the Labour Party, are overwhelmingly for staying in, because we believe the European Union has brought investment, jobs and protection for workers, consumers and the environment.'[156] This was one of the very few positive comments on the EU during the entire campaign, since the bulk of the 'remainers' preferred to subscribe to 'Project Fear', emphasising the disastrous consequences of leaving the EU. By the end of the campaign, Corbyn had made six times more media appearances than Boris Johnson, but the BBC and other media devoted much more time to Johnson than to Corbyn. It helps to be a figure of fun. In fact, in the first month of the referendum campaign, the Labour Party attracted a mere 6 per cent of the TV coverage while the Conservatives grabbed 32 per cent.[157]

Alan Johnson, a Corbyn critic who headed up the 'Labour In For Britain' [*sic*] campaign, was as ineffectual as he had been as shadow chancellor under Ed Miliband. He did not even have much of an impact in his own Hull constituency, which voted 67 per cent to leave. Of course Alan Johnson blamed Corbyn.

A few days after what turned out to be the worst mistake made by a Conservative government ever – calling a referendum on the EU *and* losing it – the Parliamentary Labour Party (PLP), far from capitalising on the Conservative defeat and Cameron's resignation, and in what must rank as one of the least intelligent moves made by any party anywhere in Europe (when the enemy is down you kick it, you do not indulge in self-harm) tabled a motion of no confidence in Corbyn as Labour leader. This motion, tabled by Margaret Hodge, was supported by a staggering 172 Labour MPs (out of 212) as well as by most of the shadow cabinet. As Tristram Hunt and Alan Lockey wrote: 'the internecine factionalism that has greeted his [Jeremy Corbyn's] election obscures a party in which *all* wings find themselves in something of an intellectual catatonia.'[158] It was their choice, as Milton put it, speaking on behalf of God: 'Freely They Stood Who Stood, And Fell Who Fell.' (*Paradise Lost*).

Catatonia, however, was far more prevalent among distressed anti-Corbynistas. A parliamentary party with an ounce of collective intelligence would have examined why there was such a huge gap between themselves and the party activists they claimed to lead. Or they would have realised that it would be impossible for a leader to win an election when he lacks the support of the overwhelming majority of his own MPs. But such an ounce was impossible to find. Corbyn refused to resign on the grounds that he had been elected by party activists and not by the PLP.

The internecine attacks continued at a higher level of idiocy. Owen Smith (unknown then and since) arose to challenge Corbyn for the leadership on the basis of considerable support in Parliament – *faute de mieux* – but very little outside it. Corbyn saw off the challenge and was re-elected as leader in September 2016, obtaining almost 62 per cent of the vote and consigning Owen Smith to well-deserved oblivion. There were more resignations, more local election problems, and an important by-election (Copeland) was lost, though Labour retained Wales and won the London mayoralty. Yet the outcry against the unelectable Corbyn continued. Nothing of similar magnitude had happened when, with Gordon Brown as prime minister, Labour had its worst results in forty years in the local elections of May 2008, ending up in third place. In the 2009 European elections, again under Gordon Brown,

Labour obtained only 16 per cent of the vote, again ending up in third place, behind the Conservatives and UKIP (though just ahead of what Ed Miliband and Corbyn obtained in, respectively, the Euro elections of 2014 and 2019). Internal dissent against Brown was minimal. Most of the Parliamentary Labour Party kept quiet, their heads, ostrich-like, solidly in the sand, heads to be raised only five years later against Jeremy Corbyn, but if heads are devoid of political intelligence, it does not matter whether they are down in the sand or up in the air.

In 2017, the general assumption was that, with Labour in such a dire state, the Conservatives would win the next election. This induced an initially reluctant Theresa May, in the midst of Brexit negotiations, to call an early election, assuming she would obtain a massive majority and thus be able to offer the country 'a strong and stable government'. This was not regarded as a major gamble since most polls gave her a secure majority. The pollsters were seriously wrong. The most laughable was that run by Lord Ashcroft, which on the eve of the election was confidently explaining that the 'Ashcroft Model' had worked out that the Tories would have a potential majority of at least sixty-four.[159]

But it was a gamble May lost, along with her majority. Fearing Corbyn, she had repositioned her party to the left (as 'New' Labour had once repositioned itself to the right in response to Thatcher's victories). The electoral manifesto of the Conservative Party, *Forward, Together: Our Plan for a Stronger Britain and a Prosperous Future*, beggared belief in its apparent ditching of all that Thatcher had stood for: the Conservatives now did 'not believe in untrammelled free markets'; rejected 'the cult of selfish individualism'; 'abhorred social division, injustice, unfairness and inequality', sought workers representation on company boards; would ensure that workers' rights conferred on British citizens from membership of the EU 'will remain'. The Conservatives now declared that public service 'is a noble vocation, one which we will celebrate'; they denounced social injustices borne by those who went to a state school, those who are working-class, those who are black ('treated more harshly by the criminal justice system' than

white), those who are born poor (for they die 'on average nine years
earlier than others), and women (for they 'earn less than a man'),
etc.[160] By appearing to suggest that the austerity policies pursued by
George Osborne (whom she had sacked) had been too harsh, May
also indirectly challenged the old mantra of Blair's New Labour,
namely that austerity was the only game in town, or indeed that
Labour would have to present a more gentle version of Thatcherism.

At the 2016 Conservative Party conference, Theresa May, having
recently become prime minister, had already committed herself to
a new populism:

> within our society today, we see division and unfairness all around
> ... Between the wealth of London and the rest of the country. But
> perhaps most of all, between the rich, the successful and the pow-
> erful – and their fellows ... But today, too many people in positions
> of power behave as though they have more in common with inter-
> national elites than with the people down the road, the people they
> employ, the people they pass in the street ... But if you believe
> you're a citizen of the world, you're a citizen of nowhere. You don't
> understand what the very word 'citizenship' means.[161]

Included in the category of 'citizens of nowhere' (in a different
era she might even have used the words 'rootless cosmopolitans')
were 'left-wing human rights lawyers' who 'harass the bravest of
the brave' (i.e. returning soldiers). Had Jeremy Corbyn used that
language he would have been decried by many in his own party as
an anti-Semite. William Davies, writing in the *London Review of
Books*, declared he was 'surprised that a speech condemning financial elites, human rights lawyers and nationless people in blanket
terms wasn't interpreted as anti-Semitic'.[162]

Totally out of sync with these developments, Corbyn's opponents in the Parliamentary Labour Party vociferously argued that
he was a throwback to the 1960s. They seemed to accept that
the only valid politics were variants of Thatcherism or, to coin
a phrase, Thatcherism with a human face. In its rhetoric if not
its deeds, the PLP even found itself by-passed on the left by the
Conservatives.

But the Conservatives' swing to the left did not fool anyone (few people read manifestos anyway). Theresa May lost her majority. The pledge to have workers on company boards was swiftly abandoned. The Social Mobility Commission – set up by the Conservative-led coalition in 2012 to monitor progress towards improving social mobility – resigned six months after the election, citing 'lack of political leadership'.

The electoral swing to Labour in 2017 (plus 9.6 per cent), though not sufficient to ensure victory, was stronger than that in any previous election since 1945. Labour did particularly well among young voters. Corbyn won the support of two-thirds of the under-twenty-fours, and over half those aged twenty-five to thirty-four, leaving the Conservatives ahead only among electors aged forty-five and older. (The Labour advance among the young was confirmed even in the disastrous election of December 2019.)

In 2017 Labour's share of support rose to 40 per cent – five points above Blair in 2005, and adding 3.5 million votes to Labour's total under Ed Miliband in 2015. Corbyn did well in working-class areas of the north such as Oldham West and Royton, where there was a swing of over 10 per cent, quite contrary to the impression Rafael Behr had sought to convey during the by-election of December 2015, when he explained that 'In Oldham, Jeremy Corbyn is just another face of "poncified" Labour' (*Guardian*, 2 December 2015). Behr recanted two years later: 'Jeremy Corbyn's supporters correctly understood that his candidacy represented a total rupture from the party's past.'[163] Pity Behr hadn't. Politicians, even intelligent ones, were no better: in August 2016 Sadiq Khan had urged Labour members to vote for Owen Smith, declaring 'We cannot win with Corbyn' (*Guardian*, 21 August 2016).

The so-called 'commentariat' also got it completely wrong, particularly those writing for the left-leaning liberal press. On 31 March 2017, the *New Statesman* intoned: 'Corbyn's failure is no excuse for fatalism.' In the same issue, Nick Pearce (Professor of Public Policy at Bath) explained to all and sundry that 'Corbynism is invisible now. It has no secrets to conceal.' On 25 February 2017, in the *Guardian*, Jonathan Freedland explained portentously that 'the glum truth is, the pressure that counts won't come from the likes of me, people who warned Corbyn would be a disaster from the start', but from the activists. In the *Observer* of 19 March 2017, Nick Cohen, in his regular mode of incandescent hysteria, screamed 'Don't tell me you weren't warned about Corbyn', and wondered whether there would be '150, 125, 100 Labour MPs' left. His advice was 'to think of a number then halve it'. Addressing himself to Corbyn supporters, just in case they had not got the point, he then added that the words 'I Told You So You Fucking Fools!' will be 'flung at you by everyone who warned that Corbyn's victory would lead to a historic defeat'. Labour won 262 seats, yet Cohen kept his job and continued his hysterical commentary unremittingly.[164] He should take a leaf (but he won't) from Peter Oborne, a centre-right journalist, who, with remarkable integrity (something seldom seen in the press), wrote a passionate *mea culpa* admitting he that he had completely underestimated the difficulties Brexit would face and that 'we must swallow our pride and think again.'[165]

The British liberal media got it wrong in 2017 because they were prisoners of their anti-leftist ideology and took their own wishes and desires as pictures of reality. The commentators, instead of thinking hard, joined the chorus. That way, if they get it wrong, they are in good company. The Labour Party establishment also got it wrong, mugged by reality, and not for the first time. This is a party which refuses to learn from history. In the 1930s it even managed to expel three politicians who turned out to be the now almost legendary architects of the modern British welfare state in the Labour government 1945–51: Stafford Cripps, later Chancellor of the Exchequer, Nye Bevan, later minister of health, and George Strauss, later minister of supply, all guilty of advocating a popular front with the Communists.

On 9 June 2017, when the UK election results came in, everyone recognised that Theresa May had been the real loser, having lost her majority. Corbyn, although he did not win, had done far better than most previous Labour leaders, and was leading a healthy party with a spectacularly large membership. According to the BBC's political editor, Laura Kuenssberg, some of the MPs who increased their majorities thanks to Corbyn had 'unashamedly promised their constituents on the doorsteps that he would be gone after the election and, more to the point, that they'd help remove him'.[166]

The Scottish Nationalists lost seats, UKIP sank into near oblivion, while the Liberal Democrats barely recovered from their appalling performance of 2015. In Northern Ireland the old establishment parties, the Ulster Unionist Party and the Social Democratic and Labour Party, were wiped out, while the DUP returned ten MPs and Sinn Féin seven.

Theresa May, still prime minister of a government that was neither strong nor stable, was forced to make a deal with the DUP, one of the most unenlightened parties in Western Europe. She set out the financial support she was prepared to offer: £200 million, plus £75 million per year to help provide ultra-fast broadband in Northern Ireland, plus £100 million per year for two years for health service transformation, etc. In total the deal will have cost the British tax-payer over £1 billion.[167] Most people would call this unashamed bribery, yet, incredibly enough, it's legal. More to the point, the increasing self-confidence of the forces of civic liberalism in the Republic of Ireland which led to victories in referendum legalis-ing same-sex marriage (May 2015) and abortion (May 2018) have highlighted how backward is Northern Ireland where both are banned, largely due to the opposition of the DUP, Theresa May's best friend.

While the Labour Party was thriving with an increased and confident membership, many in the parliamentary party and in the liberal press continued their attacks on Corbyn, in particular keeping alive the alleged anti-Semitism problem (which by then had become an unquestioned and unquestionable truth). Meanwhile the Conservatives barely existed as a party. In July 2019, Labour had 485,000 members, the Liberal Democrats 115,000, the SNP 125,000, and the Conservatives 180,000.[168] In the final ballot to elect Theresa May's successor in 2019, just under 140,000 votes were cast. In 1952, the Tory party had 2.75 million members.[169] Now it had become a party of elderly men: 71 per cent of its members are male, against 63 per cent for the Lib Dems, 57 per cent for the SNP, and 53 per cent for Labour.[170]

While the Labour establishment kept on behaving as if the Conservatives were the natural party of government, the last time the Tories had won an election decisively was in 1987 under Thatcher. In 1992 and 2015 they gained a small majority; they lost in 1997, 2001, and 2005, and failed to win an overall majority in 2010 and in 2017.

Few commentators ate humble pie after the surprise of the 2017 elections. They just readjusted their seats and went on with the same degree of arrogance as before, barely toned down. Andrew Rawnsley wrote lamely: 'It wasn't just us. Virtually no one saw it coming. The politicians, especially the politicians, didn't see it coming either. Their crystal balls were completely cracked.'[171] Perhaps journalists and academics and politicians should use their brains and leave crystal balls to the Celtic Druids. Rawnsley then went on to blame the Tories, who 'foolishly tried to make it a presidential contest, when led by someone so hopeless at retail politics that Mrs May couldn't have sold a glass of water to a man dying of thirst'. Pity he had not said this before.

Owen Smith admitted that he had been 'clearly wrong in feeling that Jeremy wouldn't be able to do this well. And I think he's proved me wrong and lots of people wrong and I take my hat off [to him].' Mandelson now recognised that Corbyn's campaign had been 'very sure-footed'. Four months earlier at an event organised by the *Jewish Chronicle* he had patiently explained that Corbyn had 'no idea in the twenty-first century how to conduct himself as a leader of a party putting itself forward in a democratic election to become the government of our country', adding that 'I work every single day in some small way to bring forward the end of his tenure in office.'[172] Strange that in 2019 Boris Johnson did not thank him for the help received. Harriet Harman tweeted that she had 'over-estimated' Theresa May and under-estimated Jeremy Corbyn. Those who, like Stephen Kinnock, Hilary Benn, and Chuka Umunna, had lambasted Corbyn now, thanks to him, retained their seats with increased majorities.[173] Stephen Kinnock, on the night of the results, was so visibly upset that Corbyn had done so well that he had to be given instructions on how to react by his obviously far more politically shrewd wife, the former Danish prime minister, Helle Thorning-Schmidt.[174]

Commentators and politicians had attempted to justify their disparagement of Corbyn in terms of his unelectability. Had they had some integrity they would have argued against his policies, instead of saying, over and over again, that he could not win. As the Roman historian Livy put it so neatly in his *Ab Urbe Condita*, 'Eventus docet: stultorum iste magister est' (Experience is the teacher of fools).[175] Of course, Corbyn didn't win, and in 2019 he lost heavily, but no Labour leader could have won against the entire press, his party establishment, and, above all, without Scotland; and Scotland had been lost before Corbyn came on the scene.

But what did Corbyn actually stand for? He stood against the renewal of the Trident nuclear weapons system (independent only in name), though he accepted that no commitment to scrapping it would be included in the party manifesto; he stood for reversing cuts in welfare and public services; renationalising some public utilities; non-interventionism in foreign affairs; abolishing the Private Finance Initiative; taxing the rich; increasing the minimum wage; recovering money lost through tax evasion; ending the charitable status of public schools; abolishing university fees, and so on. These proposals were attacked as a 'far left' programme. However, as one astute commentator wrote, 'the reality is that it proposed no more than a return to what would once have been seen as a moderate version of social democracy'.[176] Corbyn also risked upsetting his traditional working-class voters by being quite principled on immigration.

The main problem with a wish list like Corbyn's is the one encountered by virtually all politicians: how are you going to pay for this? If the answer is 'more taxes', then are there really enough rich people to pay for it all? If the answer is 'we shall borrow', then what will the consequences be? To say simply that any politician making such proposals is 'unelectable' is to refuse to deal with such issues.

In the past Corbyn had been cool towards Europe (voting against the Maastricht and Lisbon Treaties), but during the referendum

campaign he took a 'balanced' approach: yes to 'social Europe' –
pointing out that the EU had brought jobs, investment, protection
for workers, environmental regulations, etc. – but complaining
about bureaucratic control and its emphasis on deregulation.[177] The
media described these policies as 'extremist', claiming they were a
throwback to the 1970s or 1960s. In reality many of Corbyn's policies were supported by the public. A majority favoured getting rid
of nuclear weapons, particularly if the survey question mentioned
the money saved.[178] A YouGov poll in October 2016 showed that
Corbyn's policies were more popular with the public than those of
the Conservatives; 51 per cent were in favour of renationalising the
railways – unsurprisingly since they are in such a mess (companies
such as Virgin Trains have not even been penalised for running the
East Coast rail franchise into the ground) – while only 22 per cent
opposed it.[179]

Renationalising the water utilities was equally popular, particularly because water companies seem to have done everything they
can to make themselves unpopular: Thames Water, for instance,
hardly pays any taxes, its shareholders receive huge dividends, it
has enormous debts, and was fined for leaking untreated sewage
into the Thames.[180] Yet 33 per cent thought the Conservatives had
the best policies on the economy, while only 13 per cent thought
Labour did. Obviously much depended on how the questions were
asked, but what these figures show is that Corbyn's policies were
far from being unpopular.[181] Where Corbyn (and Labour) waffled
and hesitated was on Brexit, torn between taking a clear stand to
demarcate themselves from the Tory Brexiteers (and consequently
alienating some anti-EU Labour supporters), and fudging. Fudge
was the chosen strategy. Perhaps it was the only one: after the
2019 disaster some said that Labour lost because it had become a
remainer party, others because it had accepted Brexit.

A couple of days before the 2017 election, Gary Younge, one of
the few *Guardian* commentators not to have been overwhelmed by
the anti-Corbyn 'groupthink', wrote:

For the past two years, it has been received wisdom that ... the
Labour party under Corbyn was unelectable. Not simply that it

would lose, but that there was no plausible way it could compete. These were not presented as opinions but as facts. Those who questioned them were treated like climate change deniers... . To take Labour's prospects seriously under Corbyn was to abandon being taken seriously yourself.[182]

At the Glastonbury Festival, a couple of weeks after the election, the young revellers welcomed Corbyn with what had already become a famous chant (Oh, Jeremy Corbyn! to the tune of 'Seven Nation Army' by the White Stripes). The chant was heard for at least twenty minutes before he appeared on stage. He drew the biggest crowds of that year's festival. No other politician in the UK could have pulled that off. When Corbyn entered the newly elected House of Commons, his backbenchers, many of whom had spent the previous two years plotting against him, gave him a hero's welcome. Polly Toynbee, who had been less than enthusiastic about Corbyn in April 2017 ('the shockingly inept opposition leader will preside over catastrophe for his party'), by September graciously acknowledged her mistake and his success:

> Oh, Jeremy Corbyn! What a difference a year makes... . This united party are all Corbelievers now, and which lingering Labour doubters can pick a quarrel with any of this agenda? Believing he might really win has never been easier. His learning curve has been meteoric, this speech authoritative and abundant with promises both necessary and popular.[183]

Zoe Williams was one of the few to dedicate an entire column to acknowledging her mistake: 'I backed Owen Smith against Jeremy Corbyn. But I regret it now' (*Guardian*, 2 January 2018). Even Gordon Brown pronounced what amounted to a belated recognition that Jeremy Corbyn is 'a phenomenon' and that he 'expresses people's anger at what's happened'.[184] It's never too late.

It's never too late to change one's assessment – except for Philip Collins, a former speech writer for Tony Blair, now a *New Statesman* columnist, who in November 2017 compared Corbyn to Robert Mugabe and Ratko Mladić (the butcher of Srebrenica). The apparent reason, in an article devoid of any, was that Corbyn had opposed the war in Kosovo and the bombing of Belgrade (which Collins supported and which resulted in hundreds of civilian casualties). Obviously Collins could not distinguish between Srebrenica and Kosovo. His article was peppered with the kind of insults one finds in the tabloid press: Edward Herman (who co-authored books with Noam Chomsky), with whom Collins disagrees, is called an 'obscure fool', while Chomsky is described as the 'doyen of the charlatan left'. The readers' comments were overwhelmingly supportive. Collins knows his audience, a knowledge which spares him the headache of having to construct an argument.[185]

Corbyn had the enormous advantage of not being in power. But he had the enormous disadvantage of having to face a barrage of accusations from his own side. He had always played the role of the dissident outsider – not that of the insider-leader. Not at ease on television – looking too earnest in an era where bluster and cant rule, choosing not to vigorously rebut the most ludicrous of accusations (such as that of anti-Semitism), appearing to apologise constantly, unable to respond to the bullying journalists who interviewed him – he faced an electorate who, though not particularly bothered with the anti-Semitism accusation, did not regard him as a leader. Theresa May faced a similar problem. She lost her premiership because she did not have the support of her parliamentary party and because she chose to try to accommodate them instead of involving Labour in the Brexit negotiations. She resigned and Boris Johnson became prime minister. The chaos spread. Pretending to negotiate with the EU but in fact risking a no-deal exit, Johnson managed not only to unite all the opposition parties, but even to alienate many in his own party who refused to back his decision to suspend Parliament for five weeks in September 2019. As a result, having failed to suspend Parliament, Johnson expelled twenty-one of his own parliamentarians, an unprecedented and widely criticised act. The purge included Tory grandees such as Kenneth Clarke, the former chancellor Philip Hammond, and seven former Cabinet members as well as Nicholas Soames, grandson of Winston Churchill. The media stood admiringly at such audacity. Had he done anything remotely similar, Corbyn would have been called a despotic Stalinist. But then Johnson had the support of the majority of his parliamentary group. Corbyn did not, could not expel anyone, and could not even discipline Margaret Hodge who had called him a 'fucking anti-Semite'.

Once he had accepted the idea that there should be a second referendum, Corbyn was not even able to defend the policy that, if he became prime minister, he would negotiate new terms of exit with the EU and then remain neutral in the subsequent referendum. What he should have said is that everything depended on the deal achieved. He also should not have agreed to another election in November 2019. He should have let Johnson come up with a deal – impossible since he had no majority in the House of Commons.

The election of December 2019 saw a massive victory for the Conservative Party, which emerged with a spectacular eighty-seat majority. But the electoral support achieved by the Conservatives was not so spectacular. They increased their vote by only 1.2 per cent over the 2017 election. But this was enough to move them from no absolute majority to a stunning victory. The Liberal Democrats gained 4.2 percentage points but lost a seat, that of their leader, Jo Swinson. Such is the roulette of the British electoral system.

Labour lost a number of traditional working-class seats, presumably because of tactical voting by Brexiteers who had voted Labour in the past. It maintained its lead in London where the 'remainers' were exceptionally strong. But, overall, Labour went down by 7.8 points over 2017. Though Corbyn crumbled, he still did better, in percentage terms, than Ed Miliband in 2015 or Gordon Brown in 2010.

Blaming Corbyn for the loss of previous Labour 'fortresses' in the north, the so-called 'Red Wall', became the default position of many who lost their seats. Let us take three cases of Labour defeat in their strongholds.

Caroline Flint had been the MP for the Don Valley constituency in South Yorkshire for twenty-two years. In campaigning for the Brexit referendum, she had switched from 'remain' to 'leave' to court favour with her constituents. It did not work and she blamed Corbyn's commitment to remain. In 1997, when Flint was first

elected, she had 58 per cent of the vote, but then lost votes at subsequent elections under leaders Tony Blair and Gordon Brown. In
2017 her vote went up (under Corbyn). She lost her seat in 2019,
blaming Corbyn even though the loss of Labour voters in Don
Valley had been almost constant since 1997. No attempt appears
to have been made to analyse this. Much simpler to say that it was
all Corbyn's fault.

In Stoke-on-Trent, Ruth Smeeth – a former director of the pro-
Israel lobby organisation BICOM, vociferous in accusing Labour
and Corbyn of anti-Semitism – was elected in 2015 with just under
40 per cent. Labour, however, had had 65 per cent in the constituency in 1997. In 2017, under Corbyn, her share went up to almost
51 per cent, before dropping to 37 per cent in 2019. The 2017 gains
were attributed to various factors, the 2019 drop to Corbyn.

The sad saga continued in another Labour fortress, Sedgefield,
which had been won by Blair in 1997 with a staggering 71 per cent.
By 2001, Blair's vote was down to 65 per cent, and by 2005 to 59
per cent. In 2010 Phil Wilson (a former lobbyist for a gambling firm)
succeeded Blair as the local MP. He won with only 45 per cent. He
improved a little in 2015 and even more in 2017 (during the pro-
Corbyn wave), though he had explained to his voters he was not a
'Corbynista'. In 2019 his share of the vote sank once again to 47
per cent (still a little better than he had achieved in 2010) and he
lost his seat. Thus in Sedgefield too, the decrease in the Labour vote
had preceded the advent of Corbyn. This did not prevent Wilson
from declaring that 'Jeremy Corbyn lost me my seat.'[186]

One could multiply these examples of the Labour vote declining in former strongholds well before 2019. One thing is clear:
the Labour crisis will not be resolved if MPs continue to find easy
explanations for their predicament. Their prospects are dire since
they did not seem to realise that their constant sniping at the leader,
particularly at a difficult time when Britain was going through its
most serious crisis since the war, could only have negative effects.

At least in opposition life is relatively easy, since one does not have
to face the brutish realities of national and international political constraints. This was the problem Syriza had to face in Greece

when it unexpectedly won the elections in 2015. The country had been particularly damaged by the global downturn of 2007–8: the economy was structurally weak, tax evasion was widespread, the 'black' economy was absurdly large. Greece regularly infringed the eurozone stability criteria because in order to sign up for the euro, previous governments had used dubious statistics on the size of its public debt and deficit (statistics which were readily accepted by the rest of the EU for political reasons). The global downturn of 2008 led to a crisis of confidence, a growing trade deficit, a reluctance to buy Greek government bonds, and an exhausting series of tax increases requested by the IMF and the European Central Bank in exchange for a bailout.

In late 2011, with the political system in meltdown mode and amid growing popular protests, the government led by the socialist PASOK resigned. In 2009 the party had won with 44 per cent. In the first of the two elections held in 2012 its vote share crumbled to 13 per cent, in the second it lost another point. In 2015, when there were again two elections, PASOK was a dead party, collecting between 4 and 6 per cent.

The traditional conservative party, New Democracy (ND), did better, but the party that surged ahead was Syriza, a coalition of leftist radical parties. In 2009, before the crisis hit Greece, Syriza had been able to muster only 4.6 per cent (while the communists of the KKE had 7.5 per cent). By May 2012 Syriza was the second Greek party with 16.8 per cent. A month later it had climbed to 27 per cent, and in the two elections of 2015 it reached 35–6 per cent, forming a government with the support of the Eurosceptic Independent Party.

The previous coalition of socialists and conservatives (PASOK and ND) had implemented drastic austerity policies to placate the European Central Bank and the IMF, dramatically increasing poverty, unemployment, and social despair. This was the basis for Syriza's success, but the constraints had not changed. The position of extreme weakness in which the country found itself meant that the party had very little room for manoeuvre.

As Costas Douzinas, a London academic and a Syriza MP since 2015, pointed out, Syriza was not prepared for government 'in such harsh conditions' (but then without the harsh conditions it would not have been in power); 'the manifesto promises had not been accurately costed'; 'many ministers did not have a good understanding of their portfolio', etc.[187] Syriza could wave the anti-austerity banner but there was little it could do. Leaving the euro would simply mean a collapse of the new currency that would have had to be introduced instantly (unlike the euro, which was introduced after lengthy preparations). The inevitable massive devaluation of the currency would then have wiped out the savings of many Greek citizens. Greece was forced to remain in the eurozone and keep its debts.

Alexis Tsipras, Syriza's leader, had been elected prime minister on an anti-austerity platform, but cruel reality convinced him that he needed to compromise with the so-called Troika (the European Commission, the IMF, and the European Central Bank) in order to avoid being forced out of the eurozone. He called a referendum for 5 July 2015, to decide whether to accept the conditions imposed. The electorate rejected the conditions by a large majority (over 60 per cent). Some, such as the finance minister Yanis Varoufakis, sacked shortly after the referendum, believed Tsipras had hoped that the referendum would approve the bailout, though he (Tsipras) campaigned for a rejection, so that he would not be blamed when accepting the European 'diktat'.[188] The upshot was that Syriza, in order to obtain bailout funds, had to implement austerity policies similar to the ones they (and the electorate) had previously rejected.

The EU too was faced with constraints, hamstrung by treaties and regulations. To waive them for Greece would have led to protests from other countries such as Portugal, Spain, Ireland, and Cyprus which had had to accept the rules. The only alternative to accepting the EU conditions would have been for Greece to default and leave the eurozone, causing major damage to the European banking system. The Greeks could have gambled that the EU would have blinked first and helped Greece anyway (Varoufakis explained that 'It's not about who will blink first').[189] That was 'Plan B', the 'Drachma Plan' of the left faction within Syriza led by Panagiotis Lafazanis and Dimitris Stratoulis – a kind of 'if you don't do as I say I will blow myself up and everyone else along with me'.

Understandably, no one had the courage or the folly to take up this gamble. Despite its apparent radicalism, Syriza's proposed solution to the crisis was traditional Keynesianism: help us to increase public spending and eventually we will be able to pay back our debts. Syriza never seriously envisaged leaving the euro, let alone the EU. Greece might feel unsafe inside the EU but would feel even more unsafe outside it. More surprisingly, given Syriza's leftist credentials, is the fact that Greece was one of the few NATO countries to spend at least 2 per cent on defence, second only to the US (and, consequently, was warmly congratulated by Trump).[190] But fear of Turkey, once again, and the need to use military conscription to keep youth unemployment down, count here far more than do fear of Russia or loyalty to the Atlantic alliance.

Syriza's four years in power ended in a major electoral defeat in July 2019. A landslide brought the conservative New Democracy party back to power with an absolute majority, doubling its previous representation. Greek politics is as uncertain as ever.

The dilemma Syriza faced was the same as that facing all leftist forces in Europe, from Podemos to Corbyn, from Mélenchon to Portugal's Bloco de Esquerda: they operate in an interdependent and globalised capitalist world where no one can go it alone. They assume, just like politicians of the centre and of the right, that once one wins, one is in power. In reality one is only in office, and it is increasingly difficult for the left in Europe to get into office, let alone into power.

5

The American Hegemon

Today there is no international hegemon. The Soviet Union is no more. China is not strong enough (yet). Europe is in disarray. The US is in decline.

Europe is now part of the world's periphery. Europeans talk about Europe ceaselessly. They wonder about its role, where it is going, and whether the United States can continue to lead or whether some new hegemon will emerge. Yet we should not forget that it is not inevitable that one country and one country alone should 'rule the world'. In fact no one ever 'ruled the world', and hegemonic powers were hegemonic, at most, within a determinate region (Alexander's Macedonia, Ancient Rome, Imperial China, Genghis Khan's Mongol Empire, etc.). In any case the world can work equally well (or equally badly) without a 'hegemon'. What matters is what the putative hegemon does when its hegemony is threatened – a characteristic of American ideology in the era of its decline: 'blind self-satisfaction and belief in the natural rightness of dominion', as Perry Anderson put it.[1]

Britain towards the end of the eighteenth century, and for much of the nineteenth, was not a hegemon; it ruled the waves – or so it thought since it had the strongest navy in the world – and, by the end of the nineteenth century, had the largest empire ever, and was the main trading nation, but it did not control the world. The US was not a hegemon before the Second World War, though it had been the leading industrial power at least since 1900. Even after 1945, the US, though certainly the main superpower, faced the communist bloc. It could not do as it pleased. It could not prevent the communist revolution in China. It was unable to stop the division of Korea. Initially it even trailed the USSR in the space race. It suffered an unprecedented humiliation in Vietnam. It had to accept a communist state, Cuba, a few miles from the shores of Florida. It could not protect one of its chief allies in the Middle East, the Shah of Iran, from being ousted by followers of the Ayatollah Khomeini.

The total incompetence of the US military was amply demonstrated in virtually all its foreign adventures, even though its military spending almost matches the total of the next eight powers, accounting for 36 per cent of global defence spending.[2] The US was not able to defeat the Taliban in Afghanistan (one of the world's poorest states), in what has been the longest American war ever, even though it deployed, at one time, more than 100,000 troops, has lost over 2,300 soldiers, and spent more than $1 trillion.[3] Before its own involvement in the country, US decision-makers, blindly following Cold War logic, provided aid to the anti-Soviet mujahedeen, following the Soviet invasion of Afghanistan in December 1979. By 1989 the USSR under Gorbachev had withdrawn its troops without any of its war aims accomplished. By then, however, the Americans had created a situation they could not control or understand. In 1998, Zbigniew Brzezinski (President Carter's national security adviser between 1978–81) was interviewed by the French weekly *Le Nouvel Observateur*. He was asked whether he regretted providing help to the Islamic forces of the mujahedeen. He replied: 'Regret what? That secret operation was an excellent idea. It had the effect of drawing the Russians into the Afghan trap and you want me to regret it?' The interview continued:

Nouvel Observateur: And neither do you regret having supported Islamic fundamentalism, and providing weapons and advice to future terrorists?

Brzezinski: What is most important to the history of the world? The Taliban or the collapse of the Soviet empire? Some excited Muslims [*Quelques excités islamistes*] or the liberation of Central Europe and the end of the Cold War?

Nouvel Observateur: Some excited Muslims? But we heard time and time again that Islamic fundamentalism represents a world menace today.

Brzezinski: Nonsense![4]

The American objective of nation-building in Afghanistan failed completely. What emerged was a narco-state.

The US scuttled out of its 'humanitarian intervention' in Somalia in 1994 after a couple of its helicopters were shot down, resulting in the death of eighteen US soldiers. In the ensuing battle hundreds of civilians lost their lives. President Bill Clinton had previously declared that 'we came to Somalia to rescue innocent people in a burning house. We've nearly put the fire out, but some smouldering embers remain. If we leave them now, those embers will reignite into flames and people will die again.' They withdrew anyway and Somalia was left in utter chaos.

Further 'mistakes' followed. In 1998, in retaliation for terrorist attacks on US embassies in Tanzania and Kenya, Clinton ordered the bombing and destruction of the Al-Shifa pharmaceutical factory in Sudan on the basis of faulty evidence supplied by the CIA alleging that the owners had ties to al-Qaeda. The factory, a major medical supplier, was destroyed. Eventually US officials acknowledged that the evidence was not 'as solid' as it seemed at first. In fact there was no proof. No apology was proffered and no payment made.[5] As Christopher Hitchens wrote, 'Clinton needed to look "presidential" for a day ... he acted with caprice and brutality and with a complete disregard for international law, and perhaps counted on the indifference of the press and public to a negligible society like that of Sudan.'[6]

In 1999 NATO, led by the US with the full backing of Blair's Labour government, launched a war against Serbia over Kosovo. They pounded Belgrade for seventy-eight days in support of the Kosovo Liberation Army, until recently classified as a terrorist organisation (KLA) partly funded by the trade in illegal drugs. Twenty years later Kosovo was still a failed state subsidised by the West.[7]

In 2011, there was the UN-sponsored US intervention, egged on by David Cameron and Nicolas Sarkozy, in support of the rebellion in Libya against Muammar Gaddafi. Privately, President Obama called Libya a 'shit show'. The country subsequently became a haven for various kinds of Islamic terrorists.[8] Migrants blocked in Libya by the country's Coast Guard, with the support of the EU, were detained in 'horrific' and 'inhuman' conditions, according to the United Nations High Commissioner for Human Rights Zeid Raad Al Hussein.[9]

Proxy wars were even worse than direct Western intervention: the war in Yemen conducted by Saudi Arabia with Western weaponry (the US and the UK are the biggest arms exporters to Saudi Arabia) has led to massive casualties and the worst cholera outbreak in history.[10] The United Nations warned that 13 million people in Yemen were facing starvation. In October 2017, Michael Fallon, then British defence secretary, asked MPs not to criticise Saudi Arabia and thereby risk damaging the fighter jet deal that was being negotiated.

Jeremy Corbyn, as leader of the Labour Party, called for support to be withdrawn from the Saudi government bombing campaign in Yemen; 129 Labour MPs followed him but 100 did not. Had they voted, the government would have been defeated. Among those who directly or indirectly supported Saudi Arabia's bombing were former leadership contenders Andy Burnham and Liz Kendall. No liberal interventionism for Yemen, but support for Saudi Arabia's inhumane intervention. Its blockade led to what three UN agencies described as 'the worst humanitarian crisis in the world': 11 million children in need of assistance, 14.8 million people deprived of basic health care, and an outbreak of cholera which resulted in more than 900,000 suspected cases.[11]

And no humanitarian intervention either for the Rohingya Muslims in Myanmar, threatened with genocide.

The US was also unable to establish democracy in Iraq after its 'humanitarian' intervention in 2003. It has been unable (or unwilling) to resolve the Israel–Palestine conflict. After the fall of communism it looked as if the US might 'rule the world', since it was the only global power left, yet this was arguably the beginning of its decline. Every intervention left the country it 'helped' in worse shape than before – no mean accomplishment. Obama was unusual among US decision-makers for having understood the limits of American powers. His often-repeated if inelegant maxim, 'Don't do stupid shit', caused consternation among Washington hawks who would have intervened almost anywhere at the drop of a hat. In April 2008, during her first presidential campaign, Hillary Clinton – who, unlike Obama, got it wrong about Iraq – warned Iran that, if she were president, the United States would 'totally obliterate' Iran in retaliation for a nuclear strike against Israel. She did not equally warn Israel not to nuke Iran (Israel has nuclear weapons, Iran hasn't).[12]

In February 2011 Clinton (then secretary of state), Samantha Powers (US ambassador to the UN), and Power's predecessor Susan Rice had argued for air strikes in Libya against the more cautious advice of members of the Obama administration, thus precipitating the disaster.[13] It makes Trump seem not quite as weird.

The widely admired Barack Obama, however, is himself hardly a dove. At the beginning of his first term of office he had a vision of a world without nuclear weapons. The vision remained just that, since the reduction in the stockpile of nuclear weapons under Obama was far slower than under any of his three immediate predecessors.[14] He continued to send additional troops to Afghanistan, while remaining impassive as ISIS surged in Iraq, and supine before Abdel Fattah el-Sisi's murderous takeover in Egypt (against an elected president). His Affordable Care Act was a minor reform while, under his watch, the rich became even richer. When it came to authorising the killing of people, Obama was no slouch. During his 2008 presidential campaign he had been against the war in Iraq and the use of torture. Once president, he insisted that the right thing to do was for him to vet all intended drone strikes. So every week, a lengthy article in the *New York Times* explained, the security services gave Obama a list of terrorist suspects in distant lands and recommended who should die.[15] Then the president ticked boxes. This, of course, is not terrorism; it's just killing people in distant lands.

In just the first year of the Obama presidency the CIA conducted fifty-two drone strikes in Pakistan compared to forty-eight during the entire eight years of the Bush administration. In 2016 it then increased its targeted assassination programme in the Yemen. This programme was approved by the overwhelming majority of Americans (83 per cent), many of whom are probably surprised that anyone might want to kill US citizens.[16]

Obama accepted a disputed method for counting civilian casualties: all military-age males in a strike zone were to be counted as combatants. So if you were a male of the right age unlucky enough to be under al-Qaeda 'occupation', you were a combatant. This explained what officials claimed were the 'extraordinarily low' number of collateral deaths. All you had to do after a drone strike was to count the corpses and declare that x number of militants had been killed. It also ensured that no new names were added to Guantanamo, because those who might have been sent there were dead. The drone data, gathered from various sources and analysed by Micah Zenko of the Council of Foreign Relations, suggest that, during Obama's presidency, there were 324 civilians among the 3,797 people killed.[17]

In 2016 alone, Obama, the 2009 Nobel Peace Prize laureate, not heeding Abraham Lincoln's maxim 'One war at a time', dropped at least 26,171 bombs on seven Muslim countries: Syria, Iraq, Afghanistan, Libya, Yemen, Somalia, and Pakistan.[18] Donald Trump did better. Between his inauguration in January 2017 and October of that year he approved the dropping of more bombs in the Middle East than Obama had in the whole of 2016.[19] The US dropped almost eight times more bombs on Afghanistan in 2019 (7,423) than in 2015, more than at any time since 2006 when the Pentagon began counting.[20] On 13 April 2017 it dropped one of its largest non-nuclear devices, dubbed 'the mother of all bombs' (MOAB), on a tunnel complex used by so-called Islamic State militants in eastern Afghanistan. Military experts say that the use of the MOAB was strategically significant. They were, as often, quite wrong.[21]

The strikes by the US-led coalition in ISIS-controlled Raqqa, Syria, between June and September 2017 led to the death of more than 1,600 civilians, while those against Assad on 14 April 2018 – egged on by France's Macron with the somewhat unenthusiastic support of the British government – made no difference to a war Assad was winning anyway.[22] Meanwhile Saudi Arabia went on with its war in the Yemen, while Israel shot unarmed demonstrators in Gaza without a murmur of disapproval from the West.

One of the problems is that the main actor in US foreign policy is the president. Most American presidents have not had the slightest experience of foreign policy and often surround themselves with people who have very little knowledge of international relations (Brzezinski and Kissinger being the most obvious exceptions, though they only had academic knowledge before their appointment), or are too cowardly to disagree. Even though American scholarship on international relations is unsurpassed, US presidents, with a few exceptions (one can think of Nixon who was vice-president for eight years and had time to learn a thing or two), have had a very modest understanding of the 'global'.

In 1961, John F. Kennedy (and his brother Robert who had been briefly an aide to Joseph McCarthy's anti-communist witch-hunt and who, as US attorney general – appointed by his brother though he was completely unqualified – ordered the wiretapping of Martin Luther King) believed the CIA intelligence on Cuba and approved the invasion of the Bay of Pigs, the first of many failures. Paranoid about Castro and grossly over-estimating Castro's influence in Latin America (and thereby increasing it), Kennedy supported the 1962 overthrow of Arturo Frondizi, the democratically elected president of Argentina, considered intervening in Brazil to oust the democratic government of President João Goulart, and supported military coups in Guatemala and the Dominican Republic in 1963 (against Juan Bosch, its first democratically elected president).[23]

The myths surrounding Kennedy were due to his unquestioning apologists, Theodore Sorensen and Arthur Schlesinger, and to the facts that he was good-looking, had a pretty wife, and was murdered by a mad killer. His numerous liaisons with women posing security risks exposed him to blackmail by the FBI and J. Edgar Hoover, and would have led to his resignation in a country with a

less slavish press, or today under the impact of the #MeToo movement. He was also dependent on amphetamines and other drugs
needed to combat his back injuries and Addison's disease.[24] None
of this should come as a surprise to anyone who examines dispas-
sionately the hawkish Cold War rhetoric of Kennedy's bombastic
inaugural address (praised throughout the West) when he declared,
'Let every nation know, whether it wishes us well or ill, that we
shall pay any price, bear any burden, meet any hardship, support
any friend, oppose any foe to assure the survival and the success
of liberty.'[25] Had Donald Trump used similar language in 2017,
everyone in the West would have panicked and run for cover. In fact
Kennedy was a remarkably incompetent president.

Compare his warmongering rhetoric to Dwight Eisenhower's
thoughtful moral views proclaimed at the height of the Cold War.
Eisenhower was a former general and an undistinguished president, widely believed to have encouraged (along with the British)
the assassination by the Belgians of the democratically elected
Congolese leader Patrice Lumumba in January 1961.[26] However,
Eisenhower is also remembered for denouncing the 'industrial-
military complex', in his Farewell Speech of 17 January 1961, in
terms which make him sound almost a pacifist: 'we must guard
against the acquisition of unwarranted influence, whether sought
or unsought, by the military-industrial complex. The potential for
the disastrous rise of misplaced power exists and will persist.' But
he should equally be remembered for saying, at the start of his presidency, in what came to be known as 'The Chance for Peace Speech':

> Every gun that is made, every warship launched, every rocket fired
> signifies, in the final sense, a theft from those who hunger and are
> not fed, those who are cold and are not clothed.
>
> This world in arms is not spending money alone. It is spending
> the sweat of its laborers, the genius of its scientists, the hopes of its
> children. The cost of one modern heavy bomber is this: a modern
> brick school in more than 30 cities. It is two electric power plants
> ... It is two fine, fully equipped hospitals ... This is not a way of
> life at all, in any true sense. Under the cloud of threatening war, it
> is humanity hanging from a cross of iron.[27]

None of this seemed to perturb Kennedy. The 1962 Cuban missile crisis, his 'finest moment', when he was 'eyeball to eyeball' with the Kremlin, originated with the deployment of American Jupiter missiles (regarded as 'first strike' weapons) in Turkey, within range of major Russian cities. Understandably alarmed, the Soviets retaliated by deploying nuclear-armed missiles in Cuba. Kennedy, needing to look tough, declared the Soviet move a threat to peace and security. Everyone panicked. The president looked presidential. Eventually the USSR withdrew its missiles and Kennedy withdrew his from Turkey (and promised never to invade Cuba). That was done on the quiet: the Soviets understood he needed to save face.

Kennedy's most serious foreign policy mistake (he accomplished virtually nothing domestically) was to believe his generals over Vietnam, thus initiating the most serious foreign policy disaster in American history. Kennedy, always a Cold War hawk, had appointed Robert McNamara as his defense secretary, a man who had spent most of his life in corporate roles in the Midwest, as if that gave one any insight in international politics. Much later, McNamara acknowledged as 'a weakness of our form of government' that, while in Europe ministers will often have spent time in opposition acquiring experience, 'I, in contrast, came to Washington from having served as President of Ford Motor Company.'[28] Bad habits continue: Donald Trump's hapless secretary of state, Rex Tillerson, sacked in March 2018 and described in *The Atlantic*, somewhat unfairly since the competition is keen, as 'The Worst Secretary of State in Living Memory', was the boss of ExxonMobil, a leader in climate change denial.[29] Trump's main advisers in March 2018 were all former generals: John Kelly (White House chief of staff who left office at the end of 2018), James 'Mad Dog' Mattis (secretary of defence, forced out in December 2018, Trump used the 'mad dog' nickname when he appointed him), and H. R. McMaster (national security adviser, sacked at the end of March 2018 in favour of the appalling John Bolton). In no previous Western democracy have all key foreign policy decision-makers been ex-generals. Mattis was succeeded by Patrick Shanahan who had spent most of his life working for Boeing – a real product of the 'military-industrial complex'– and was investigated though ultimately cleared for continuing to favour Boeing's business while deputy secretary of defense.

McNamara failed in everything he tried. Under his and Kennedy's watch, 500,000 American soldiers went to Vietnam, where 58,000 of them died, along with Vietnamese casualties (both civilian and military) estimated as ranging between 882,000 and 1,050,000.[30] It took thirty years for McNamara to admit, in his memoirs, the enormity of his 'mistakes': 'I want to put Vietnam in context ... Yet we were wrong, terribly wrong. We owe it to future generations to explain why. I truly believe that we made an error not of values and intentions but of judgement and capabilities.'[31]

McNamara's lack of grasp of international affairs was shown in his naive belief in the mantra that 'If Laos is lost to the Free World, in the long run we will lose all of Southeast Asia.' This is what Eisenhower had told him, and he repeated it to Kennedy in a secret memo on 24 January 1961.[32] Dean Rusk, secretary of state under Kennedy and Johnson, was convinced that Vietnam was a mere puppet of China. Such appalling ignorance was one of the side-effects of McCarthy's purge from the State Department of 'leftists' who knew a thing or two about Asia.

Kennedy's successor, Lyndon Johnson, was a shrewd and clever man with massive experience in Congress, but he knew little about foreign policy. By 1966 even McNamara began to doubt the US's ability to win. In a telephone conversation with Johnson on 28 June 1966, he said 'We're taking ... soldiers, with God knows how many airplanes, helicopters and firepower and going after a bunch of half-starved beggars ... we need to look at it that they can keep that up almost indefinitely.'[33] General William Westmoreland, the self-deluded commander of US forces in Vietnam (1964–68) – described by David Halberstam, author of the best account of the war, iron-ically entitled *The Best and the Brightest*, as 'not brilliant' – had been equally puzzled: he referred to the Vietnamese he was fighting as 'termites' in a lengthy metaphor with racial overtones.[34] This was the language of the common American soldier. As the British war correspondent Max Hastings reported, US soldiers regularly referred to the Vietnamese, whether friend or foe, as 'gooks or dinks'. Many expressed their sympathy for the plight of Lieutenant William Calley, responsible for the My Lai massacre of 16 March 1968, when between 300 and 500 peasants, including women and children, were murdered, some of the women having been raped before being killed. Major Colin Powell, later US secretary of state, produced a report on My Lai which was 'an uncompromising whitewash'. By 1971, as Hastings (not a man of the left) later wrote, 'most correspondents of all nationalities had despaired of the American cause'.[35]

Westmoreland, however, never accepted that the US had lost.[36] His strategy consisted in trying to kill as many North Vietnamese and Vietcong soldiers as possible until what he called a 'crossover point' was reached, where casualties were more than the enemy could sustain. To put it even more simply, the 'strategy' consisted in killing as many people as possible. Between 1965 and 1967 the US and its allies dropped over 1 million tons of bombs on the South.[37] When the reporter Neil Sheehan, 'embedded' with the US Army, warned Westmoreland of the enormity of civilian casualties, the general replied, 'Yes, but it does deprive the enemy of the population, doesn't it?'[38] Between 1965 and 1972 they used napalm, a jelly-like substance that sticks to the human body, burning it in an unbearably painful way and almost always killing its victims. In the same period the Americans also used Agent Orange, a toxic chemical intended to deprive Vietnamese farmers of clean food and water and to make the enemy visible (it had previously been used by the British in Malaya).

This was all to no avail. Johnson tried to involve other countries in the Vietnam quagmire, notably Great Britain, but Harold Wilson, far, far shrewder than Tony Blair, turned down the request.

As Norman Dixon wrote in his *On the Psychology of Military Incompetence*, 'In this most ill-conceived and horrible of wars', Lyndon Johnson and his advisers selected targets 'at a nice safe distance of 12,000 miles' while the man on the spot, Westmoreland, was 'bemused by the sheer weight of destructive energy'. Together Johnson and Westmoreland 'produced a pattern of martial lunacy so abject and appalling that it eventually did for both of them'.[39] The problem with Johnson, McNamara and co. is not just that they were not in control but that they did not even realise that they were not in control. The Vietnamese knew time was on their side. As Pham Van Dong, prime minister of North Vietnam, told the *New York Times* in 1966: 'And how long do you Americans want to fight ... one year? Two years? Three years? Five years? Ten Years? Twenty Years? We will be glad to accommodate you.'[40]

The North Vietnamese and the Vietcong had no air force but they had been fighting for decades, were fighting for their own land, and were infinitely more experienced than the Americans. This is why they won. Force is not everything in military matters. As Horace explained almost 2,000 years ago, 'Vis, consili expers, mole ruit sua' (Force, without wisdom, collapses under its own weight) (*Odes*, Book III, Chapter 4).

Johnson should have listened to Hans Morgenthau, the eminent political scientist of the so-called 'realist' school, who had realised that America was bound to lose. As Morgenthau titled an article in the *New York Times* magazine (18 April 1965): 'We Are Deluding Ourselves in Vietnam.'[41] He was duly dismissed as a consultant by Lyndon Johnson.

Matters improved (slightly) under Nixon who, advised by Henry Kissinger, was sufficiently alert to accept Chinese entreaties. These led to the recognition of China, and the dumping by the Americans of their erstwhile ally Taiwan, as well as South Vietnam. It had taken years for the Americans to extricate themselves from Vietnam, partly to avoid acknowledging they had lost.

Nixon and Kissinger had invaded Cambodia, savagely bombed Laos and North Vietnam, supported the Pinochet coup in Chile, allowed Saddam Hussein a free hand with the Kurds, and supported the Pakistani military in their mass slaughter in Bangladesh. Yet Nixon and Kissinger were foreign policy professionals. After them foreign policy was back in the hands of dilettantes such as the hapless Gerald Ford, the House minority leader, who had been drafted in as vice-president when Spiro Agnew was forced to resign for tax fraud, and then found himself president when Nixon resigned in August 1974 in the wake of the Watergate scandal. Ford kept Kissinger as secretary of state, and Kissinger spent much time in the so-called shuttle diplomacy in the Middle East, solving short-term problems and creating longer-term ones, while supporting Indonesia's slaughter in East Timor.

Ford was followed by Jimmy Carter, who had previously been state senator for Georgia and then governor of Georgia (hardly a training ground for ruling the world). Carter was followed by Ronald Reagan whose main political experience, after a period as a second-rate Hollywood actor, was as governor of California. Reagan's successor was George Bush senior, who at least had been US ambassador to the UN, then envoy to China, and then, but for less than a year, director of the CIA. Then it was the turn of another amateur: Bill Clinton, whose main experience was as governor of Arkansas, one of the poorest and most under-educated states in the country, with a population of 3 million people. Then there was George Bush Junior, former governor of Texas, and finally Barack Obama, the junior senator from Illinois, who promised and failed to close Guantanamo during the eight years of his presidency, presumably so no one would think he was soft on terrorism.[42]

Last but not least in this sorry line is Donald Trump, who never understood the limits of presidential power and will remain a universal laughing stock. During his presidential campaign Trump declared pompously that he would stop China from 'raping' the US economy. Once elected, on a visit to Beijing in November 2017, he almost genuflected to a self-confident Xi Jinping and behaved with uncharacteristic modesty and respect. He did not mention anything which might offend the Chinese – Taiwan, Tibet, Tiananmen Square – and did not blame China for the American trade deficit. As he might have put it in one of his numerous silly tweets: 'Sad!'

In July 2017, during a visit to Poland, home of one of the most right-wing governments in Europe, Trump was introduced by his wife Melania and began his speech with a toe-curling tribute to her: 'there is truly no better ambassador for our country than our beautiful First Lady, Melania. Thank you, Melania. That was very nice.' Most of the rest of the speech was a turgid pandering to Polish nationalism of no great significance to anyone except Polish nationalists. Stuff like 'The triumph of the Polish spirit over centuries of hardship gives us all hope for a future in which good conquers evil, and peace achieves victory over war … in the Polish people we see the soul of Europe.' Then it was down to business, with Trump the salesman thanking Poland for acquiring from the United States 'the battle-tested Patriot air and missile defense system – the best anywhere in the world'.[43]

The amateurish style of American politics is further exemplified by the (brief) surge in support for Oprah Winfrey's improbable candidacy as the next president of the United States, on the basis of an eight-minute speech at the Golden Globe Awards in January 2018. It was a well-delivered speech of the utmost banality in which, following tradition, she thanked the various people who have helped her in her career: 'it is a privilege to share the evening with … the incredible men and women who have inspired me', and ended by mentioning the struggle against racism, Rosa Parks, and looking forward to 'a new day … on the horizon!'[44] One is tempted to dismiss this as simply another instance of celebrity culture gone mad, but with Trump as president, 'Oprah for president' did not sound quite so ludicrous, since American politics has become spellbound by the power of the spectacle.[45]

Trump's presidency took international approval ratings for the US to a new low across 134 countries, at 30 per cent (it had been 48 per cent in Obama's last year in office). The only states where the approval ratings increased with Trump were Belarus, Israel, Macedonia, and Liberia. In Europe, approval ratings for Trump were high only in Kosovo (75 per cent) and Albania (72 per cent). In Poland it was 56 per cent (probably because of his visit) and in Italy, the fourth country, with an inexplicable 45 per cent. In the UK, notwithstanding the 'special relationship', it was 33 per cent, in France 25 and in Germany 22. Making America 'great again' is going to be an uphill task. Those surveyed were also asked to rate three other countries: China got 31 per cent, Russia 27 per cent, and Germany did best with 41 per cent.[46] No one was asked to rate the UK in spite of Gordon Brown's conviction that British creativity could make the twenty-first century 'a British century'.

American global political influence had been waning for some time, but this was completely lost on Tony Blair who, in typical prostrate position, addressing the joint houses of Congress on 13

July 2003, explained that 'the most dangerous political theory' was that the power of the US needed to be balanced with that of another power, adding, just to endear himself to historians, that there had never been a time 'when the study of history provides so little instruction for our present day'.[47] Like all his predecessors and, no doubt, all his successors, he felt the need to mention the fabled 'special relationship' between the US and the UK. This 'relationship' is one of the more embarrassing aspects of British foreign policy. In so far as it exists at all it is confined to the sharing of intelligence and to American support for Britain's 'independent' nuclear weapons. It should be called a 'relationship of dependence'. The 'special relationship' is taken seriously only in the UK, while in the US it is mentioned only when a British prime minister lands in Washington, almost as if to please an elderly and somewhat potty uncle basking in their out-of-date illusions.

When it comes to Trump, however, Blair is probably right in his remarks about history: historically there has been nothing quite like Trump. He has been an embarrassment to all supporters of the US. European conservatives cringe when he speaks, and his tweeting has been unpredictable, making uncertainty the hallmark of his presidency. His famous but vague promise to 'Make America Great Again' (a slogan similar to one previously used by Ronald Reagan in 1980), though it suggests that the country is no longer 'great', elides the fact that America was never 'great'. US military interventions, almost all useless from the point of view of its own national interests, have, as we have seen, almost always resulted in disaster. One of the many reasons for this, in addition to chronic military incompetence, is that ordinary Americans, not unreasonably, do not wish to die for their country, particularly when they do not understand why. US soldiers may believe that the US is a beacon of hope for the planet but they did not understand what they were doing in Korea, Vietnam, Cuba, Afghanistan, Iraq, Libya, etc. 'Stopping the spread of communism' was not very convincing since it entailed assuming that communism, if not halted in Laos or Cambodia or Vietnam, would somehow have reached Palm Beach or Atlantic City. As Niall Ferguson put it: Americans 'would rather consume than conquer'.[48] This means that soldiers cannot be deployed for long, and are soon replaced by equally inexperienced soldiers (unlike the Vietnamese or the Taliban who fought and fight for years).

America's 'greatness', if one wants to use the term, lies in the field of popular culture (music, films, etc.), in software (Apple, Microsoft, etc.), and in social media (Facebook, Twitter, etc.). Examples of what Joseph Nye, in his *Bound to Lead: The Changing Nature of American Power* (1990), called 'soft power'. Here the US dominates and will go on dominating for some time; but who knows for how long? In China the internet and technology conglomerate Tencent, one of the largest corporations in the world, dominates the world's largest digital market. Behind Tencent are other Chinese internet giants such as JD.com, Alibaba, and Baidu. There is plenty for Facebook, Amazon, Netflix, and Google to worry about.

The United States is not an exemplary society, as most intelligent Americans realise only too well. The race divide is still as deep as it was before the election of a black president. An enormous proportion of blacks are killed by the police, or are in prison, or are poor. Mass shootings have become the norm. According to a study by the US Department of Education, 32 million adults in the US can't read.[49] In 2016 life expectancy fell for the first time since 1993. Every day, more than ninety Americans die after overdosing on opioids such as pain relievers, heroin, and fentanyl.[50] This opioid crisis can be traced back to the early 1990s and the over-prescription of powerful painkillers (at the time this problem existed in the UK as well: at the Gosport War Memorial hospital more than 450 patients died due to opioid drugs policy). By 2011, painkiller prescriptions had tripled. In 2016, there were 63,000 fatal overdoses – more than the total number of Americans killed in Vietnam.[51]

According to the World Bank, American neonatal mortality rates in 2016 were higher than those of Cuba, and of most Western nations. At four per thousand live births, it is just ahead of 'communist' China (five). Inequalities have increased dramatically. There is a greater gap than usual between leaders and led: Congress has become a club that consists of 245 millionaires (out of 535 voting members): 66 per cent of senators are millionaires (you need millions to fight for a seat), as are 41 per cent of members of the House, compared to just 1 per cent of Americans.[52] Political divisions are stronger than ever; bipartisanship in Congress became a thing of the past in the years of Clinton and Obama.[53]

Donald Trump, in his sparsely attended inaugural address of 20 January 2017, having promised that 'From this day forward, it's going to be only America first, America first', saw no cause for optimism: 'Mothers and children trapped in poverty in our inner cities; rusted-out factories scattered like tombstones across the landscape of our nation; ... and the crime and gangs and drugs that have stolen too many lives and robbed our country of so much unrealised potential. This American carnage stops right here and stops right now.'

In reality the 'carnage' had been decreasing for years. The US homicide rate declined by nearly half between 1992 and 2011. From 2002 to 2011, male victims of homicides were 3.6 times the number of female victims; the rate for blacks was 6.3 times higher than that for whites.[54] In 2017, 15,613 people were intentionally killed by shooting – more than five times the number killed in the

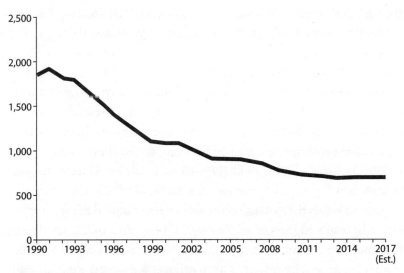

Figure 3 Violent crimes per 100,000 people in the 30 largest US cities (1990–2017)

Source: Ames C. Grawert and James Cullen, 'Crime in 2017: A Preliminary Analysis', Brennan Center for Justice at NYU School of Law, 6 September 2017, p. 2.

four coordinated terrorist attacks of 11 September 2001 (when 2,996 died).[55]

The US annual rate for homicide per 100,000 was, in 2016, 5.4, higher than in North Korea (4.4) and Cuba (4.9), much lower than El Salvador (82, the highest in the world), Venezuela (56), and South Africa (34). But the US rate is far higher than that in comparable 'advanced' countries such as Japan (0.3), South Korea (0.7), Italy (0.7, Mafia notwithstanding), Germany (1.2), New Zealand (1), the United Kingdom (1.2), France (1.3), or Canada (1.7). Some US cities have a homicide rate comparable to the worst in the so-called Third World: in 2018 St Louis topped the American league with 61 homicides per 100,000, followed by Baltimore (51). These two cities were respectively fifteenth and twenty-third in the world league for worst crime rates. The top ten are all in Latin America.[56] There were no European, Asian, or Middle Eastern cities in the top fifty. Most European countries are at the lower end of the international league table for homicide levels. China conformed to the European level: 1 per 100,000.[57]

Internationally the United States is increasingly isolated, particularly on issues such as the Middle East and global warming (which Trump regards as a Chinese hoax, 'created by and for the Chinese in order to make US manufacturing non-competitive'.)[58]

Not so long ago the US was also extremely 'backward' in the field of civil rights, and to some extent still is. Long civil rights battles had to be fought to ensure that blacks could vote in Southern states. It was only in 1967 that the Supreme Court declared the so-called anti-miscegenation laws prevailing in some Southern states to be unconstitutional. The verdict (known as *Loving vs Virginia*) originated when Richard Loving (white) married Mildred Jeter (black) in 1958 in Washington DC, where mixed marriages were legal. They then returned to Virginia where they had always lived. A few weeks later they were arrested in the middle of the night, prosecuted, and sentenced to a year in jail. The sentence was suspended on condition that the couple lived outside Virginia. By 1964, frustrated at not being able to visit their relatives in Virginia together, they appealed. The Circuit Court judge, Leon Bazile, refused to vacate the sentence, declaring that 'Almighty God created the races, white, black, yellow, Malay, and red and placed them on separate continents ... The fact that he separated the races shows that he did not intend the races to mix.'[59] Eventually the Supreme Court intervened and, in 1967, declared the miscegenation laws unconstitutional. But it took a long time for all Southern states to comply. Alabama, the last state to change its laws, did so in 2000, well after apartheid had been abolished in South Africa. None of this should surprise those who are aware that between 1877 and 1950 over 4,000 racial lynchings took place in twelve Southern states.[60]

Those who today complain about the 'nanny state' should consider that, in 1914, thirteen US states were not allowing those with epilepsy to marry. In 1927, the US Supreme Court (in *Buck vs Bell*) ruled by eight to one that it was permissible for states to forcibly sterilise 'mental defectives', which included epileptics. Over the following thirty years some 50,000 epileptics were sterilised. In the United Kingdom it was hardly better: the Matrimonial Causes Act of 1937 decreed that a marriage could be annulled if 'either party to the marriage was at the time of the marriage ... subject to recurrent fits of insanity or epilepsy'. This clause was repealed only in 1971 with the Nullity of Marriage Act.[61] In Japan an estimated 16,500 people were sterilised without their consent under a eugenics law introduced in 1948 and in force until 1996.[62] Of course, elsewhere it was worse: in Nazi Germany the mentally disabled were murdered.

There are times when a 'nanny state' is preferable to being at the mercy of one's parents. In 2019, in California, David and Louise Turpin were condemned to life imprisonment for having kept twelve of their thirteen children, aged two to twenty-nine, imprisoned since birth, often chained in appalling conditions and given only one meal a day, abusing and torturing them. Their home was registered as a private school, with David Turpin listed as the principal. In California private schools are not licensed by the state education department and no agency regulates or oversees them. They were only required to file a report once a year. California, not being a 'nanny state', lacks the authority to monitor, inspect, or oversee private schools.[63]

There are times when one desperately needs a 'nanny state', as long as the nanny is not Donald Trump. This was cruelly exposed in the White House's response to the coronavirus pandemic. On 24 February 2020, Trump had tweeted that the situation was 'very much under control'. On 11 March he declared, to the astonishment of most experts, that America was deploying 'the most aggressive and comprehensive effort to confront a foreign virus in modern history'. In modern history! And not just a virus: a *foreign*, a *Chinese* virus, as if viruses had passports. Then the inevitable bluster: 'No nation is more prepared or more resilient than the United States.' An absurd statement since the lack of universal medical coverage meant that many Americans will be reluctant to have themselves tested.[64] As Trump was speaking, the virus had spread to forty-four states involving at least 1,920 patients. After Trump's address, David Litt, a former Obama speechwriter, declared 'my careful rhetorical analysis is that he's gonna get us all killed'. Two weeks later the front page of the *New York Times* lamented: 'Job Losses Soar, US Virus Cases Top the World' (27 March). As Robert Reich pointed out, since the US has no real public health system, the coronavirus had a clear run.[65]

Trump blamed other countries, not only China but also the European Union, banning travellers from the EU from entering the US. At first the United Kingdom was excluded – no one understood why.[66] The already depressed markets dropped by a further 10 per cent.

In the *New Yorker*, Susan Glasser, in her regular 'Letter from Trump's Washington', pointed out that at first Trump denied the seriousness of the coronavirus outbreak and was still insisting that it carried 'very, very low risk' for Americans, before adopting a 'militaristic and nationalistic tone' which 'sounded scary and ignorant and utterly inadequate at a time when the country [was] being radically upended'. She added: 'Trump was detached from the unfolding reality of a global crisis that is unlike any in memory.' Of the 1,049 tweets Trump had sent in the previous five weeks, only forty-eight mentioned coronavirus, Glasser pointed out. The first was on 24 February 2020, in which he declared that the virus was 'very much under control in the USA'.[67] In fact, the preparations for confronting the virus were inadequate compared to those of South

Korea, and the US seemed to have learned little from China or Italy. Trump's budgets had made deep cuts to science, including cuts to funding for the Centers for Disease Control and Prevention and the National Institutes of Health. In 2018, Trump fired his homeland security adviser, Tom Bossert, whose job included coordinating the response to global pandemics. Bossert was not replaced. In 2019, Tim Ziemer, director for global health security at the National Security Council, left the council and was not replaced. Dr Luciana Borio, the National Security Council director for medical and biodefence preparedness had left in May 2018 and was also not replaced.[68] By November 2020, the death toll in the US had reached 240,000, the highest in the world.

A February 2020 White House briefing entitled 'Freedoms and Promoting American Values' declared glibly that 'in America, we believe in the majesty of freedom and the dignity of the individual'.[69] That may well be so, but when one talks about values (American, British, French, or whatever) one should be aware that this is not an unquestioned field. There are constant disagreements within every society. Once many thought homosexuals should be jailed, women should stay at home, criminals should be hanged, blacks should know their place, and that it was perfectly rational to torture prisoners of war to extract information. This is not a past to be proud of. Making America 'great' might involve revisiting history and not using the word 'again' again.

6

European Narratives

Values come and go. European values are a construct used by those who want to promote certain values and discredit others as 'non-European'. The idea of a unified set of principles and values which one could call 'European' only existed in the imagination of intellectuals as a programme for the future, not a reality. There were no uniform values: not in France, not in Britain, not in Italy, not even during the Renaissance, and not during the Enlightenment. Yet many invoke recently accepted 'values' as if they are ancient. The idea of there being 'common European values' is fairly recent, invented in the eighteenth century.

The idea of European unity is even more recent. One hundred and fifty years ago Europeans were busy uniting states, not Europe. Over 150 years ago Italy was being united, as was Germany. No one was talking about a united Europe, not even Giuseppe Mazzini, founder of the association Giovine Europa, who assumed that a united Europe would only come about once each national state had come into being. Giovine Europa was one of Mazzini's many fantasies, only a dream (*non è che un sogno mio*), as he himself admitted later, in a letter written on 22 June 1835, his birthday. But then, as Eric Hobsbawm remarked about Mazzini's political initiatives, his 'mere presence' would have been enough 'to ensure their total ineffectiveness'.[1]

Europe was so divided that when Europeans thought about wars, they thought mainly about waging wars against other Europeans. By the end of the nineteenth century the British and the French were worried about the Germans, the Italians about the Austrians, the Poles about the Germans, the peoples of the Balkans about each other, the Ottomans about Europe, and the Russians – the Russians were worried about everything, as they are now.

Far from uniting, Europeans were preparing for the worst internecine wars of their history, worse than the Hundred Years War or the Thirty Years War, worse than the Napoleonic Wars. Just over a century ago, the First World War (fought mainly in Europe) destroyed the possibility of global European supremacy. By the time the war was over, the more percipient among Europeans realised that their continent was no longer the centre of the universe. But many Europeans continued cultivating their illusions throughout the 1920s and 1930s. There are still some French and British who go on behaving as if they have empires.

The British believed they were carrying the 'white man's burden', though Rudyard Kipling, who coined the expression, thought that burden should be carried by the US. The French had a *mission civilisatrice*; the Portuguese, much earlier, their own, rather ridiculous *missão civilizadora*.

Others too had illusions. In 1917 the Russians started an extraordinarily ambitious experiment: the construction of a powerful industrial society which would become a model for the rest of the world, since it would lead to a just and equal society without classes or private property. The experiment failed miserably, at enormous human cost. That failure led to Russia being dominated by mafia-like plutocrats in what has become one of the most unequal economies in the world, with the top 10 per cent owning 77 per cent of the wealth.[2]

The Germans under Adolf Hitler dreamt that Europe could be united under their leadership, and cleansed of undesirable elements such as Jews, Romani, and Slavs. And let's not forget Mussolini and his pathetic dreams of a return to Roman glories.

Smaller countries had fewer illusions, one of the unremarkable benefits of being small and weak. As Paul-Henri Spaak, a former socialist prime minister of Belgium and one of the founding fathers of European integration, is supposed to have said, there are only two kind of states in Europe, small states and small states that have not realised they are small. France and Great Britain obviously belong to the second category.

The Second World War added another 50 million dead to the 20 million of the first and completed the task of taking Europe from the centre of the world to its periphery. In the twenty years following the end of the war, the French and the British lost their empires. Europe itself was divided between East and West. Germany was sliced into two and remained so until 1990, its new generations only too aware of the horror of war and determined to abandon any bellicose project, a lesson expensively learnt. The communist dream embodied in the USSR collapsed unexpectedly in 1989–91. The situation we face today and which we will continue to face is largely determined by this momentous event.

But to return to the question of so-called European supremacy: Europe in the nineteenth century may well have been the 'centre of the universe', but that was not so before the eighteenth century. A spaceship loaded with social scientists from Mars or Jupiter, on a fact-finding mission to Planet Earth during, say, the sixteenth or the seventeenth century, would not have noted much in the way of European supremacy except in some scientific domains such as astronomy and cartography (the Chinese had invented earlier than the Europeans the compass, the plough, gunpowder, the stirrup, and printing).

China, Mughal India, and perhaps even Japan were politically more advanced, with a more sophisticated bureaucracy, superior medicine, and artistic achievements on a par with much Renaissance art (most of which was confined to central and northern Italy, the Netherlands, and Germany). There was also little doubt that barbarity and intolerance were far more pronounced in Europe than elsewhere. Before the eighteenth century it was certainly much safer to live under Islam or Buddhism or Confucianism than in Christian Europe. And Europeans settling outside Europe were not particularly enlightened – just think of the fate of the Native Americans or the indigenous Australians. European barbarism and intolerance continued well into the twentieth century, as Auschwitz and the Gulag should remind us.

The assumption of European superiority was developed in the eighteenth and nineteenth centuries. In the former it was based on the intellectual achievements of the Enlightenment, its rationality and its triumph over clerical obscurantism. This feeling of superiority was further enhanced in the nineteenth century when European supremacy was anchored on a stronger material basis: the development of a technological and industrial capitalist society. However, those who talked about the superiority of Europe – a beacon of modernity, the cradle of civilisation – did not mean 'Europe' as a geographical reality stretching from the western coasts of Ireland and of the Iberian peninsula to the Caucasus and Constantinople, and from the icy wastes of Finland, Sweden, and Norway to the warmer climate of Sicily. They meant Western Europe, defined differently at different times, according to whoever was writing. The great historian Leopold von Ranke, in his *History of the Latin and Teutonic Peoples from 1494 to 1514* (1824), explicitly excluded the Hungarians and the Slavs, who 'long vacillated between the Romish and the Greek form of worship ... It will not be said that these peoples belong also to the unity of our nations [i.e. the Latin and Teutonic peoples]; their manners and their constitution have ever severed them from it.'[3]

The opposition between East and West is not new. The identification of 'Europe' with Western Europe and the negative view of the East had been commonplace for a long time. Voltaire, in his *Histoire de Charles XII* – one of the bestsellers of the eighteenth century – assumed, not entirely wrongly, that his readers would live in civilised Western Europe and not in the North or in Eastern Europe.[4] In his *Histoire de l'Empire de Russie sous Pierre le Grand*, Voltaire noted that reformers such as Tsar Peter did not try to emulate distant countries, such as Persia or Turkey, but looked for a model in *notre partie de l'Europe* (our part of Europe), 'where all kind of talents are celebrated for eternity'.[5] The West meant enlightenment, progress, secularism, and human rights, and even the rights of women (not that such rights really existed in Europe, East or West).

That which is not 'Europe' is barbarian territory: Montesquieu in his *De L'Esprit des lois* asserted that it was in Asia that 'despotism feels so natural' (*naturalisé*).[6] Since then, and down to the present, Eastern European countries have struggled to be regarded as part of Europe. The Poles stress the divide between themselves and 'barbaric' Russia; the Hungarians, the Poles, and the Czechs insist they are part of 'Central' rather than 'Eastern' Europe. (Western) Ukrainian nationalists constantly redefine Ukraine as part of the West and its liberal tradition, in spite of the historical fact that most Ukrainians and Russians are bound together ethnically and culturally by an ancient common history.

Some members of the elites of the Ottoman Empire, China, and Japan displayed the same sentiment. They might have wanted to preserve their 'souls', their culture, and their tradition, but they also wanted modernity, thinking that the fabled Western package could be dismantled into its various components and that one could pick and choose. They had become admirers of Europe only when Europe had become militarily superior and threatened to colonise them.

This humility was new. Before, East had looked down on West or, rather, had not bothered to look at all, since there was nothing to learn from it. The Chinese regarded Europeans as barbarians, distinguishing between Hua (Chinese) and Yi (foreign barbarians). The West, however, at least in the seventeenth and eighteenth centuries, was transfixed by the Far East and particularly by Qing China: its gardens and pagodas decorated Kew and Tivoli; porcelain and lacquered cabinets were imported or imitated; Rococo artists were inspired by Chinese motifs; Chinese 'wisdom' (there is always a good deal of fantasy in this kind of worship) was admired by the thinkers of the age. They built on reports dating from the sixteenth century, written by Jesuits such as Matteo Ricci (1552–1610), who had gone to convert heathens only to discover wealth and taste, culture and art, an astonishing bureaucracy, and benevolent and tolerant rulers. Ricci, known to the Chinese as Li Madou, lived in China for twenty-seven years, and translated into Latin the Confucian Four Books. His diaries, *De Christiana expeditione apud Sinas* (On the Christian Mission among the Chinese), posthumously published in the West in 1615, expressed his admiration for Confucius (though not for Buddhism). He was accused of having 'gone native', to use an expression favoured later in British circles to censure colonial officials who had become too enamoured of local cultures. Voltaire and Leibniz too admired the teaching of Confucius.[7] Hegel, though he knew little about China, declared it 'is this wondrously unique empire that astonished Europeans, and has continued to do so'.[8]

By the middle of the nineteenth century the situation had reversed: Europe thought it had nothing to learn; Asia, everything. The Chinese Imperial Court, having done its best to pre-empt reforms, reluctantly decided to embrace 'the new'. In 1901, a letter eliciting proposals from officials of the vast empire received various responses. Zhang Zhidong, governor of Shanxi, advocated rebuilding China on the basis of 'Western methods' so as to attain 'wealth and strength'.[9]

Japan too, and earlier than China, was swept by a wave of enthusiasm for Western progress. The Meiji leaders resembled contemporary elites in the Third World, torn between admiration for the West and detestation of it. At first, in the 1850s, the impact with the West had sparked off a xenophobic movement of rejection. But, in the 1870s and 1880s this gave way to a general pro-Western enthusiasm. The era when Japan regarded itself as singular among nations was over. The Japanese would have to learn to become like Europeans to avoid succumbing to them. Now East looked to West with fear and admiration.

Two world wars later, it was the turn of Europe to look further west, to the United States, with fear and admiration. This Europe, this *Western* Europe, felt small, threatened, divided, humbled, and humiliated. The terrible war had been largely caused by Western European powers (Germany and Italy). Europe had been saved by the USSR, that is to say by the 'wrong side of Europe', and by the US ('the wrong side of the Atlantic'). It was largely in response to the Second World War that the European Economic Community (EEC), as it was initially called, was born. A puny enterprise compared to the enormous catastrophe which had preceded its creation, it was initially a small free-trade area involving only six states (the Benelux countries, West Germany, France, and Italy) and a minority of the inhabitants of the continent. But it soon became, however imperfectly, the focus for the dreams of unity that many Europeans harboured.

In some cases such dreams were those of a return to a glory they thought had existed previously. In others, it was a way of defending Europe against the new 'West', that of the United States. In yet others it was just a question of prosperity. Many have claimed that European unity was a way of preventing a new internecine conflict, as if there were ever a serious prospect that, in the years following the Second World War, Germany, divided and chastened, would start another one by invading France, or Poland, or Belgium, or that France and Great Britain would go to war. Yet the idea that peace in Europe was a central objective of the European Economic Community was constantly reiterated, as if economic matters were too sordid to be the glue holding Europe together. As Jacques Delors, president of the European Commission, mused in his speech at the European Parliament on 17 January 1989: *On ne tombe pas amoureux d'un grand marché* ('nobody can fall in love with a large market').[10]

Pacifist rhetoric had been deployed earlier, on 9 May 1950, the anniversary of the end of the Second World War in Europe, by the French foreign minister, Robert Schuman. He proposed a European Coal and Steel Community (ECSC), harbinger of the EEC, adding, with typical Franco-nationalist bombast, that France had for more than twenty years been a champion of a united Europe, and that it had always had serving peace, *servir la paix*, as its essential aim. The words were uttered while France was waging a bitter and quite useless colonial war in Indochina with American backing. And only a few years earlier French foreign policy objectives, as embodied in the Monnet Plan of 1946, included keeping Germany weak and annexing the Saar (and its mineral resources). An earlier plan, drafted in 1944 by Henry Morgenthau, then US secretary of the Treasury, proposed to destroy Germany's key industries. Under Roosevelt's successor, Harry Truman, the American administration, quite rightly, thwarted such vindictive plans and devised instead the Marshall Plan. Better help Germany and Western Europe to be rich and anti-communist than poor and open to Soviet entreaties.

Unable to subjugate Germany, the French decided that it was preferable to hold her in a tight embrace.

In 1993 the EEC had become the European Union. The original six members became, in stages, the twenty-eight (twenty-seven after the UK's departure). Each step from the six to the twenty-eight has been described as a step towards European unity. Of course things are more complicated than that.

The Europe of the European Union has remained profoundly divided. This is not surprising. Europe has never existed as a united entity. No conqueror, no country, has ever been able to impose its rule over the whole continent – not Trajan (under whom the Roman Empire reached its greatest extent), not Charlemagne, not Napoleon, not Hitler.

The development of the European Union reflects this historical disunity. States joined for different reasons and never because they became enamoured of the European ideal, though political rhetoric dictated that ideals should be invoked whenever possible. It was the Community's economic success that eventually convinced the British, whose economy had performed so poorly in the 1960s, to join in 1973 (having failed to do so earlier because of the opposition of de Gaulle). The Danes and the Irish joined at the same time because their economies were then highly intertwined with that of the United Kingdom. Greece joined in 1981 and Spain and Portugal in 1986, to put the past of their dictatorships behind them. In 1995, Sweden, Austria, and Finland joined largely for economic reasons. And then, between 2004 and 2013, almost everyone else: not only Malta and Cyprus, which did not wish to remain isolated small countries, but also many of the former communist countries (outside the USSR), because they needed respectability and recognition, because they wanted to establish a clear barrier between themselves and the history of communism, because they were scared of Russia, and, above all, because they hoped to become prosperous like the countries of Western Europe.

That the dominant ethos of the European Union should be market-oriented will not surprise any observer of its history. Its goal has always been the abolition of intra-economic barriers and the creation of a single market with a single currency. Welfare legislation has always remained solidly in the hands of nation-states. And so has taxation, the main instrument of economic decision-making. Some social provisions were thrown in to keep the unions on board. Some human rights tenets were added to keep liberals happy.

In any case, economics is not enough to construct an identity. Can one construct a European identity? Should one construct it? What would it entail? The only model we have for this is the construction of national identity. This takes us back to the nineteenth century, when History, then barely established as a subject of study in the academy, was becoming important. The Romantic revolution had recentred it as the master narrative in which the people could read their own biography. Heroes could still be kings and queens but only because they represented the 'genius' of one's nation. Historians, for centuries the lackeys of sovereigns, the chroniclers of lies, now acquired a 'democratic' role and, with this, an important market. The British historians of the nineteenth century, such as Thomas Babington Macaulay, G. M. Trevelyan, and Bishop William Stubbs, presented a rosy and entirely comforting view of the development of British history. It was the history of a succession of intelligent reforms based on pragmatism. Even Cromwell, the civil wars, and the execution of Charles I were drafted into a story of constant peaceful progress towards greater democracy and constitutional rights. An enlightened and astute ruling class gave in to popular pressure just at the right time, before the masses turned to violent revolution. Unlike the rebellious French, the confused but well-meaning Italians, the militaristic Germans, and the hopelessly romantic Poles, the British did everything right. This cliché still dominates the British view of themselves.

In France too, history was used as the pre-eminent terrain where national identity could be forged. A people who did not know its own history, it was believed, would always be at the mercy of despots by whom they would be hoodwinked and cheated. The people had to be told the 'truth' about themselves. This was the task of historians, the new priests of the secular order. This is what the great historian Jules Michelet believed. In 1846 he wrote that France was the only country whose interests were mixed with those of the rest of humanity, because its great national legend 'is the only one which is complete ... it is an immense, uninterrupted stream of light, a true milky way, upon which the world has ever its eyes fixed' (*une trainée de lumière immense, non interrompue, véritable voie lactée sur laquelle le monde eut toujours les yeux*). Unlucky Germany and England, on the other hand, remained strangers to *la grande tradition du monde, romano-chrétienne et démocratique* (the great Romano-Christian and democratic tradition of the world).[11]

More than fifty years later, Ernest Lavisse, holder of the chair of modern history at the Sorbonne, wrote a multi-volume text, *Histoire de France depuis les origines jusqu'à la Révolution* (1901), as well as books and lectures aimed at teachers of history in the schools of the Republic. He felt that children should be instructed that their duty was to avenge the defeat of Sedan in 1870 by Prussia (the bellicose element was toned down gradually), and to defend the values of the French Revolution against all those who sought to re-establish the Ancien Régime. In his entry ('L'histoire') for the *Nouveau Dictionnaire de Pédagogie et d'instruction primaire* (1911) he wrote: 'There is in the most distant past a poem which must be instilled in young souls to strengthen their patriotic spirit. Let's lead them to love our ancestors the Gauls ... Charles Martel at Poitiers, Roland at Roncevaux, Godfrey of Bouillon, Jeanne d'Arc ... all our heroes of the past, even if enveloped in legends.'[12]

'Legend' is the right word. Charles Martel did not stop Islam at Poitiers in 732. Roland who died a hero at Ronceveaux was not fighting the Muslims – as the celebrated epic poem *La Chanson de Roland* would have it – but the Basques. Godfrey of Bouillon was only one of the many leaders of the First Crusade, etc.

Nowadays such embellished history has been toned down and French schoolchildren are no longer compelled to recite, as had been compulsory for decades, the absurd notion that their 'ancestors' were the Gauls and that Clovis, the first 'Christian' king, was the first king of France. In the ranks of the few who would wish to go back to this facile indoctrination was François Fillon, the defeated candidate of the centre-right at the presidential elections of 2017. He had promised, in a speech in August 2016, that if elected he would appoint a commission of 'respectable historians' to produce a new history for schools which would constitute a 'national narrative' (*récit national*), just like Michelet in 1846. Emmanuel Macron also celebrated the *récit national* during his electoral campaign by declaring that there are elements in the *roman national* 'which help to constitute ourselves as a nation', and then trotting out the usual *grandes figures françaises*: Clovis, Jeanne d'Arc, etc.[13]

Some British politicians have echoed these attempts to inculcate nationalism at school. Michael Gove, as secretary of state for education, speaking in the House of Commons on 9 June 2014, promised that he would require all schools 'actively to promote British values'.[14] Back in October 2010, Gove, an overrated 'intellectual', bemoaned the lack of emphasis on Churchill, eminent Victorians, and 'Britain and her empire' in the history curriculum. 'This trashing of our past has to stop', he said, complaining that 'The current approach we have to history denies children the opportunity to hear our island story.'[15]

Gove thought he had the backing of the 2002 Education Act, enacted by a Labour government, seeking to compel schools to teach 'British values'. A cursory reading of the relevant section of this Act (section 78) shows that there is no mention of 'British' values; all it says is that schools should promote 'the spiritual, moral, cultural, mental and physical development of pupils'. This is so vague and anodyne that liberals as well as jihadists – indeed most people – would agree that 'spiritual development' is a Good Thing, though they would disagree as to what form it might take. The website of the school inspectorate Ofsted, however, does mention as fundamental 'British' values 'democracy, the rule of law, individual liberty and mutual respect for and tolerance of those with different faiths and beliefs and for those without faith'. It is not clear why these values are peculiarly British.[16]

Another politician to wax lyrical about British values was Gordon Brown. In February 2007, speaking at the Commonwealth Club in London just a few months before succeeding Tony Blair as prime minister, Brown declared that 'Britain' has a 'unique history', as if other countries had all the same history, and as if the component parts of the UK, which Brown duly listed, had the same history. He then extolled 'British values' (again, tolerance, belief in liberty, fair play, etc.): 'Even before America said in its constitution it was the land of liberty ... Britain can lay claim to the idea of liberty', which 'has emerged from the long tidal flows of British history – from the 2,000 years of successive waves of invasion, immigration, assimilation and trading partnerships, from the uniquely rich, open and outward looking culture'.[17] Not bad for a Scot with a PhD in history to assume that Scotland and England have shared the same 'British' history for the last 2,000 years, or even existed for that long.

One is reminded of George Bernard Shaw's sarcastic comment written as the First World War got under way: 'I have spent so much of my life in trying to make the English understand that we are cursed with a fatal intellectual laziness, an evil inheritance', which he attributed to the luck of having had a monopoly of coal and iron which, for a while, made Britain supreme.[18] One hundred years later the same intellectual laziness endures though the coal has gone.

As for British values: should one add colonialism, racism, and the slave trade; that the death penalty was abolished in Great Britain only in 1965 (and in Northern Ireland in 1973), after Portugal, Denmark, Italy, Germany, Austria, Switzerland, Finland, Sweden, and many others; that male homosexuality was a crime in the UK until 1967 (preserved in Scotland until 1981, and in Northern Ireland until 1982), while its criminalisation had been abolished in France in 1791, in the Netherlands in 1811, in Brazil in 1831, in Portugal in 1852, in the Ottoman Empire in 1858 (at the time when someone could still be hanged in Britain for 'buggery'), in Japan in 1880, in Italy in 1889, in Denmark in 1933, in Iceland, Switzerland, and Sweden in the 1940s, in Greece and Jordan in 1951, in Thailand in 1956, in Czechoslovakia and Hungary in 1961, and in Israel in 1963; that Jews were accepted at the University of Padua in 1222 but only in 1856 at the University of Oxford. Corporal punishment was banned in Polish schools in 1783, in France in the first half of the nineteenth century, in Russia in 1917 (after the revolution), in the Netherlands in 1920, and in Italy in 1928 (under fascism!). In England and Wales corporal punishment was outlawed only in 1986, and only in state schools; if your parents paid, you could be beaten in private schools until 1998 in England and Wales, 2000 in

Scotland, and 2003 in Northern Ireland – always the last when it comes to human rights.

As recently as 1970–1, as documented in a 1977 letter from the then Labour home secretary, Merlyn Rees, to the prime minister, James Callaghan, Conservative ministers had given permission for the use of torture against internees in Northern Ireland, evidence that was reportedly withheld from the European Court of Human Rights.[19] In 2018 the parliamentary Intelligence and Security Committee (chaired by the Conservative MP Dominic Grieve) revealed that British intelligence agencies were involved in the torture and kidnap of terrorism suspects after 9/11, when Tony Blair was PM and Jack Straw was foreign secretary.[20]

British values? Tolerance? Fair play?

Still, remarkable progress has been made in the West towards tolerance. A report by the International Lesbian, Gay, Bisexual, Trans and Intersex Association (ILGA) reveals that there are still seventy-two states that criminalise same-sex relations (37 per cent of all UN states). Thirty-two are in Africa, ten in the Americas (almost all in the Caribbean), twenty-three in Asia (including both India and Pakistan, but not China). In some states only the 'promotion' of homosexuality is forbidden, as in Russia and Lithuania (and as was the case in the UK with Clause 28 of the Local Government Act 1988, finally repealed in 2003 after initially successful opposition in the Lords). On the whole, Western Europe emerges with a clean bill of health when it comes to the legal status of homosexuals.[21]

The common European experience is a mythology of progress and civilising mission (ignoring the heavy borrowing from the Orient), as well as a bloody history of warfare and genocide. One could stress the positive and tone down the negative, but, fortunately, historians nowadays are unlikely to do that. Having gained their professional freedom, historians of integrity are not about to tailor their teaching and writing to the requirements of 'a common European identity'.

Both nations and nationalism are too strong to be ignored in the European project. Indeed, all the documents of the European Union, whenever they mention the need for more coherence and a common identity, are careful to mention the necessity of avoiding fragmentation, chaos, and conflict, and the desirability of achieving cohesion, solidarity, subsidiarity, and cooperation, and of respecting the existing national identities of the member states.

I don't think a European identity can be taught. I don't think that one can make Europe a nation-state of nation-states – which is not to say that the slow and painful construction of the European Union, in spite of all the problems, the mistakes, the silly rules, the democratic deficit, and the low turnout at elections, is not a Good Thing. Besides, elements of a European identity have evolved in some countries, thanks to a common currency, the abolition of passport controls in the Schengen area, and the university exchange known as the Erasmus programme. What is certainly not taught, or not taught enough, is the history of other European countries.

But let us not forget that most people's idea of history is not based purely on what they were taught at school. They learn their history partly from the distorted recollections and prejudices of parents and grandparents, partly from the inchoate references to the past they glean from broadcast news, newspapers, books (particularly novels), and, above all, from television and films.

Politicians too contribute to the distortions of history whenever they use the past to justify their policies. It is now an axiom that if you wish to invade a country ruled by a dictator the default position is to compare the dictator to Adolf Hitler. In April 1999, Ken Livingstone, then an MP and not yet mayor of London, compared Milošević to Hitler (*Independent*, 20 April 1999) when calling for 'humanitarian' intervention against Serbia – i.e. bombing Belgrade and its civilian population. He was not the only one. Bill Clinton did the same, while implicitly comparing himself to Churchill. In August 2002, Donald Rumsfeld, US secretary of state for defense, warned his audience against being 'soft' on Saddam Hussein as Europe had been with Hitler.[22] In 2003 (just before the invasion of Iraq) Tony Blair said exactly the same thing. Perhaps it was better to be less interventionist. In November 2015 Jeremy Corbyn, by then leader of the Labour Party, decided that the party should oppose air strikes in Syria. Sixty-six Labour MPs, led by the shadow foreign secretary Hilary Benn, voted against him. Yet in 2013 David Cameron had lost a government motion by 272 votes to 285, with thirty Tory MPs joining forces with Labour, led by Ed Miliband, and including Hilary Benn, to block a British intervention in Syria.

Hilary Benn's 2015 speech in favour of intervention was widely praised as 'impassioned' (*Daily Mirror*), 'the speech of a true leader' (*Daily Telegraph*). In a litany of absurd historical parallels, Benn, foaming at the mouth, compared the jihadists of ISIS to Nazi Germany and Fascist Italy: 'we are here faced by fascists ... And what we know about fascists is that they need to be defeated ... It's why this entire House stood up against Hitler and Mussolini.'[23]

Needless to say this was pure bombast. The British have been marginal in the war against ISIS in Syria, as confirmed in a scathing report by the House of Commons Defence Committee. In it we read that between September 2014 and May 2016, UK air strikes in Iraq were only 7 per cent of the total and only 4 per cent between December 2015 and May 2016. Mark Carleton-Smith, deputy chief of defence staff, admitted to the Committee that in Syria the UK was only 'marginally engaged'.[24] And it could contemplate only air strikes because the British Army was barely functional. It finds it so difficult to recruit soldiers that it now tries to encourage women, gays, and ethnic minorities to join the fewer than 80,000 regulars. Young people with reasonable qualifications, explained a gay recruit, can do better 'than get paid £17,000 to crawl through mud in the rain in North Yorkshire'.[25]

The defeat of ISIS was due to a combination of Russian air power, Iraqi-backed Shia militias on the ground, Iran-backed Hezbollah, the Syrian army, and Kurdish forces backed by the Americans from the air. The retaking of Mosul from ISIS in July 2017 was achieved by Iraqi government forces backed by US air power with marginal contribution from the British who, presumably, also contributed to the frighteningly high number of civilian casualties.[26] In October 2017, Raqqa, the so-called capital of the so-called caliphate, was re-taken by Kurdish Syrian troops supported by US air strikes. A city which once had 200,000 inhabitants now lay 'in pieces' according to *Time* magazine, 'with nearly every building damaged or destroyed'.[27] An Amnesty International report of 5

June 2018 established that the US-led coalition forces destroyed the city, killing hundreds of civilians in the process of 'liberating' them from ISIS.[28] So much for humanitarian intervention. Wars such as these inevitably lead to considerable civilian casualties, as Major-General Rupert Jones, once Britain's top military commander in Iraq, explained: 'War is "hell" and it is impossible to defeat ISIS without killing civilians.'[29]

The conflict in the region continued and became ever more complex with further Turkish intervention, while the US increasingly wavered under its ever wavering president.

. In all this the British have been (and will continue to be) as irrelevant as Hilary Benn and his silly comparisons of ISIS with Hitler.

Such comparisons are old hat. In 1956 the British prime minister Antony Eden and the leader of the opposition Hugh Gaitskell both compared Nasser to Hitler for having had the temerity to nationalise the Suez Canal. At a World Affairs Council session in Boston on 15 February 1984, US secretary of state George Shultz said that Nicaragua 'feels like Nazi Germany'. In March 2014, Hillary Clinton, no longer US secretary of state, but still a foreign-policy hawk, compared Putin's occupation of Crimea to Hitler's occupation of the Sudetenland in 1938. There are, of course, similarities, but the word 'Hitler' conjures up not just the Sudetenland but also Auschwitz, world war, and genocide, and those who make the comparison are perfectly aware of the effect that the mere mention of Hitler's name has. A bit like telling a vegetarian, 'Oh, a vegetarian, like Hitler.'

In Oslo on 10 December 2009, during his Nobel Lecture, Barack Obama compared al-Qaeda's leaders to Hitler.[30] More recently, in March 2018, following the attempted murder of Sergei Skripal (a Russian who spied for Britain and was then exchanged for Russian spies in the West) and his daughter in Salisbury, allegedly by Russia, Boris Johnson (speaking to the Foreign Affairs Select Committee and responding to prompts from the Labour MP Ian Austin) called for England to pull out of the World Cup to be held in Russia, and agreed, with characteristic understatement, that Putin was going to use the competition the way Hitler used the 1936 Olympics. This, of course, turned out to be one of Johnson's many absurd statements. In an article in the *Daily Mail*, Iain Duncan Smith drew a comparison between the CBI stance on appeasing Hitler in the 1930s and its present opposition to Brexit.[31] (The Tories, at the time, were the main proponents of appeasement, but does history matter when one is trying to score debating points?) Madeleine Albright, no more impressive as an historian than she was as US secretary of state, calls anyone she doesn't like a 'fascist', from the North Korean dictator, Kim Jong-un, to (potentially) Trump.[32] Last but far from least, Prince Mohammed bin Salman, the de facto ruler of Saudi Arabia, declared that the 'Iranian supreme leader makes Hitler look good'.[33]

All this only confirms what has come to be known as Godwin's Law, after the American attorney Mike Godwin's assertion that, as a political discussion develops, the probability of a comparison involving Hitler increases, Hitler being little more than a metaphor for 'the worst person you can think of and whom everyone has heard of'. In the Middle Ages it was Satan. At least the Führer really did exist.

Hitler aside, the typical history taught in schools in most of Europe consists of a fundamental pillar: the history of one's own country. To this pillar is added a smattering of Greek and Roman history, allegedly 'our' common heritage (a notion invented in previous centuries), some major events (the Black Death, the French Revolution), and some landmark periods such as the Renaissance or the Enlightenment (usually heavily geared to one's own country).

The peoples of the European nation-states did not choose their nation. They have had nationhood and nation-building thrust upon them. Eventually they became British, German, French, Italian, Spanish, or Belgian, etc. They may have felt themselves to be Scottish or Cornish, Gascon or Breton, Bavarian or Prussian, Sicilian or Piedmontese. Many still do, but – thanks to a bureaucracy and an education system which gave them a common language and a 'common' history; thanks to wars, national anthems, sporting tournaments, Eurovision song contests, national broadcasters, and a host of other initiatives – most Europeans have learned to identify with a particular set of political institutions they call the 'nation'.

In many cases fortuitous political circumstances led inhabitants of a particular region to develop a 'national' spirit. The people of Nice are French today, and many are probably proud of it, but until 1860 Nice was part of the Kingdom of Sardinia (Piedmont). The inhabitants spoke the local patois, the *niçois* (a kind of Occitan). In 1860, Emperor Napoleon III obtained Nice and its surrounding territory from the Kingdom of Sardinia in return for the military help he had given it during the 1859 war against Austria. Nice and its inhabitants were now 'French' and, no doubt, soon felt as patriotic as if they had been born in Lille (which became 'French' only in 1668) or Lyons. Had that not happened, the Italian Riviera would have been much more extensive, with tourists enjoying *zuppa di pesce* instead of the *bouillabaisse*, and its inhabitants supporting Italy's national football team rather than that of France.

Let me conjure up a contemporary example. Imagine something terrible happened to the United Kingdom, for instance a major collapse of the economy due to Brexit and/or the coronavirus epidemic, which persuaded the Scottish, the Irish, and even the Welsh that they would be better off if they seceded. England would be left on its own. Imagine further that the collapse was so serious that regions of England decided they too wanted independence, Cornwall for instance. Today a Cornish nationalist party exists, but it is generally regarded as joke. But then so were the Scottish nationalists once. Imagine Cornwall as an independent country. This is not so unrealistic since it has a population of over 530,000 (the same as Luxembourg) and an area of 3,563 km² (bigger than Luxembourg). The new nationalist government would immediately start constructing a Cornish identity and a Cornish culture. Right now it seems only 3,000 people, at best, can speak Cornish (or *Kerneweg*). But the new government could force schools to teach Cornish. After all, in 2002 the then Labour government, perhaps in a desperate attempt to ingratiate itself with local voters (there are very few Labour supporters in Cornwall), requested that Cornish be included in the European Charter for Regional or Minority Languages. Since the EU promotes regional identities, in 2005 it allocated £80,000 for the promotion of Cornish – not a princely sum, but enough to cover the salaries of a couple of school teachers. In 2014 the EU recognised the Cornish as a national minority group.

Cornwall is one of the poorest regions in the UK, indeed in the EU, and is a recipient of EU funds. Not that this stopped it voting in favour of Brexit in 2016, probably under the illusion, once the UK is out, that London will fund the revival of the Cornish economy.[34]

But, in our fictional example, the new independent Cornish government could make it a condition of public employment that people should be able to speak Cornish or willing to learn it. It could subsidise a newspaper in Cornish (even now one of the local papers has the occasional article in Cornish). There is no literature in Cornish to speak of, but this does not mean that the new government could not annex literary figures with connections to Cornwall, for instance the Nobel Laureate William Golding of *The Lord of the Flies* fame, or D. M. Thomas, poet and author of *The White Hotel*, who were both born there, as well as some who were not, such as Daphne Du Maurier, who lived in Cornwall and most of whose novels are set there. In her last novel, *Rule Britannia*, Du Maurier even imagines a Cornish secessionist movement repressed by an American expeditionary force.[35] Independent Cornwall could also appropriate ancient folk stories such as that of Tristan and Isolde, much of which takes place in Cornwall and on which Wagner based his famous opera, having borrowed the story from a thirteenth-century German, Gottfried von Strassburg, who, in turn, borrowed it from Thomas of Britain, probably a Norman who settled in England, who had written it in old French. Not much Cornish here.

After a few decades of this kind of systematic public intervention, perhaps even earlier, Cornwall would have become a proud nation – just like all the others.

To construct a nation, it is necessary to have a state, to raise taxes, to control education and the media, and to have a police force and an army. The European Union lacks such mechanisms and few would want it to have them. It is impossible to build a European identity the way the French or British or German identities were built.

Moreover, right now, while the nation-state remains the main focus of identity, an increasing proportion of Europeans are angry with their conventional politicians and either vote for 'anti-system' Eurosceptic parties of the right, parties that raise the spectre of the dangers of immigration, or don't vote at all. They also vote for people who have never been politicians, as if jobs in, say, real estate and TV (Donald Trump and Silvio Berlusconi), banking (Emmanuel Macron), comedy (Beppe Grillo), or the food industry (the Czech leader Andrej Babiš) offer greater guarantees of political integrity. Even in the case of Jeremy Corbyn, his obvious lack of interest in conventional party politics, in spite of a lifetime in politics, was an advantage.

Commentators have noted that 'the people' are angry with the 'elites'. More time should be spent examining why the quality of political personnel in the West has degenerated so much. I hope it is not a harking back to 'the good old days' to compare, favourably, the old leaders – Harold Macmillan, Harold Wilson, even Margaret Thatcher; Helmut Schmidt, Willy Brandt, and Konrad Adenauer; Alcide de Gasperi, Giulio Andreotti, Enrico Berlinguer, and Aldo Moro; Charles de Gaulle and François Mitterrand; Adolfo Suárez and Felipe González; Andreas Papandreou and his father Giorgios – to their successors. But it is not great men (and women) who make a difference; it is circumstances. Where would de Gaulle or Churchill have been without the Second World War? Or FDR without the Great Crash of 1929? So many Russians would not have lamented the death of Stalin in 1953 had he not been regarded as the victor of the war rather than a paranoid murderer. In morbid times the Latin metaphor *nanos gigantum humeris insidentes* (standing on the shoulders of giants) does not hold. This is a time of pygmies who have no memory of giants.

7

Europe Imploding?

So far the European Union has failed every test of 'European solidarity': the 2008 global downturn, the crisis in the Middle East,
the Arab Spring, and, more recently, the spread of the coronavirus
epidemic. This is not entirely surprising since, in spite of the bluster
about European values and the Eurosceptics' depiction of the EU
as a monolithic bloc from which one should 'take back control', the
powers of Brussels are extremely limited. So when there is a crisis,
such as that of the coronavirus, it is every nation for itself.

There was alarm in Europe when Trump imposed his ban on
travellers from Europe, but borders were closed elsewhere too, even
though for a virus the whole world is like Schengen: it does not stop
at the borders. Exports of medical supplies have been restricted in
spite of the commitment to a single market. On 12 March 2020 nine
medical experts from China arrived in Italy with 31 tons of medical
supplies, including intensive care unit equipment, medical protec-
tive gear, and antiviral drugs. 'By contrast, in a shameful abdication
of responsibility, fellow countries in the European Union failed to
give prompt medical assistance and supplies to Italy.'[1] Early on,
Austria and Slovenia closed their borders to Italians in spite of
Schengen. Others followed, including Germany shutting its borders
with France, Austria, and Switzerland. And that, at least by April
2020, was the 'collective' European response to the pandemic: each
state to its own.

But then Europeans had not been looking to the European Union
for guidance and leadership for a while. In theory one might have

expected that, disappointed with national politics, they would turn to the EU, but their frustration with their own political class turned into opposition to the pan-European project of their established national leaders.

But why are so many angry or, at the very least, disappointed? Europeans have never been richer, and have never experienced such a long period of prosperity and peace. In the present difficult economic climate the European Union may be an irrelevancy, a side issue or an obstacle, but the EU did not cause the global downturns of 2008 or 2020, nor the shift of manufacturing jobs to China and elsewhere (on the contrary it tried to stem the flow), nor the growing power of finance and of the banks. Neither did it cause inequalities. Perhaps it is not surprising that the European project has failed to conquer the hearts and minds of so many. To become central to political life the EU would need far more powers than it possesses at present. But to acquire more power it needs the backing of Europeans. It needs to conquer hearts and minds. And this is the vicious circle in which the Union finds itself.

Did people want an ever closer union? Obviously not. Did they want an even more 'market-oriented' Europe? Probably not. Do people want a 'social' Europe? Certainly yes – and unsurprisingly so, since no one wants lower pensions, expensive health care, long working hours, and a lack of provision for young families.

An attempt was made to provide the EU with a constitution in the hope that Europeans would see in this a unifying charter. But the problems multiplied. The constitution became a factor of disunity. Napoleon is alleged to have said that a constitution should be *courte et obscure* – brief and obscure. The aborted and now forgotten Euro-constitution of 2005 passed half the Napoleonic test. It was obscure, but it was also far too long (almost 400 pages, divided into 448 articles). Ambiguity is a double-edged sword. It can unite those who want to be united and find something positive in the text, and divide those determined to come to a negative verdict. This was what happened with the proposed constitution rejected by the French and Dutch in referendums held in 2005, and later reborn as the Treaty of Lisbon signed in 2007 and coming in force after 2009. There is no denying that the driving ethos of the failed constitution (as of most EU initiatives) was 'market' Europe rather than 'social' Europe.

The winning idea, expressed by virtually all conservatives and even by some on the left, was that the main impediments to economic progress in Europe are labour market rigidities and excessive social provisions, and that deregulation and privatisation, within limits, would widen opportunities and resolve problems. Thus the neoliberal view was firmly at the centre of the economic discourse of the main European political parties. It declared that true freedom resides in the market, a notion Marx sarcastically denounced when he wrote that the market, where 'Mr. Moneybags and the possessor of labour-power' (i.e. the worker) encounter each other, 'is in fact a very Eden of the innate rights of man. There alone rule Freedom, Equality, Property and Bentham.' Freedom, because the two parties 'are constrained only by their own free will. They contract as free agents'; Equality, because each 'exchange equivalent for equivalent', i.e. wages in exchange for labour; Property, because 'each disposes only of what is his own. And Bentham, because each looks only to himself.' Marx continued: 'no one troubles himself about the rest', and eventually all works out for the best 'for the common weal and in the interest of all'.[2]

This became the central global narrative of our age, not because it worked, but because it was advanced by the hegemonic players in the world financial system, from Washington and London to the IMF and the World Bank. The people who ran the world financial system were fairly incompetent. To take just one name: Robert Rubin, US Treasury secretary, and one of the architects of Clinton's deregulation and of the repeal of the Glass–Steagall Act. Here was a 'master of the universe', a man who worked for Goldman Sachs for twenty-six years (and became its chairman), who later became chairman of Citigroup, and yet who failed to notice the brewing sub-prime mortgage crisis – not that this stopped him from enjoying, upon retirement, a bonus of $126 million in cash and stock. Citigroup, of course, had to be bailed out by the US Treasury to the tune of $476.2 billion in cash and guarantees.[3] As the *New York Times* caustically wrote, 'The Citi may never sleep, but he [Rubin] snored.'[4] And, alas, he was not the only incompetent in charge of the 'universe'.

Joseph Stiglitz, Nouriel Roubini, and others such as the hedge-fund manager Michael J. Burry had seen the coming catastrophe; and so did even Doris Dungey, who worked in the mortgage industry and who blogged under the pseudonym of Tanta. Doris, unfortunately, was not in charge of the universe, unlike Bob Rubin and his friends.

At first, the crisis of 2007–8, which some compared to the 1929 crash, barely dented the universal commitment to a neo-liberal market economy. The triumph of capitalism seemed to be confirmed. A social system can be deemed to have triumphed not when everything is going well but when it is in crisis and everyone attempts to save it. All remained united around the idea that a cap-italism freed from regulation was for the best (as if markets did not require states). This is not a platform around which one can con-struct political unity. Unity is about agreed rules, not the absence of rules. Neoliberal Europe is an oxymoron.

Nor could European unity and identity be constructed on military and power-politics competition. In most international affairs – whether the crisis which destroyed the former Yugoslavia, the multiple crises afflicting the Middle East, the wars in Iraq and in Afghanistan, the civil war in Syria, the catastrophe which befell Libya after the fall of Gaddafi – there could never be and never was a common European position, or, if one was found, it was ineffectual.

The Iraq War was a particularly dramatic instance of the difficulty of establishing a united European position. The two countries regarded as the axis of European integration, France and Germany, were both against intervention, but they failed to aggregate the majority of European countries. Opinion polls regularly demon-strated that a majority of European public opinion was against the war even before the extent of the Iraqi disaster was known. Perhaps they were citizens of what Rumsfeld pejoratively labelled 'Old Europe' (i.e. those countries, such as France and Germany, which refused to toe his line) and not of 'New Europe' (those that did, mainly countries seeking US protection against Russia). Britain was completely behind the Americans, with Blair standing 'shoulder to shoulder' with George W. Bush, and later repeating the same mantra – 'I thought it was the right thing to do' – well after everyone else had accepted that it was the wrong thing to do. Iraq presented no threat, had no weapons of mass destruction, and the UN inspectors had not even completed their task (and anyway found nothing). No one knows how many Iraqis died, though we know that 4,000 Americans died, that more than 2 million Iraqis fled abroad, and that 1.5 million were displaced. Car bombs, suicide attacks, sectarian killings, and disproportionate US counter-insurgency tactics and air strikes produced a major humanitarian catastrophe.[5] The country never recovered, while Blair still thinks 'it was the right thing to do'.

Virtually all Sunnis viewed the invasion as a humiliation aimed at putting the majority Shia Arabs in power.[6] The US authorities failed completely to understand the importance and the dynamics of local politics in Iraq, which is why their subsequent attempts at nation-building failed miserably.[7] Britain was just as bad. Nowhere in the mass of declassified material presented at the Chilcot Inquiry into the Iraq War is there an analysis of the likely consequences of an invasion.[8] Gordon Brown, full of rancour against Tony Blair, and suggesting that he himself had nothing to do with the decision, lamely wrote in his memoirs that, 'having reviewed all the information *now* available' (my emphasis, he was writing in 2017), 'we were all misled on the existence of WMDs'.[9]

In January 2003, with the same lack of diplomatic savoir-faire which would be further developed by Trump, Rumsfeld had declared: 'If you look at the entire NATO Europe today, the centre of gravity is shifting to the east and there are a lot of new members. The vast numbers of other countries in Europe, they're not with France and Germany, they're with the United States.' France and Germany were outraged.[10] At the same time, the American neo-con and political commentator Robert Kagan, in his *Of Paradise and Power: America and Europe in the New World Order*, came up with the felicitous formula (in the sense that journalists could just repeat it without bothering to read the book) that 'Americans are from Mars and Europeans are from Venus', adding 'They agree on little and understand each other less and less.'[11]

Kagan's analysis was, at least in part, common sense: if one has little power one is less likely to start a war. Americans, he explained, admitting this was a caricature, think they live in 'an anarchic Hobbesian world' where one is safe only if one can clobber everyone else; Europeans are 'Kantian' and seek to live in a world of laws and rules of negotiation and cooperation.[12] Europeans might take this as a compliment, confirming their idea that while they are sophisticated and subtle diplomats who have read their Machiavelli, the Americans are mindless warmongering bullies. Americans are then, to paraphrase Abraham Maslow, like people with a hammer for whom all problems become nails.[13]

Kagan's formula was interpreted by many in Washington as meaning that the Europeans could not be relied upon to help police the world. The US had to do the job on its own. The poor opinion some US government advisers had of the European Union was unwittingly confirmed by Victoria Nuland (US assistant secretary of state and, as it happens, wife of Robert Kagan) when, in a leaked phone conversation with the US ambassador to Ukraine during the 2014 crisis in that country, she exclaimed: 'Fuck the EU!'[14] This attitude towards Europe was taken to new heights by Donald Trump, as the coronavirus catastrophe, having started in China, was engulfing the rest of the world.

When it comes to the main issues in international affairs there is no European 'Venus' to counterpose to the American 'Mars', no single European position, no single European initiative, no single European solution. No one turns to Europe for advice. The appointment of a European 'foreign minister', essentially a powerless politician acting as a mediator, revealed the fantasy behind a common European foreign policy. As the then Belgian foreign minister Mark Eyskens declared in 1991, just as the first war against Iraq was getting under way, paraphrasing a widely known quote: 'Europe is an economic giant, a political dwarf, and, even worse, a worm until it concerns itself with elaborating a defence capability.'

How could it be otherwise? Europeans know little about each other. They do not even know each other's pop songs, bestseller, or television programmes. The one country every European national knows better than all other European countries is the US. Films, novels, and songs contribute to this, but the news media too play their part. Elections in European countries are barely covered by the media in the others, only the French and the British and occasionally the German get some attention. On the BBC News at Ten, on 5 March 2018, the important Italian general election which had just taken place – which saw the obliteration of the centre-left, the humiliation of Berlusconi, and the victory of the xenophobic Lega and of the Eurosceptic Movimento Cinque Stelle – was the seventh item on the news agenda and was dealt with in three minutes. So it is not strange if most Europeans would be quite unable to name the prime minister of most other European countries, including big ones such as Italy. US elections, on the other hand, are systematically examined, discussed, dissected, and commented on. This extensive coverage is not unjustified: who the next president of the US will be matters more to most of us, and for obvious reasons, than who the next prime minister of Belgium or Romania will be, but it does not justify the lack of interest in other countries.

So what can Europe do? It should look less to the past and more towards the kind of future it wants and, above all, what it can show the world. This is the spectacle of an association of twenty-seven countries which have different histories, different languages and, in some ways, not that much in common, but which, nevertheless, against the odds, have tried to find a way of coexisting. Europe could try to show the other 200 or so countries in the world that while coexistence may be difficult, there is no alternative to cooperation. Attempting to establish a New World Order (to quote the phrase used by George Bush senior on 11 September 1990 to a joint session of Congress just before the First Gulf War) is a project from a different age. We have seen the shallowness of this kind of thinking. There has been no order, new or old, for Iraq, or for Afghanistan, or for Syria, or for Libya.

We have learned the hard way that there is no grand plan for Europe, no magic wand. There is only the hard work of establishing rules of coexistence, and at least thereby modestly building on something real, something Europeans have tried in the past and will continue, one hopes, to try in the future. What is distinctive in Europe, or at least in Western Europe, is a kind of social capitalism, though that too is in grave danger. What made European nation-states different from the other two main models of advanced capitalism – the American and the Japanese – were relatively strong trade unions and social democratic parties; but, as we have seen, their powers and ambitions have been much reduced. Perhaps they are doomed. Besides, since much of social Europe is anchored to the nation-state – by a main source of identity – the European Union cannot be seen as the foundation of a social Europe.

There are, of course, important social elements in today's European Union, especially when it comes to workers' rights, education, health, and environmental regulation. These have had the positive function of enabling many on the social democratic left to accept integration and give up their narrow and futile vision of building socialism – or rather, as one should say today, social capitalism – in one country. The result is that Western Europe, along with Japan and Singapore, has surpassed the US in having the highest material standards in the world.

The social elements of the Union, however, were always meant to be functional in relation to competition. Their purpose was to establish a level playing field inside the European markets, reducing the worst forms of social dumping by moving towards an equalisation of the length of the working day or ensuring a minimum wage. Even here, as mentioned earlier, there is no uniformity, and some member states, such as the Scandinavian countries (which have relatively strong trade unions), as well as Austria, Italy, and Cyprus, do not have a minimum wage set by the government. Germany introduced a statutory minimum wage as late as January 2015.

The electorates of states with advanced welfare states do not wish to reduce social provisions. Their health-care arrangements are better than those in the United States and so are their levels of environmental protection. However, the countries with limited welfare states – this includes most of the new members – know that their unique competitive advantage lies in low wages, low taxes, and low social provisions. They are forced into further tax cuts and more privatisation. Social inequalities between the different member states thus remain a constitutive part of the European Union. Take the minimum wage, where the differences are remarkable: the statutory minimum monthly wage in Bulgaria is 260.76 euro, in Romania 407.86 euro, in Portugal 676.67, in the UK 1,400.99, in France 1,498.47, and in Luxembourg 1,998.59.[15] Only when the economic gap between the more advanced countries and the laggards has narrowed might there be a more balanced social Europe. That day is far off.

Like many nebulous concepts whose meaning is almost impossible to define, 'European identity' is a warm, comforting phrase. Most people can be European and something else. Only a few strident nationalists fear European identity. And we all know where nationalism has taken Europe: into mass murder, genocide, conquest, oppression. So European identity suggests a process in which Europe turns its back on the bad old days and looks towards a future of peaceful coexistence between peoples who maintain their languages, local cuisines, and other pleasing aspects of their national identity.

There is an urban myth according to which 12 per cent of Americans, when asked who Joan of Arc was, reply that she must have been Noah's wife.[16] This, after all, makes perfect sense since if you have not heard of Joan of Arc (and why should you if you live in a small town in the middle of Iowa?) you would at least have heard of Noah's Ark and, since all the animals were paired, Noah too must have had a wife ... and since the Bible does not name her, Joan is as good a name as Rebecca or Nefertiti. This story is one of the many told by Europeans (and educated Americans) with a feeling of intellectual superiority: Americans may be richer, technologically more advanced, militarily all-powerful, or just better at popular culture, but when it comes to Culture with a capital 'C', then Europeans are best.

But are they, really? The cultural formation of Europeans (like that of Americans) is largely determined by what they learn at school and through the media. In the vast majority of European schools what students are taught is largely their own national history and their national literature. To make this knowledge stick it must be regularly reinforced later in life by their own reading, or by what they watch on television or hear on the radio. Otherwise they will forget. Repetition is the name of the game. An American child may be taught about Thomas Jefferson, but the name will soon be forgotten unless it is mentioned again and again by politicians, in films or on TV, or because streets are named after him, or his face is on the two-dollar bill. Alexander Hamilton is far more famous now because of the successful musical about him – in which his enormous contribution to the establishment of the American financial system is barely mentioned. Every celebrity knows that, to paraphrase Verdi's *Rigoletto*, the public *è mobile qual piuma al vento* (is fickle like a feather in the wind) and that only constant repetition ensures the durability of one's fame. Many people know who Shakespeare was because the world they live in is full of cultural references to him, but many, even in Great Britain, no longer remember or even know who John Milton was (*Paradise Lost,* had it been a thrilling novel adaptable by Hollywood, would have had greater fame) or Christopher Marlowe, whose mistake was to get killed at the age of twenty-nine. The plays Marlowe wrote were as good as any Shakespeare had written by the same age. Had Shakespeare died at twenty-nine we would not have had *Romeo and Juliet, The Merchant of Venice, The Merry Wives of Windsor, Hamlet, Othello, Macbeth, King Lear*, etc. Today, through a combination of talent and luck, Shakespeare is an international icon; Marlowe and Milton are not.

There is, of course, an international class of cosmopolitan intellectuals who speak various languages (especially English), travel, and have friends across several continents with whom they share ideas and knowledge. They are the equivalent of the medieval men of learning who had in common a religion (Christianity), a language (Latin), and a culture (Greek and Roman classics), while most Europeans were illiterate and could barely see beyond their own village.

Today this international class, though certainly far larger than that of the Middle Ages, is a small minority. The others are still enclosed in their village, except that now the village is their own nation even though they also live in a global world. Provincialism and globalism coexist, as can be seen in the success of popular

TV shows such as *Who Wants to Be a Millionaire?* This has been syndicated in over a hundred countries, making it the most internationally successful TV quiz of all time. The format is remarkably similar: the winner wins at least 1 million in the local currency, questions are in ascending order of difficulty, competitors stuck for an answer can use a limited number of escape routes (phoning a friend or asking the public). The game would never work if the questions were not adapted to national cultures. This is not just dictated by considerations of language, but also because there is very little truly global knowledge. The question 'Who wrote *I promessi sposi?*' (*The Betrothed*) would be elementary in Italy but extremely difficult in Illinois, and quite hard even in France or England, where Manzoni is almost unknown. Global knowledge is limited to international popular culture: singers, actors, politicians, and some sportspeople.

Evidence for this global ignorance comes from a survey conducted in 2008 by the French Ministry of Culture.[17] The aim was to establish how much Germans, Italians, and French knew of each other's cultures, the kind of culture one is taught at school. The results were alarming. When asked to name at least two major political figures who had a significant impact on the history of Germany before 1900, 70 per cent of Italians and 72 per cent of French people could not name a single one, not even Bismarck. Seven per cent named Hitler, unaware that in 1900 he was only eleven. Seventy per cent of French and 63 per cent of Germans could not name a single protagonist of Italian history before 1900 – not even Garibaldi. French history did a little better thanks to Napoleon (mentioned by about one-third of Italians and Germans), but 32 per cent of Germans and 40 per cent of Italians could not recollect a single French historical figure – not even Joan of Arc, let alone her husband.

Only 10 per cent of French people knew that Dante was the author of the *Divine Comedy*, though most Europeans have probably heard of Pinocchio (thanks to Walt Disney). The French and Italian communist parties were for a long time the strongest in Western Europe, but their failure is evident: only 33 per cent of Italians and 16 per cent of French could identify Karl Marx as the author of *Das Kapital*. Pavarotti was, by far, the best-known dead

Italian, but only 10 per cent of the French knew that Verdi had composed *Rigoletto*. Hardly anyone outside Italy (and not that many in Italy) had read Italo Calvino or Elsa Morante, Sciascia or D'Annunzio.

We could go on but the point is made. De Gaulle was right, unfortunately: Europe is really *l'Europe des patries*. Everyone knows a little about their little national garden but not much about those of the others. This is not because people are 'ignorant' but because the mechanism of cultural reinforcement is almost completely dominated by national media. It is a vicious circle.

The media, private or public, must give its public what it wants and the public wants what it already knows. And what it knows is its own (national) village plus America. There are plenty of 'small' exceptions to this – The Beatles were global as is Harry Potter (performing and writing in English helps) – but the US is still the only country able to export vast amounts of its own cultural output, facilitated by the fact that, as a land of immigrants, its own culture is a mixture of many cultures.

The persistence of provincialism and low-level nationalism is only one of the reasons for the relative failure of the European project. Euroscepticism has increased remarkably in the last twenty years, as have Eurosceptic parties, even in Italy, a former euro-enthusiastic country, where Eurosceptic parties have grown enormously. In 2004, 50 per cent of Europeans trusted the EU, but by 2016 the figure was down to 32 per cent (converging with the dismal percentage of those trusting their national governments, which hovers around 31–2 per cent mark).[18]

Apart from Greece (understandably enough), the most Eurosceptic country was Britain which, on 23 June 2016, voted to leave the EU by a majority of 52 per cent to 48 per cent. There were significant regional variations. Scotland wanted to remain (62 per cent) as did Northern Ireland (56 per cent) while a majority in Wales, as in England, voted to leave. The 'Brexiteers' were overwhelmingly concentrated in the smaller towns of England. Some major cities such as Birmingham and Sheffield too had a small majority for 'leave' but Bristol, Leeds, Liverpool, and Manchester, as well as Brighton,

Oxford, Cambridge, and Reading wanted to remain. London was solidly for remaining (60 per cent) with huge majorities in inner London: over 78 per cent in Lambeth and Hackney and about 75 per cent in Camden and Islington. There were other cleavages: 70 per cent of voters whose educational attainment was GCSE level or lower voted to leave, while 68 per cent of voters with a university degree voted to remain in the EU. A large majority of the young (defined as those under twenty-five) voted to remain (71 per cent), while a large majority of the old (over sixty-five) voted to leave (64 per cent).[19] Among Conservative voters 58 per cent wanted to leave, but only 37 per cent of Labour and 30 per cent of Liberal supporters.[20]

In other words, it is not an outlandish caricature to suggest that the 'typical' Brexiteers were elderly, poorly educated, conservative provincials. They will be the main victims of Brexit. They decided the destiny of the United Kingdom, perhaps the destiny of Europe. The establishment was strongly pro-remain, including the financial sector, the entrepreneurs, the trade unions (the TUC), and the majority of MPs of all parties, not least, of course, the prime minister David Cameron who called the referendum (as well as his successor Theresa May). The Bank of England, the OECD, the IMF, the London School of Economics, the US government-funded Rand Corporation, and the National Institute of Economic and Social Research have investigated the economic consequences of Brexit and all came to the conclusion that the impact will be negative.[21] A report by the think-tank Global Future, written by the economist Jonathan Portes, examined four likely scenarios for a post-Brexit Britain ('like Norway', 'like Canada', 'WTO rules', and 'bespoke'). All of them are economically damaging: the least worst being the Norway scenario in which Britain would be subject to EU rules over which it would have no control.[22]

Understandably, the British debacle on Europe has been blamed on the losers, on the lower classes, on ignorant voters who believed that, once freed from the 'tyranny' of Brussels' faceless bureaucrats, manna would fall from the heavens, freedom would arrive, and 'we' (who were never in control) would be back in control, master of our own home in this ever globalised world. Yet in 1975 an earlier referendum had confirmed British entry into the EEC by a solid majority (67 per cent), and in 1975 there were plenty of elderly uneducated provincials. The real culprits were not 'the losers' but successive British prime ministers. With the exception of Edward Heath (the only true Europeanist and the person who negotiated the original entry in 1973), they all exhibited a narrow view of the European Union. As David Marquand wrote more than ten years ago, the UK has 'deliberately stood aside from virtually all the crucial developments in the EU since the early nineties'. Britain is not in the Euro and not in Schengen. 'It has deliberately turned itself into a marginal, offshore island, irrelevant to the concerns and future of the European mainland.'[23]

Harold Wilson was in favour of entry because it suited the British economy (then in a particularly poor state). Vision was not his 'thing'. James Callaghan, even though he was foreign secretary and hence one of the protagonists of British renegotiations leading to the referendum, appeared more than reluctant to support the 'yes' vote. In a radio phone-in on 27 May 1975, he declared, to the astonishment of Robin Day who was presenting the programme, that he was neither pro nor anti, adding, thus distancing himself in an extraordinary manner from the key issue:

I am here, and the Prime Minister has taken the same line; it is our job to advise the British people on what we think is the right result. Now there are a lot of other people who've always been emotionally committed to the Market. A lot of other people have been always totally opposed to the Market. I don't think the Prime Minister or myself have ever been in either category and that is not our position today. I'm trying to present the facts as I see them and why we have come down in favour of – now Britain is in, we should stay in.[24]

Margaret Thatcher saw the European Union as an entity from which one should try to get the maximum out while putting the minimum in. Even though she was one of the architects of the Single European Act of February 1986, and therefore of the development of European integration, her view of the EU was the same as that taken by many recent Brexiteers: Brussels was an expensive and bloated bureaucracy that needed to be kept at a safe distance. She fought like a tiger to cut British contributions: 'I want my money back', she demanded in 1980. In Bruges in 1988 she declared, 'We have not successfully rolled back the frontiers of the state in Britain, only to see them re-imposed at a European level, with a European super-state exercising a new dominance from Brussels.' In 1986 she fought against Michael Heseltine, then defence secretary, who wanted the British helicopter company Westland to be bought by a European consortium, preferring instead the US-based Sikorsky. She won, he quit in a huff. She became increasingly anti-European. Immediately after an EEC summit in Rome (28 October 1990) she thundered: 'If anyone is suggesting that I would go to Parliament and suggest the abolition of the pound sterling – no! … We have made it quite clear that we will not have a single currency imposed on us.'[25]

Two days later she rejected the proposal by the president of the European Commission, Jacques Delors, to democratise the European Community, by declaring firmly and famously that Delors 'wanted the European Parliament to be the democratic body of the Community, he wanted the Commission to be the Executive and he wanted the Council of Ministers to be the Senate. No. No. No.'[26]

The pro-European deputy prime minister, Geoffrey Howe, could not take any more. A couple of weeks later he gave a resignation speech to the House of Commons, employing a cricket metaphor which few in Europe could possibly have understood: 'It is rather like sending your opening batsmen to the crease, only for them to find, as the first balls are being bowled, that their bats have been broken before the game by the team captain.' He accused Thatcher of conjuring up a 'nightmare image' of Europe as 'a continent that is positively teeming with ill-intentioned people, scheming, in her words, to "extinguish democracy", to dissolve our national identities and to lead us through the back-door into a federal Europe'.[27] With dwindling support within her own ranks, Thatcher was forced out of office.

Her successor, John Major, promised to keep Britain 'at the very heart of Europe', yet he confined the country at the periphery by opting out of the Social Chapter and single currency aspects of the Maastricht Treaty (1992) and succeeding in keeping the dreaded term 'federal' out of it. This was barely enough to contain the hard-core of anti-EU Conservatives, who, in an unguarded moment, were referred to as 'bastards' by the exasperated prime minister.[28]

Tony Blair was less hamstrung: he was a convinced 'European' (by British standards), he had a solid majority, his party had made its peace with the EU, and the Conservatives were in disarray and led by a succession of ineffectual Eurosceptics from William Hague (1997–2001), to Iain Duncan Smith (2001–3) and Michael Howard (2003–5) – all men of remarkably narrow vision. Blair's ambition was, once again, to be at the 'heart of Europe' (the much used expression betraying a vainglorious harking back to a past of greatness). His greatest success was abandoning the UK's opt-out from the Social Chapter. Blair, though, failed to make the case for Europe in Britain (in fact British public opinion seems to have become more anti-European during his term of office) because he failed to argue for a more integrated Europe, failed to make the case for adopting a single currency (here the main problem was Gordon Brown's opposition), and failed to distance himself from the US. His departing speech as prime minister on 10 May 2007 was an extraordinarily pedestrian series of soundbites ending with:

> This country is a blessed nation.
> The British are special.
> The world knows it.
> In our innermost thoughts, we know it.
> This is the greatest nation on earth.[29]

Gordon Brown, though far less Europhile, was certainly not a Eurosceptic either. His view on Europe was that if only Europeans were more like the British, i.e. if they agreed to deregulate their labour market, be less 'inward-looking', and more open to globalisation, matters would work out for the best.

Since the share of national income going to working people has declined throughout the OECD countries, it should be no surprise that so many believe the global economy is working for the few, not the many. Globalisation comes in various forms: when it works well, standards of living and productivity improve, but not necessarily employment.[30]

The intelligent thing to do is to ensure that the losers from globalisation do not lose too much. The losers, after all, are those most likely to destabilise a system that has not turned them into winners. Here, as in much else, international cooperation is called for. From Brown's perspective, like that of his predecessors, cooperation is not what matters. What matters is to be 'at the heart' of everything that matters: 'Britain brings the influence that comes from being right at the heart of great international institutions and alliances – the EU, NATO, the UN, the Commonwealth, the G8 and G20.'[31] Other countries are 'members'; Britain can only be 'at the heart'. And Brown was at one with Blair in thinking that the UK's 'most important bilateral relationship' was that with the US.[32]

Brown resisted tax harmonisation, proudly explaining in his memoirs that, 'Even when in a minority of one, I stood firm at countless European finance ministers' meetings when under pressure to accept a compromise; I insisted that a one-size-fits-all savings tax would simply shift savings out of Europe.'[33] In reality all the British wanted from Europe was to use it to improve their economic position. There was never an attempt on their part to develop Europe politically, let alone deepen the process of integration. They wanted an economic union as long as the EU remained a political dwarf. Britain was always ready to ask for derogation or prorogations, insisting the UK was a special case. The British took part in the negotiations setting up the euro in order to make it weak, with as few rules as possible, but remained determined not to become a part of it. They have always been keen to stop the democratisation of the EU and the strengthening of the European Parliament. They accepted all the new members with alacrity because they knew that enlarging the Union would be an impediment to deepening it. All that mattered in the Maastricht Treaty was the single market. The British government was relieved when the treaties of Nice and Amsterdam failed.

❧

In perfect continuity with previous Labour governments, David Cameron (in alliance with the allegedly Europhile Liberal Democrat Party) joined the Czech Republic in not signing the 2012 European Fiscal Compact. Like John Major, Cameron faced the same problems with the 'bastards' (i.e. Eurosceptics) within his own party. In 2013 he promised that, should he obtain a parliamentary majority at the 2015 general election, he would negotiate new terms for continuing British membership of the EU and would then hold a referendum on whether or not Britain should stay in. He probably calculated that (as was widely predicted) he would not win a majority at the election or that, if he did, he would win the referendum. He was wrong on both counts.

Having obtained in 2015, to the surprise of most, a parliamentary majority, Cameron did try to renegotiate terms, though anyone with a minimal knowledge of the workings of the EU could have told him that the other twenty-seven members were never going to accept any form of immigration control, or additional powers for national parliaments to veto proposed EU legislation, or any diminution of the powers of the European Court of Justice. His subsequent move, to hold a referendum on membership of the EU, will rank as the least intelligent political initiative since 1066. The referendum inevitably forced many Eurosceptics, most of whom never seriously envisaged that the UK might leave the EU, to campaign in favour of Brexit. So, just in order to resolve a pathetic internal problem of party unity – the kind of problem any party leader is frequently faced with – Cameron endangered the future of the United Kingdom and of Europe while leaving his party more divided than ever, united only by an insatiable 'appetite for power'.[34]

Cameron's hapless successor, Theresa May, had to entrust the negotiations over leaving the EU to the most incompetent team one could imagine. The minister in charge of Brexit, David Davis, was so jejune in matters of trade negotiation that he assumed Britain could 'breeze out' of the EU and that the US, Australia, China, and India would line up to enter into trade deals with the UK. He expected May 'to immediately trigger a large round of global trade deals with all our most favoured trade partners', with the certainty that the negotiation phase would be concluded 'within between twelve and twenty-four months'.[35]

Davis did not realise that the UK could not negotiate any trade deal while still in the EU, that is, not until at least two years after March 2017, when Article 50 was invoked. He did not realise that half of British trade is outside the EU, but under trade deals negotiated through the EU, so the chances that, as he claimed, 'we can negotiate a free trade area massively larger than the EU' are fairly remote. Nor did he seem to realise, though he had been warned of this by Michel Barnier, the EU's chief negotiator, that it would be difficult to find a solution that would not require a border between the Republic of Ireland and Northern Ireland if the UK left the single market.

On 7 December 2017, a blustering Davis admitted to the Brexit select committee that the fifty-eight impact studies he had previously claimed had been undertaken – and which contained in 'excruciating detail' an analysis of the likely consequences of different departure scenarios for various sectors of the economy – did not, in fact, exist.[36] In July 2018 Davis eventually resigned, along with Boris Johnson, in opposition to the so-called 'Chequers Plan' devised by Theresa May.

In comparison to the other members of the Brexit team, Liam Fox (overseas trade) and Boris Johnson (then foreign secretary), David Davis emerged as a monument of economic competence. Johnson, who owed his worldwide renown to the art of buffoonery of which he is a master, dismissed talks of a large payment to the EU with a shrug. They can 'go and whistle', he declared in the House of Commons in July 2017, before the enormity of the task ahead dawned on him. 'There is no plan for no deal because we are going to get a great deal', he announced with evident self-satisfaction (though Davis, a month earlier, had told the BBC that the government had worked up a 'no deal' plan in detail).

Liam Fox was equally and blissfully unaware of something called reality (a common predicament in today's politics). This is a man who had fiddled his parliamentary expenses and used public money to pay for a friend to accompany him on official trips; a man who blamed 'lazy and fat' businesspeople for Britain's poor export performance, and who claimed that Britain shared values with Rodrigo Duterte, the president of the Philippines – notorious for encouraging extrajudicial killings (see above). Now Fox appeared to think that the British government could agree forty free trade deals with other non-EU countries 'the minute' the UK left the European Union in 2019, though this, he acknowledged, could only occur by 'copying and pasting all 40 of the EU's external trade deals' already in existence (on the assumption that everyone agreed to this). On 20 July 2017 he had declared 'The free trade agreement that we will have to do with the EU should be one of the easiest in human history.'[37] In *human history*? A few months later, on 5 September, David Davis, speaking in the House of Commons, declared, 'No one has ever pretended this will be simple or easy. I have always said this negotiation will be tough, complex and, at times, confrontational'.[38] He should have talked, at least occasionally, to his colleague Liam Fox.

On 6 July 2018, Theresa May obtained the approval of her cabinet for a new proposal which appeared to make concessions to the EU. It would be a not-too-hard Brexit, but a not-too-soft one either. Davis and Johnson at first appeared to be on side, but dealing with the EU proved more difficult than the Eurosceptics had ever envisaged. This was not surprising: May had to satisfy twenty-seven countries, the European Commission, the British Parliament in which she did not have a majority, her own party, and the small and recalcitrant Democratic Unionist Party (DUP) on whose support she had to rely. She even had to take seriously backbenchers such as Jacob Rees-Mogg, whom hardly anyone, until recently, took seriously. When in December 2017 May appeared to have reached the first stage of a deal with the European Commission's president, Jean-Claude Juncker, it turned out, embarrassingly, that she had not cleared it with her allies in the DUP.

A leaked document from the Irish ministry revealed that the British negotiating team had become a laughing stock. Boris was found 'unimpressive' by the Czechs, who 'felt sorry for British ambassadors' unable to communicate a coherent message. Latvia said UK ministers had made 'a poor impression'. Ian Forrester, a British judge in the European Court of Justice, is reported to have complained about the poor quality of politicians in Westminster. Everyone was alarmed by the 'chaos in the Conservative government'.[39]

The idea that the EU would be so terrified of Brexit that they would give in to the UK's demands pervaded the British political establishment, the pathetic remnant of an imperial mentality which makes foreigners smile. One of the least intelligent British newspapers, Murdoch's *Sun*, welcoming Article 50 and the formal declaration that the UK wanted to leave the EU, reinterpreted May's original letter as threatening that unless the EU provided a good deal, the UK would not help in the fight against terrorism. The delirious *Sun* headline was 'Your Money or Your Lives – Trade With Us and We'll Help Fight Terror' (30 March 2017). On the same day the *Daily Mail* heralded 'Cheers to a Great British Future', next to a large photo of Nigel Farage with his regular bovine grin, holding the inevitable glass of beer and sporting a pair of Union Jack socks. The *New York Times* was more realistic: the Brexit news was at the bottom of the front page, while China and the Middle East were given far greater prominence.

Some of the arch-Eurosceptics in the Conservative Party had been ridiculously unrealistic. Former cabinet minister Owen Paterson, prey to self-delusion, had previously declared (on 28 October 2015) that if Britain voted to leave it would be 'inconceivable we won't come to a satisfactory trade deal'.[40] John Redwood, once thought to be a possible Tory leader, wrote on 17 July 2016 that 'Getting out of the EU can be quick and easy – the UK holds most of the cards in any negotiation.'[41] Yet, a year later, now wearing his hat as the 'chief global strategist' for the investment firm Charles Stanley (on £180,000 a year while allegedly representing his Wokingham constituents who voted to remain), he advised investors 'to look further afield as [the] UK economy hits the brakes'.[42]

Part of the difficulty facing the country was the interpretation given to the results of the referendum on leaving the EU. The Conservatives chose to interpret the results as signifying that 'the British people' (i.e. just under 52 per cent of those who voted) wanted to leave the customs union and the single market, sever all connections with the European Court of Justice, and restrict immigration from the EU. A reasonable compromise between the 52 per cent and the 48 per cent would have been to leave the EU but negotiate terms for remaining in the single market (including free movement of labour) – a position similar to that of Norway. In fact, by joining the European Free Trade Association (EFTA), like Iceland, Norway, and Switzerland, the UK would be inside the single market, but disputes over its rules would be settled by the EFTA court and not the European Court of Justice. This would have been a compromise between leavers and remainers, but would also have risked splitting the Conservative Party, since the Eurosceptics, now emboldened, would not have accepted it. So, once again, major decisions on the future of the United Kingdom were subordinate to the interests of the future of the Conservative Party. Putting party above country remained the default position of the pseudo-patriotic Tories.

Britain was now isolated and split, out of Europe and at the mercy of a somewhat deranged American president, and led by an incompetent prime minister, Boris Johnson. But Europe too was disunited, unable to reach an agreement on refugees, and facing a growing tide of Euroscepticism, illiberal regimes in Eastern Europe, and the possible break-up of Spain.

Eighteen months after the referendum, Theresa May tweeted: 'There's more to do, but we should be proud that manufacturing output is at the highest level in 10 years.' Since the global downturn had started ten years earlier, what the prime minister was actually saying was that it had taken a decade to get back to the level of 2008 (achieved, incidentally, largely because the collapse of sterling had helped exports). As David Blanchflower, a former member of the Bank of England's Monetary Policy Committee, pointed out in a tweet, this means that it was the slowest recovery in 300 years.[43] What's more, average workers were earning less in real terms than they did in 2008, while top incomes had shot up. To add to the misplaced boast, it turned out that the UK growth figure for 2017 was 1.8 per cent, compared with the eurozone's 2.2 per cent.[44] There is a basis for the electorate's deep mistrust of politicians.

As the Irish political scientist Peter Mair noted back in 2006, politics and politicians seem to have become increasingly irrelevant to many ordinary citizens. Fewer and fewer people vote.[45] Fewer join political parties (unless, he might have added had he been writing ten years later, there was something to excite them, as was the case with Corbyn after 2015). Parties matter less and they are not as solid as they used to be, hence the rise of 'anti-politics' parties. Mair noted that through each of the four decades from the 1950s to the 1980s, average turnout levels in Western Europe scarcely altered, increasing marginally from 84.3 per cent in the 1950s to 84.9 per cent in the 1960s, and then falling slightly in the 1970s and 1980s. By the 1990s average turnout fell significantly, dipping below the 80 per cent mark. In the twenty-first century it dropped further, 'a striking indicator of the growing enfeeblement of the electoral process'.[46] The trend is unmistakable. Turnout in Austria, France, Finland, Germany, Ireland, Italy, Switzerland, the UK, and the Netherlands dropped significantly, although not so much in the Scandinavian countries (see table).

In the post-dictatorship countries of southern Europe, after years of oppression, the first elections in the 1970s were marked by high turnouts of around or over 80 per cent; by 2015–16, the turnout

Table 1. Turnout at elections: Western Europe

	1950s	2000s
Austria	95	80
Denmark	81	86
Finland	76	67
France	80	61
Germany	86	75
Ireland	74	64
Italy	93	79
Norway	78	76
Sweden	78	82
Switzerland	68	46
Netherlands	95	79
UK	80	60

Source: Pascal Delwit, 'The End of Voters in Europe? Electoral Turnout in Europe since WWII', *Open Journal of Political Science* 3:1 (2013).
Note: Belgium and Luxembourg have been left out because in these countries voting is compulsory.

was down to 55.8 per cent in Portugal, 66.5 per cent in Spain, and 56.6 per cent in Greece. In the post-communist democracies, political participation, already low in the 1990s, had sunk even lower.[47] And electoral turnout has also declined steadily throughout the West.[48]

For obvious reasons, politicians care more for voters than for party members (whose main use is that of getting the voters out). Party members, precisely because they are in a party, are not like normal people. They are fascinated by politics, and are willing to spend evenings in dismal settings arguing about political issues, instead of watching television or having a drink with friends or reading a book. As Oscar Wilde once remarked, 'The trouble with socialism is that it takes up too many evenings.'

Leaders remember party activists only at party conferences, when they subject them to rousing speeches. But the growth of social media has made traditional ways of addressing the electorate less relevant than in the past. Emmanuel Macron and Donald Trump did not need canvassers or party activists to win.

Politicians claim to listen to their constituents, but in fact the main way they know what people think is through opinion polls, since the constituents they are in touch with are usually those with a grievance, or a bee in their bonnet, or a cause – people all as 'abnormal' as party activists. The vast majority of people don't even know who their MP is and don't care. It is remarkable, for instance, that Kate Hoey, a vociferous Labour Brexiteer – who had no problems campaigning alongside the UKIP leader and embracing (in Brixton!) typical countryside causes such as fox-hunting with dogs – was returned in 2017 with an increased majority in one of the most urban constituencies in the country, in a London borough (Lambeth) which had the highest pro-remain vote in the UK (78.6 per cent), and with a large ethnic minority population. People voted Labour, not 'Brexit Hoey'.

But politicians appropriate the meaning and significance of votes, interpreting them any way they like. Voters can only vote. Once their vote is cast, they have given up their powers, their aims, their desires, to someone they hope they can trust. Voting, unavoidably, is an abdication of power. One votes and then one can go home and vent one's fury on one's loved ones or the cat. There is no other way. Power, inevitably, resides in the few. The issue is how those few are selected: brute force, rank, status, birth, or elections.

Of course, outside the polling booth, in what we call a democracy, one can influence others by demonstrating, writing, replying to pollsters, campaigning, or by becoming a personality, a celebrity, or a terrorist. But outside the polling booth is the reign of unequal power and unequal influence. Inside it is one person, one vote, and hence powerlessness. Even when elected, politicians are faced with the limitations on their power. There is no remedy. Modern politics is largely about failing; and most political lives, 'unless they are cut off in midstream at a happy juncture', as Enoch Powell famously wrote, 'end in failure, because that is the nature of politics and of human affairs'.[49]

8

Lost Hopes?

O speranze, speranze; ameni inganni
della mia prima età!
(Oh hopes, hopes; sweet deceptions
of my early age!)

Giacomo Leopardi, *Le Ricordanze*, 1829

People do not trust governments. This is hardly a novelty. Despair about the ruling classes is as old as the ruling classes themselves. In his *Florentine Histories* (1532), written partly to ingratiate himself with the Medici family, Machiavelli examined the morbid symptoms of the second half of the fourteenth century, and recorded a startling denunciation of bickering elites (the Ricci and Albizzi families) by a spokesman for 'concerned citizens', mainly merchants and prosperous guildsmen, assembled in the church of Saint Piero Scherraggio (located where the Uffizi now stands). The anonymous speaker, presumably expressing Machiavelli's own thoughts, addressed himself to the *magnifici Signori* (the Magnificent Lords, Florence's main ruling body). He complained, as people have done throughout the ages, that standards of behaviour are deteriorating and that 'oaths and promises have lost their validity, and are kept as long as it is found expedient and are adopted only as a means of deception':

And certainly in the cities of Italy all that is corruptible and corrupting is assembled. The young are idle, the old lascivious, each

sex and every age is plagued by revolting habits ... from this follow
hatred, enmities, quarrels, and factions resulting in deaths, banish-
ments, the affliction of good men, the preferment of the wicked ...
And most lamentable is it to see how faction leaders sanctify their
vile designs with words full of piety and ostensible honesty; the
word liberty is constantly on their lips, but their deeds prove them
to be liberty's greatest enemies.

Personal corruption has engulfed everything:

The reward they seek is not the glory of having brought freedom
to the city, but the satisfaction of having vanquished others, and of
becoming rulers; and to attain their end, nothing is too unjust, or
too cruel, or too avaricious. Thus laws and rules, peace, wars, and
treaties are adopted and pursued, not for the public good, not for
the common glory of the state, but for the convenience or advantage of a few individuals.

But the spokesman maintains some hope:

We have not dwelt upon our corrupt habits ... to occasion you
alarm, but to remind you of their causes; to show that as you
doubtless are aware of them, we also keep them in view, and to
remind you that their results ought not to make you diffident of
your power to repress the disorders of the present time.

There is hope, because an old world is decaying: 'the empire has
lost its ascendancy, the pope is no longer formidable, and the whole
of Italy is reduced to a state of the most complete equality'. All it
takes is for the *magnifici Signori* to resolve the situation for 'no
other motive than the love of our country'. He added:

the corruption of the country is vast, and much discretion will be
required to defeat it; but do not impute past disorders to the nature
of men, but to the times, which, being changed, give reasonable
ground to hope that, with better government, our city will have
better fortune in the future; for the malignity of the people will be

overcome by ... adopting only such principles as are conformable to true civil liberty.[1]

So what is wrong is not human nature, but 'the times', the circumstances, and these can change as long as one can trust the 'Magnificent Lords' to do the right thing. They must be trusted, there is no other way, and one must hope for more favourable times.

As Machiavelli explained in *The Prince* (Chapter 6), there are two conditions for a positive change: there must a combination of *fortuna*, that is to say 'luck' or propitious circumstances, and there must be leaders with the required *virtù*, that is to say, the capacity and skill to exploit such circumstances.

One cannot do much about *fortuna*. In an ever more integrated world no single actor can change the world, but one can always hope that there will be leaders, parties, groups, classes, able to do their best within existing constraints.

This is our present problem. We have lost hope that such leaders and parties will emerge and guide us, if not to salvation, at least towards less morbid times. Twenty years ago, a political science book entitled *Why People Don't Trust Government* lamented that confidence in American governments has been declining for three decades. The decline has continued. In 1964 three-quarters of Americans trusted the federal government to do 'the right thing'. In 1997 only a quarter did.[2] In 1972, 26 per cent of Americans did not trust the government 'very much', and 3 per cent 'not at all'; by 2017, the figures were 34 per cent and 13 per cent.[3] It may be consoling that a majority still trusts the government. But we can't be sure: a Pew poll taken a few months after the inauguration of Donald Trump established that 80 per cent of Americans did not trust the system.[4] No surprises here, since Trump voters voted for Trump precisely because they did not trust the federal government, while the anti-Trump voters were reeling under the shock of waking up with Trump in the White House.

Of course, polling depends on when and how the question is asked. An October 2017 Pew poll on voter dissatisfaction had Greece, unsurprisingly, topping the list, and Russia, surprisingly, doing rather well, with Germany doing best of the countries polled (see table overleaf).[5]

Table 2. Percentage dissatisfied with the way democracy is working in their country

Greece	79%
Spain	74%
Italy	67%
France	65%
US	51%
Israel	47%
UK	47%
Japan	47%
Russia	36%
Germany	26%

Source: Pew Research Center, 'Many unhappy with current political system,' 16 October 2017

The issue of trust is bound up with how politicians present themselves. They cannot but make promises. It's part of the job description. Few would dare to say 'there is not much I can do, but vote for me anyway'. Once in power they claim that all the good things that happened, were thanks to them, and blame their opponents or previous governments for all the bad things. This is normal. And of course, it is not just politicians we do not trust. We do not trust bankers, journalists, lawyers, real estate agents. According to a British poll, those we trust the most are doctors, teachers, judges, scientists, and hairdressers. Trust in priests is declining, particularly after the cover-ups of a spate of ecclesiastical sex scandals.[6]

Trust depends on what is happening. In 2006, 49 per cent of Americans had 'a great deal' or 'quite a lot' of confidence in banks. By 2016, confidence in banks, understandably, had dropped to 27 per cent.[7] If things go well, there is more trust. If things go badly, there is less. If there is a war, trust may increase out of collective solidarity. If the war goes badly and/or the threat is not taken seriously, trust declines. Trust in Stalin, Roosevelt, and Churchill probably increased as the war proceeded. It does not require a polling agency to establish that, by 1945, trust in Hitler and Mussolini in Germany and Italy must have collapsed.

Trust is all the more volatile where there are a large number of news sources. In the past, controlling the press and the media probably helped governments. In the era of the internet and the multiplication of news sources, control is more difficult to maintain, and people tend to seek news which confirms their views.

Yet in the West, since 1945, there has never been a time when there has been so much disenchantment with the political establishment. Such discontent, such unease, may be long-lasting. They are the morbid symptoms of an old world that is dying. In the West, this old world, the world that emerged from the Second World War, was a world of growth and stability, of educational expansion, a world in which the young could confidently assume that they would be better off than their parents, freer, less hamstrung by moral conventions. It was a world in which many could feel 'at home'; a world in which expectations were broadly fulfilled. Though it constantly changed, it changed for the better. It seemed a secure world, a world we knew and perhaps cherished.

The rebels of 1968, a minority about whom so much has been written, *enjoyed* their rebellion. They were full of hope, not despair. They thought they could build a better world. They were the children of the prosperous post-war era. They did not worry about getting a job, about the end of welfare, or the collapse of social services. They thought welfare and social services would go on forever. They did not foresee a future with climate change and without antibiotics. In the 1970s and 1980s, the rebels of '68 fought, with partial success, against misogyny, against racism, against homophobia.

And now? What do they expect? Or I should say, what do we expect? How happy are we? Has the 'pursuit of happiness' – an 'unalienable right' enshrined in the American Declaration of Independence along with 'Life' and 'Liberty' – come to an end? This is difficult to quantify, but brave pollsters try anyway, though the results can be puzzling. The Gallup report *What Happiness Today Tells Us about the World Tomorrow* compared how people in different countries were feeling ten years after the global downturn of 2007, and established a 'thriving' index. Russia, Egypt, Colombia, and India were at the bottom of the league: they definitively felt matters were far worse for them. Responses in Greece and Spain were, understandably, bad: down, respectively, by 25 per cent and 22 per cent. Even prosperous countries were less 'thriving': New Zealand and the US were down by 10–11 per cent, Singapore had dropped by 15 per cent, and Belgium by 14 per cent. What had happened?

It is not obvious why the largest increase of those 'thriving' since 2007 should have been in countries such as El Salvador (+27 per cent), Latvia (+21), Liberia (+20), and Honduras (+18). In El Salvador and Honduras there were fewer people killed between 2007 and 2017, but their homicide rates remained among the highest in the world. Perhaps people were just glad they were going down. In Liberia, after the civil war ended in 2003, an increase in happiness was almost inevitable, but it is surprising that it continued so steeply into 2017. The high score for Latvia is also puzzling since in April 2010 the country had the highest unemployment rate in the EU (22.5 per cent). True, matters have since improved, but the young in Latvia are certainly not thriving: youth unemployment was much lower in 2007 (7.6 per cent) than in 2010 (a staggering 41 per cent).

After Latvia, the EU country that showed more people 'thriving' in 2017 than in 2007 was Germany. So why have the two main German parties – the Social Democrats and the Christian Democrats – done so poorly and the far-right AfD so well? Maybe people don't know what's good for them, maybe 'it's not the economy, stupid', or maybe these polls are not worth much.[8] Why is it that in Finland the far-right Finns Party is doing so well (17.7 per cent in 2015, making it the second-largest party) when Finland tops most well-being indices: stability, safety, freedom, lack of corruption, wealth, 'happiest country in the world', fourth in gender equality, fourth in lowest poverty rate, and top in education among OECD countries.[9]

The Gallup survey measured improvement. The United Nations *World Happiness Report 2018* ranked countries in a league table of happiness. It is edited by distinguished economists such as John F. Helliwell, Richard Layard, and Jeffrey Sachs. They confirmed that the happiest country was Finland. New Zealand, which did not do well in the 'thriving' index, was the eighth 'happiest' country in the world, just below Canada and just above Sweden and Australia. Israel was eleventh (presumably this included Israeli Arabs but not stateless Palestinians). The UK was nineteenth, just below the US. France twenty-third, squeezed between Malta and Mexico. Astonishingly, Libya was the happiest country in Africa, and happier than Turkey, Hungary, and Portugal.[10]

In the UK, David Cameron, when prime minister, instructed the Office of National Statistics not to limit itself to easily quantifiable data such as GNP and employment rates but to measure 'well-being', including 'personal well-being'. This was done in the only way possible: by asking people to evaluate how satisfied they are with their life overall, whether they feel their life has a 'meaning' and a 'purpose'. The result is a 'well-being index', though it could be called the whinging index. To measure personal well-being, people were asked to answer four questions and rank their responses on a scale 0 to 10:[11]

- Overall, how satisfied are you with your life nowadays?
- Overall, to what extent do you feel the things you do in your life are worthwhile?
- Overall, how happy did you feel yesterday?
- Overall, how anxious did you feel yesterday?

One can only sympathise with statisticians asked to do impossible things, and then to try to do them by asking silly questions. Yesterday you might have felt miserable because your cat died or you had the flu. Tomorrow you may be happy because your team won the match or you won the lottery. Such questions tell us little about society and make comparisons impossible. In any case very little changed in the UK between 2016 and 2017: people were just as anxious or just as satisfied with their well-being.[12] The Brexit referendum, the 2017 election and the Corbyn surge, the election of Trump, and, in 2019, the advent of Boris Johnson, had, unsurprisingly, very little impact on 'well-being'.

Most historians would agree that, in the West at least, the world today looks better than it did yesterday – if 'yesterday' is 1945 or earlier. But 1945 is a long time ago. The past, to quote the famous opening line of L. P. Hartley's *The Go-Between*, 'is a foreign country'.

Optimism should prevail when we compare the present situation with that of the first half of the twentieth century. Steven Pinker's book *The Better Angels of Our Nature: Why Violence Has Declined* (2011) may use dubious statistics when comparing the ancient world and ours, but in the West since 1945 matters have improved: fewer crimes, fewer thefts, less violence, even less pollution (the smog in London of December 1952 killed 8,000 people).[13]

Outside the West, things do not look all that good. And I am not just thinking of the homicide rate in El Salvador, or the wars constantly in the news such as those in Syria, Libya, Yemen, and Afghanistan, but of the number of deaths during the Congo Civil War of 1998–2003, estimates of which range between 2.7 million and 5.5 million.[14] This was one of the greatest losses of life since the Second World War, but it was far away and the victims were not white and the big powers were not involved, so few in the West cared and the media barely mentioned the conflict.

The further back one goes in time the worse it gets, in the West as elsewhere. It was a world of wars, poverty, hunger, disease, genocide, as it still is for many who have not had the good fortune to be born in the West. But it is no use telling people that the old days were terrible, that our ancestors, even as recently as the nineteenth century, lived miserably, that most were poor, worked constantly, and died young. What matters is not how people see the past but what they expect of the future.

The phrase 'a revolution of rising expectations', coined in the 1950s, could not have been used in earlier centuries. The idea of progress may date back to the Enlightenment, but only a few intellectuals believed in it. The peasants tilling the land near to where Voltaire or Condorcet wrote their books, or the plantation slaves not far from Benjamin Franklin, did not notice any 'progress'. The same days followed the same nights and all they could hope for was the absence of war or of natural catastrophes.

Today's morbid symptoms are connected to the previous decades of growth and prosperity. To a large extent the present discontent is bound up with disillusion, with the loss of hope, which slogans like the 'The Audacity of Hope' cannot restore. This phrase, used by Barack Obama at the 2004 Democratic Convention and then as the title of his successful book, was borrowed from a sermon by

the Chicago pastor, Jeremiah Wright, who was in turn inspired by a painting by the English artist George Frederic Watts, *Hope* (1886). The painting represents a blindfolded woman, poorly dressed, sitting on a globe, listening to the faint sound of a lyre with a single string. Her situation is hopeless; perhaps the sound is of some comfort.

This is not how hope is normally represented. More often there is a dawn, 'where in sparkling majesty, a star / Gilds the bright summit of some gloomy cloud' (John Keats). Or there is a Jerusalem to be built 'In England's green and pleasant Land' (William Blake). Hope, in Emily Dickinson's words, 'is the thing with feathers / That perches in the soul / And sings the tune without the words'. Hope is the Promised Land, what the patriots called the 'Land of Hope and Glory, Mother of the Free', or what the socialists called the classless society, a society in which 'each can become accomplished in any branch he wishes', thus making it possible to do one thing today and another tomorrow, or 'to hunt in the morning, fish in the afternoon, rear cattle in the evening, criticise after dinner'.[15]

Jeremiah Wright, the pastor who inspired Obama, who officiated at his marriage and baptised his daughters, may not have lost hope, but he had little hope for America. In various sermons he accused the federal government of giving black people drugs, building bigger prisons, passing a three-strike law, and then expecting 'us to sing "God Bless America." No, no, no, God damn America ... for killing innocent people ... God damn America for treating our citizens as less than human. God damn America for as long as she acts like she is God and she is supreme.'

It was worse on 16 September 2001, the Sunday after 9/11 when, in his church, he thundered:

> We bombed Hiroshima, we bombed Nagasaki, and we nuked far more than the thousands in New York and the Pentagon, and we never batted an eye. We have supported state terrorism against the Palestinians and black South Africans, and now we are indignant because the stuff we have done overseas is now brought right back to our own front yards. America's chickens are coming home to roost.[16]

Obama and his family broke all links with the good pastor. Unlike Jeremiah Wright, Obama did not give up hope and became president of the US. Perhaps one should never abandon hope for fear of entering hell, on whose gate, as Dante wrote, is the terrible inscription: *Lasciate ogni speranza voi ch'entrate* (Abandon all hope you who enter here).

Socialists once thought the future was in the hands of the workers. In 1931 the communist poet Louis Aragon, about to commit himself, with no qualms, to Stalin's Russia, could write

J'assiste à l'écrasement d'un monde hors d'usage
J'assiste avec enivrement au pilonnage des bourgeois
I witness the destruction of a world past its use
I witness, intoxicated, the elimination of the bourgeois[17]

He was wrong but he had hope. Today, such hopes are confined to religious fanatics, and it is hard to maintain a 'normal' hope in the face of growing xenophobia and inequality, political uncertainties, climate change, environmental degradation, a global pandemic, crazy politicians. Today, the International does not 'unite the human race' as it does in the socialist anthem:

> Arise wretched of the earth
> Arise prisoners of want ...
> Of the past let us make a clean slate.
> Servile masses, arise, arise.
> The old world will die ...
> This is the final struggle,
> Let us rally, and tomorrow, the International
> will be the human race.

Today, what is 'international' is not the 'human race' but the globalised market. This has resulted in corporations and wealthy individuals playing one country off against another to avoid paying taxes, while weakening trade unions and decrying government interference, creating a race to the bottom in which each nation seeks to attract investment away from another.[18] As Martin Wolf wrote in his *Financial Times* column, 'The liberal international order is crumbling, in part because it does not satisfy the people of our societies.'[19]

Economists once believed, Pangloss-like, that the economy would eventually come good and that all would be for the best in the best of all possible worlds, *Die beste aller möglichen Welten* (Leibniz). Today we are not so sure. Yet we do not abandon hope, and we still hope that hell is not just round the corner. After all, if matters have improved over the previous centuries, it is precisely thanks to those who did not lose hope, who did not give up, and who fought on and on, however morbid the times.

Notes

1. The Old Is Dying

1 Antonio Gramsci, *Quaderni del Carcere*, Quaderno 3 (XX), par. 34.

2 For the statistics on the 'Spanish' flu see Peter Spreeuwenberg, Madelon Kroneman, and John Paget, 'Reassessing the Global Mortality Burden of the 1918 Influenza Pandemic', *American Journal of Epidemiology* 187: 12 (2018); see also Samuel K. Cohn, *Epidemics: Hate and Compassion from the Plague of Athens to Aids*, Oxford University Press, 2018, Chapter 22.

3 Robert Shogan, *The Battle of Blair Mountain: The Story of America's Largest Labor Uprising*, Westview Press, 2004, p. 4.

4 Angus Maddison, *Phases of Capitalist Development*, Oxford University Press, 1982, p. 206. Figures have been rounded up or down.

5 World Bank estimates on the basis of ILO data. For youth unemployment see the OECD data reported in the *Financial Times*, 15 December 2017.

6 Jeremy Rifkin, *The European Dream: How Europe's Vision of the Future is Quietly Eclipsing the American Dream*, Penguin, 2004.

7 'Is India really the most dangerous country for women?', BBC News, 28 June 2018.

8 On Trump's 'warm rapport' with Duterte see CNN report, 31 October 2017; see also 'The human toll of the Philippines war on drugs', *Economist*, 15 September 2016; 'Police have killed dozens of children in Philippines war on drugs, Amnesty says', *Guardian*, 4 December 2017.

9 'Mexico drug war fast facts', CNN Editorial Research, 3 April 2020; '"The training stays with you": the elite Mexican soldiers recruited by cartels', *Guardian*, 10 February 2018.

10 'Dozens of candidates killed ahead of Sunday's elections in Mexico', BBC Podcast, 28 June 2018, and 'Mexico goes to the polls this weekend. 132 politicians have been killed since campaigning began, per one count', CNN, 2 July 2018.

11 Médecins Sans Frontières survey, 12 December 2017; see also 'Going along with a pogrom', *Economist*, 9 September 2017; and the heart-breaking film made by the BBC *Newsnight* programme on the Tula Toli massacre: 'Rohingya crisis: The Tula Toli massacre', broadcast on 13 November 2017, now on YouTube.

12 'Fatalities in Terrorist Violence in Pakistan 2000–2019', at satp.org.

13 Nadifa Mohamed, 'How many dead Somalis does it take for us to care?', *Guardian*, 23 October 2017.

14 'Bronx fire: twelve die in New York apartment block blaze', BBC News, 29 December 2017.

2. The Rise of Xenophobia

1 Source: UNHCR, Figures at a Glance, 19 June 2018, at unhcr.org.

2 Figures from the International Organization for Migration, special report, 'Fatal Journeys, Volume 3 – Part 1'.

3 '46 years of terrorist attacks in Europe, visualized', *Washington Post*, 17 July 2017, citing sources collected by the University of Maryland National Consortium for the Study of Terrorism in their Global Terrorism Database.

4 See Ulster University 'Fact sheet on the conflict in and about Northern Ireland', at cain.ulst.ac.uk.

5 'Timeline: Lockerbie bombing', BBC News, 10 March 2020.

6 Frederick W. Kagan, *Finding the Target: The Transformation of American Policy*, Encounter Books, 2006, p. 358.

7 'Trump says tougher gun laws would have made Texas church shooting worse', *Guardian*, 7 November 2017; 'Texas attorney general: congregations should be armed after church shooting', *Guardian*, 6 November 2017.

8 The full list can be found in David Leonhardt, Ian Prasad Philbrick, and Stuart A. Thompson, 'Thoughts and prayers and NRA funding', *New York Times*, 4 October 2017.

9 Nouriel Roubini, @Nouriel, tweet, 15 February 2018.

10 'Alleged shooter at Texas high school spared people he liked', CNN, 19 May 2018.

11 'President Donald J. Trump's State of the Union Address', 5 February 2019. For crime rate in El Paso see 'Trump earlier this year

infuriated El Paso with lies about its crime rate', *Huffington Post*, 8 May 2019.

12 2015–16 figures. Sources: FBI, UK Home Office, *Small Arms Survey*.

13 Sarah Champion, 'British Pakistani men ARE raping and exploiting white girls … and it's time we faced up to it', *Sun*, 10 August 2017.

14 'Finsbury Park attacker "wanted to kill as many Muslims as possible"', *Guardian*, 22 January 2018.

15 'Men only: inside the charity fundraiser where hostesses are put on show', *Financial Times*, 24 January 2018.

16 Athena R. Kolbe, Royce Hutson, Harry Shannon et al., 'Mortality, Crime and Access to Basic Needs Before and After the Haiti Earthquake: A Random Survey of Port-au-Prince Households', *Medicine, Conflict and Survival* 26: 4 (2010).

17 'Thousands of children sexually exploited each year, inquiry says', *Guardian*, 21 November 2012.

18 Shirley Joshi and Bob Carter, 'The Role of Labour in the Creation of a Racist Britain', *Race and Class* 25: 3 (1984), p. 61, quoting a secret cabinet document 'Immigration of British Subjects into the United Kingdom', CAB 129/44.

19 Stuart Jeffries, 'Britain's most racist election: the story of Smethwick, 50 years on', *Guardian*, 15 October 2014.

20 The full Birmingham speech can be found on the *Daily Telegraph* website.

21 Peter Wilby, 'Exposing Enoch Powell's racist lies in a second, almost forgotten speech', *New Statesman*, 12 April 2018.

22 Martin Fletcher, 'Thalidomide 50 years on: "Justice has never been done and it burns away"', *Daily Telegraph*, 8 February 2018.

23 Harold Evans, *My Paper Chase: True Stories of Vanished Times*, Hachette Digital, 2009.

24 Dominic Sandbrook, *White Heat: A History of Britain in the Swinging Sixties*, Abacus, 2006, p. 262. See also Richard Norton-Taylor and Seumas Milne, 'Racism: Extremists led Powell marches', *Guardian*, 1 January 1999.

25 Simon Heffer, 'A prophet yet an outcast', *Daily Mail*, 13 June 2012.

26 'More than six million refugees are waiting in North Africa, Jordan, and Turkey to travel to Europe', *Daily Mail*, 24 May 2017.

27 *Daily Mail*, 20 August 1938, cited in William Maley, *What is a Refugee?*, Oxford University Press, 2016, p. 61.

28 J. Ramsay MacDonald, *A Socialist in Palestine*, Jewish Socialist Labour Confederation Poale-Zion, 1922, p. 6.

29 Paul Kelemen, *The British Left and Zionism: The History of a Divorce*, Manchester University Press, 2012, p. 20.

30 *The Letters of Virginia Woolf*, Vol. IV 1929–1931, Harcourt Brace Jovanovich, 1979, pp. 47, 195.

31 Quoted in Diana Kay and Robert Miles, *Refugees or Migrant Workers? European Volunteer Workers in Britain 1946–1951*, Routledge, 1992, pp. 116–17.

32 See Stephen Smith, *La Ruée vers l'Europe. La Jeune Afrique en route pour le Vieux Continent*, Grasset, 2018; Alain Finkielkraut, *L'Identité malheureuse*, Stock, 2013; and Renaud Camus, *Le Grand replacement*, David Reinharc, 2011.

33 Niall Ferguson, 'The way we live now: 4-4-04; Eurabia?', *New York Times* magazine, 4 April 2004.

34 Mark Steyn, *America Alone: The End of the World as We Know It*, Regnery Publishing, 2006, p. 134.

35 'Demographic portrait of Muslim Americans', Pew Research Center, 26 July 2017, and 'A new estimate of the US Muslim population', Pew Research Center, 6 January 2016.

36 For the Pew prediction see Besheer Mohamed, 'New estimates show US Muslim population continues to grow', Pew Research Center, 3 January 2018.

37 'Portrait of American Orthodox Jews', Pew Research Center, 26 August 2015.

38 See report by L. Daniel Staetsky and Jonathan Boyd, *Strictly Orthodox Rising: What the Demography of British Jews Tells us About the Future of the Community*, Institute for Jewish Policy Research, October 2015.

39 See also Mark Steyn, 'It's the demography, stupid', *Wall Street Journal*, 4 January 2006.

40 'Europe's growing Muslim population', Pew Research Center, 29 November 2017.

41 Joseph Nevins, *Operation Gatekeeper: The Rise of the 'Illegal Alien' and the Making of the US–Mexico Boundary*, Routledge, p. 120.

42 'Trump defends separating immigrant families amid outcry', BBC News, 19 June 2018.

43 Laura Bush, 'Separating children from their parents at the border "breaks my heart"', *Washington Post*, 17 June 2018.

44 'Trump ramps up rhetoric on undocumented immigrants', *USA Today*, 15 December 2019.

45 'Migrant kids are "child actors," Ann Coulter says on Fox News, telling Trump not to be fooled', *Washington Post*, 19 June 2018, which also shows the Fox News clip.

46 'Japan had 20,000 applications for asylum in 2017. It accepted 20', *Guardian*, 16 February 2016.

47 'Only 11 Syrian refugees have been taken in by the US this year',

Independent, 14 April 2018, quoting US State Department figures.

48 Figures from Full Fact, the UK's independent fact-checking charity.

49 Source: UN High Commission on Refugees.

50 *Guardian*, 19 October 2016, and *Daily Telegraph*, 20 October 2016.

51 Thomas Meaney, 'In the centre of the centre', *London Review of Books*, 21 September 2017.

52 '5 facts about the Muslim population in Europe', Pew Research Center, 29 November 2017.

53 Jamie Grierson and Pamela Duncan, 'Britons most positive in Europe on benefits of immigration. Findings contradict assumption UK is more hostile than European neighbours', *Guardian*, 2 May 2019.

54 Richard Hofstader, 'The Paranoid Style in American Politics', *Harper's Magazine*, November 1964.

55 See CNN report, 'US ambassador apologizes for 2015 remarks he had called "fake news"', 23 December 2017.

56 Public Religion Research Institute, 'Emerging consensus on LGBT issues: findings from the 2017 American Values', 1 May 2018.

57 Max Weber, 'The Nation State and Economic Policy', in Peter Lassman and Ronald Speirs (eds), *Weber: Political Writings*, Cambridge University Press, 1994, p. 12.

58 'The Clash of Civilizations?' was an article published in *Foreign Affairs* in the summer of 1993. By 1996 it had become a book.

59 Mehrdad Payander, 'Fragmentation within International Human Rights Law', in Mads Andenas and Eirik Bjorge (eds), *A Farewell to Fragmentation: Reassertion and Convergence in International Law*, Cambridge University Press, 2015, p. 313.

60 'Schadet sich die SPD mit ihrem Sarrazin-Kurs?', FOCUS Magazin, 1 May 2011.

61 Perry Anderson, *The H-Word. The Peripeteia of Hegemony*, Verso, 2017, pp. 169–74.

62 Philip Oltermann, 'AfD leaders vow to "hound Angela Merkel" after strong showing at polls', *Guardian*, 24 September 2017.

63 Interview in *Bild am Sonntag*, reported in 'AfD will ab 2021 mitregieren', *Spiegel Online*, 29 October 2017.

64 See 'Cosmopolitan lesbian turns far-right agitator', *Handelsblatt Today*, 20 September 2017.

65 Les Back, Tim Crabbe, and John Solomos, '"Lions and black skins": Race, nation and local patriotism in football', in Ben Carrington and Ian McDonald, (eds). *Race, Sport and British Society*, Routledge, London, 2002, p.94.

66 Video at 'Tavecchio, che gaffe: "Qui gioca chi prima mangiava banane …"', *La Repubblica*, 25 July 2014.

67 Paolo Fantauzzi, 'Kyenge pare un orango, il Pd salva Calderoli.

Per il Senato non c'è discriminazione razziale', *L'Espresso*, 16 September 2015; 'Calderoli: "Una Francia fatta di negri e islamici"', *Il Giornale*, 11 July 2006.

68   'Putin's party signs deal with Italy's far-right Lega Nord', *Financial Times*, 6 March 2017.

69   'Migranti, Berlusconi: "Bomba sociale, in 600mila non hanno diritto di restare"', *Il Fatto Quotidiano*, 4 February 2018.

70   See Shlomo Sand, *The End of the French Intellectual: From Zola to Houellebecq*, Verso, 2018, pp. 215–16.

71   Daniel Boffey, 'Dutch "burqa ban" rendered largely unworkable on first day', *Guardian*, 1 August 2019.

72   'Le financement public des religions en France', International Free Thought, 9 June 2012.

73   On Valls and the kippah see *Le Monde*, 24 September 2012; on Laurence Rossignol see 'Laurence Rossignol veut combattre le burkini "sans arrière-pensées"', *Le Figaro*, 16 August 2016; more generally, see *Midi Libre*, 19 August 2016.

74   'Burkini: une victoire de l'Etat de droit', *Le Monde*, 27 August 2016.

75   Matthieu Goar, 'Laurent Wauquiez élu président du parti Les Républicains', *Le Monde*, 10 December 2017.

76   'Maryam Pougetoux, responsable de l'UNEF, répond aux critiques sur son voile', *Le Monde*, 20 May 2018; @Charlie_Hebdo_, tweet, 23 May 2018.

77   'Denmark: Face veil ban a discriminatory violation of women's rights', Amnesty International, 31 May 2018.

78   'Bavarian leader sparks outrage over crucifixes in public buildings', *Handelsblatt*, 3 May 2018.

79   See the 29 July 2018 issue of *Famiglia Cristiana*.

80   Gustave Le Bon, *La Psychologie politique et la défense sociale*, Flammarion, 1910, pp. 227–8, 232, 241.

81   Édouard Drumont, *La France juive*, Vol. 1, Éditions du Trident, 1986, pp. 19, 34.

82   Jérôme Dupuis, '*Le Camp des Saints*, de Jean Raspail, un succès de librairie raciste?' *L'Express*, 6 April 2011.

83   Irma Gadient and Pauline Milani, 'Letter from Switzerland', *The Political Quarterly* 86: 4 (2015), pp. 468–71.

84   Brian Levin and Kevin Grisham, *Hate Crime in the United States*, Center for the Study of Hate and Extremism, California State University at San Bernardino, 2016, pp. 6 and 15.

85   David Kertzer, *The Popes Against the Jews: The Vatican's Role in the Rise of Modern Anti-Semitism*, Knopf, 2001, pp. 136–7.

86   Craig Storti, *Incident at Bitter Creek: The Story of the Rock Springs*

Chinese Massacre, Iowa State University Press, 1991, pp. 23–4.

87   Alexander Saxton, *The Indispensable Enemy: Labor and the Anti-Chinese Movement in California*, University of California Press, 1971, p. 273.

88   Henry George, 'The Chinese in California', *New York Daily Tribune*, 1 May 1869.

89   François Bédarida, 'Perspectives sur le mouvement ouvrier et l'impérialisme en France au temps de la conquête coloniale', *Le Mouvement Social* 86 (January–March 1974), p. 38.

90   Alain Dewerpe, *Le Monde du travail en France 1800–1950*, Armand Colin, 1989, p. 100.

91   Michelle Perrot, *Les Ouvriers en grève*, Vol. 1, Mouton, 1974, pp. 171–5.

92   Sascha Auerbach, *Race, Law and 'The Chinese Puzzle' in Imperial Britain*, Macmillan, 2009, p. 39.

93   Auerbach, *Race, Law and 'The Chinese Puzzle'*, p. 52.

94   See Alessandro Barbero's *Carlo Magno: Un padre dell'Europa*, Laterza, 2004 (Chapter 1), and Franco Cardini's *Europa e Islam: Storia di un malinteso*, Laterza, 2015.

95   World Bank data 2016.

96   Andreas Kossert, 'Founding Father of Modern Poland and Nationalist Antisemite: Roman Dmowski', in Rebecca Haynes and Martyn Rady (eds), *In the Shadow of Hitler*, I. B. Tauris, 2011, p. 98.

97   Reuters report, 'Waffen SS veterans commemorate Latvia's checkered past', 16 March 2013.

98   For Obama's intervention see his speech on International Holocaust Day on 28 January 2016, at Whitehouse archives.

99   On Orbán see 'Hungarian prime minister says migrants are "poison" and "not needed"', *Guardian*, 27 July 2016.

100 Yuri Levada Analytical Center, Survey, 10 June 2016.

101 Anna Mudeva, 'Special report: in Eastern Europe, people pine for socialism', Reuters, 8 November 2009.

102 For the Council of Europe report on human trafficking, see 'Kosovo rejects Hashim Thaci organ-trafficking claims', BBC News, 15 December 2010.

103 'Federica Mogherini fischiata e contestata dai parlamentari serbi radicali', euronews, 3 March 2017.

104 Filip Milačić, 'Divide and Rule: Ethnic Tensions in the Western Balkans are on the Rise as the Prospect of EU Membership Fades', *International Politics and Society*, 23 June 2017.

105 Ian Black, 'Why Israel is quietly cosying up to Gulf monarchies', *Guardian*, 19 March 2019.

106 'Israeli ministers to ban use of speakers for Muslim call to prayer',

Independent, 14 November 2016.

107 'Israeli extremist group leader calls for torching of churches', *Haaretz*, 6 August 2015.

108 'Jewish extremists taunt "Ali's on the grill" at slain toddler's relatives', *Times of Israel*, 19 June 2018.

109 Jewish Voice for Peace, 'Poetry is not a crime'.

110 '"We won't take part in Occupation": dozens of teens refuse to enlist in Israeli Army in letter to Netanyahu', *Haaretz*, 28 December 2017.

111 'Hundreds of Israelis demonstrate against home sale to Arab family', *Haaretz*, 14 June 2018.

112 'In Israeli maternity wards, Jewish and Arab segregation is the default,' *Haaretz*, 18 May 2018.

113 'Israeli taxi app gets sued for allegedly letting Jerusalem users filter out Arab drivers', *Haaretz*, 21 February 2020.

114 'Israel in turmoil over bill allowing Jews and Arabs to be segregated', *Guardian*, 15 July 2018.

115 'Israel passes controversial Jewish nation-state bill after stormy Debate', *Haaretz*, 19 July 2018.

116 'The Israel you know just ended. You can thank Netanyahu', *Haaretz*, 19 July 2018.

117 Daniel Barenboim, 'This racist new law makes me ashamed to be Israeli', *Guardian*, 23 July 2018.

118 'Hodge attacked for "BNP language"', BBC News, 25 May 2007.

119 Matthew Norman, 'Margaret Hodge's deranged hyperbole clouds the real fear that many British Jews do live in', *Independent*, 19 August 2018.

120 See, among many others, Ilan Pappe's *The Biggest Prison on Earth: A History of Occupied Palestine*, Oneworld, 2017; Donal MacIntyre, *Gaza: Preparing for Dawn*, Oneworld, 2017, and Ahdaf Soueif and Omar Robert Hamilton (eds), *This is Not a Border: Reportage and Reflection from the Palestine Festival of Literature*, Bloomsbury, 2017.

121 See the report by the Israeli human rights organisation B'Tselem, *By Hook and by Crook: Israeli Settlement Policy in the West Bank*, July 2010; see also Nur Arafeh, Samia al-Botmeh, and Leila Farsakh, 'How Israeli settlements stifle Palestine's economy', *Al-Shabaka*, 15 December 2015.

122 'Israel's religiously divided society', Pew Research Center, 8 March 2016, p. 153.

123 'Thousands at Tel Aviv rally call for release of IDF soldier charged in Hebron shooting', *Jerusalem Post*, 19 April 2016.

124 Ella Shohat, *On the Arab-Jew, Palestine, and Other Displacements:*

Selected Writings, Pluto Press, 2017, pp. 40–1.

125 Andrew Norfolk, 'Christian child forced into Muslim foster care', *The Times*, 28 August 2017; Gaby Hinsliff, 'The Muslim fostering row is a culture war in action', *Guardian*, 31 August 2017; Jamie Grierson, 'Inquiry rejects press claims about "Christian" girl fostered by Muslims', *Guardian*, 1 November 2017.

126 See the report by Brian Cathcart and Paddy French, *Unmasked: Andrew Norfolk, The Times Newspaper and Anti-Muslim Reporting – A Case to Answer*, Independent Publishing Network, June 2019.

127 'Corrections and clarifications', *Daily Telegraph*, 9 May 2018.

128 'Just 22 mosques given funding for hate crime security last year', *Observer*, 30 June 2019.

129 'What does "British jobs" pledge mean?', BBC News, 16 November 2016. For the TUC speech in full, see 'Brown speech in full', BBC News, 10 September 2007.

130 Anthony Barnett, *The Lure of Greatness: England's Brexit and America's Trump. Why 2016 Blew Away the World Order and How We Must Respond*, Unbound, 2017, p. 136.

131 'Worldwide broadband speed league 2019', cable.co.uk.

132 'Army chief calls for investment to keep up with Russia', BBC News, 22 January 2018.

133 David Shariatmadari, 'UK defence spending is national narcissism', *Guardian*, 26 June 2018.

134 'The migration fuelling George Osborne's "comeback country"', *Guardian*, 19 March 2015.

135 'Pret a Manger: just one in 50 job applicants are British, says HR boss', *Guardian*, 9 March 2017.

136 British Hospitality Association, *Labour Migration in the Hospitality Sector*, March 2017, esp. pp. 13ff.

137 Home Builders Federation, *Home Building Workforce Census 2017*, see esp. pp. 22, 29, 34–9; see also 'The government's Brexit immigration plan could push Britain's housebuilding industry into a staffing crisis', *Business Insider*, 5 December 2017.

138 'Profile', Russell Group, May 2016, p. 18.

139 'Medical transplants. Where staff come from', NHS staff graphic, at static.guim.co.uk.

140 'Fruit and veg farmers facing migrant labour shortages', BBC News, 22 June 2017.

141 IMF, *World Economic Outlook*, October 2016, Chapter 4, and *World Economic Outlook*, April 2018, Chapter 2.

142 Ciaran Devlin, Olivia Bolt, Dhiren Patel, David Harding, and Ishtiaq Hussain, *Impacts of Migration on UK Native Employment: An Analytical Review of the Evidence*, Department for Business,

Innovation and Skills, Occasional Paper 109, March 2014.

143 Christian Dustmann and Tommaso Frattini, 'The Fiscal Effects of Immigration to the UK', *Economic Journal* 124: 580 (2014), F593–F643. A review of the literature confirms such findings: 'How immigrants affect jobs and wages', Full Fact, 15 May 2017.

144 'UK needs migration "because native Britons are bloody stupid", says pro-EU Lord', *Independent*, 18 November 2016.

145 Dudley Baines, 'Europe Labor's Markets, Emigration and Internal Migration, 1850–1913', in Timothy J. Hatton and Jeffrey G. Williamson (eds), *Migration and the International Labor Market 1850–1939*, Routledge, 1994, p. 43.

146 'Ghana: median age of the population from 1950 to 2050', statista. com; see also Office of National Statistics, 'Overview of the UK population: July 2017'.

147 'Hard Labour: NZ's Ardern takes tougher line on immigration', Reuters, 22 August 2017.

148 'New Zealand child poverty a source of deep concern, says UN', *Guardian*, 7 October 2017.

149 Richard Prebble, 'Jacinda Ardern will regret this coalition of losers', *New Zealand Herald*, 20 October 2017.

150 Edmund Barton to the House of Representatives, discussing the 'Immigration Restriction Bill', House of Representatives, Debates, 12 September 1901, p. 48, cited in David Dutton, *One of Us? A Century of Australian Citizenship*, UNSW Press, 2002, p. 28.

151 'Australia built a hell for refugees on Manus. The shame will outlive us all', *Guardian*, 24 November 2017.

152 'Malcolm Fraser backs Greens senator', *Sydney Morning Herald*, 6 July 2013.

153 On the cost and more generally on anti-immigration policies, see Sasha Polakow-Suransky's brilliant *Go Back to Where You Came From: The Backlash Against Immigration and the Fate of Western Democracy*, Hurst, 2017, p. 89.

154 'Israel PM: illegal African immigrants threaten identity of Jewish state', *Guardian*, 20 May 2012.

155 Jonathan Freedland, 'Benjamin Netanyahu's appalling betrayal of Jewish values', *Jewish Chronicle*, 8 February 2018.

156 'ADL slams chief rabbi for likening black people to monkeys', *Times of Israel*, 21 March 2018.

157 Tweet, @CNNTonight (Don Lemon), May 2018.

158 'We US Jews promised to protect Darfur's genocide survivors. Now Israel's expelling them, and we don't care', *Haaretz*, 27 November 2017.

159 B. Michael, 'The sick historical precedent for Israel's asylum-seeker expulsion push', *Haaretz*, 11 January 2018.

160 'El Al Pilots say they won't fly deported asylum seekers to Africa', *Haaretz*, 22 January 2018.

161 Editorial, *Guardian*, 8 July 2018.

3. The Waning of Welfare

1 Gabriel Zucman, 'The desperate inequality behind global tax dodging', *Guardian*, 8 November 2017.

2 Jean Fourastié, *Les Trente Glorieuses, ou la révolution invisible de 1946 à 1975*, Fayard, 1979.

3 Estimates produced by the Nuffield Trust; see 'Ageing Britain: two-fifths of the NHS budget is spent on over-65s', *Guardian*, 1 February 2016.

4 Until 1989 there were no data for individual taxpayers; but see Tom Clark and Andrew Dilnot, *Long-Term Trends in British Taxation and Spending*, Institute for Fiscal Studies, Briefing Note No. 25, 2002; for data for individual taxpayers see HM Revenue & Customs, Survey of Personal Incomes, 'Number of individual income taxpayers by marginal rate, gender and age, 1990–91 to 2019–20', 2020.

5 See Ha-Joon Chang, 'The myths about money that British voters should reject', *Guardian*, 1 June 2017.

6 Franklin D. Roosevelt, Address at Madison Square Garden, New York City, 31 October 1936.

7 Terry H. Anderson, *The Pursuit of Fairness: A History of Affirmative Action*, Oxford University Press, 2004, p. 124.

8 See the video 'George Bush senior giving his famous read my lips, no new taxes,' speech YouTube.

9 Peter Edelman, 'The Worst Thing Bill Clinton Has Done', *Atlantic Monthly* 279: 3 (1997). The author was assistant secretary in the Clinton administration and resigned in protest when Clinton signed the bill.

10 Bill Ayres, 'The poorest of the poor: the Clinton legacy?', *Huffington Post*, blog of 22 April 2016.

11 Joseph Stiglitz, 'Capitalist fools', *Vanity Fair*, January 2009.

12 'Clinton crime bill: why is it so controversial?', BBC News, 18 April 2016. For prison data see the World Prison database at the Institute for Criminal Policy Research at Birkbeck, University of London.

13 George Klosko, *The Transformation of American Liberalism*, Oxford University Press, 2017, p. 229; the entire book is an excellent survey

of the development of welfare policies in the USA and its philosophical implications.

14 Lawrence Mishel and Jessica Schieder, 'CEO pay remains high relative to the pay of typical workers and high-wage earners', Economic Policy Institute, 20 July 2017; see also Diane Ravitch, 'Big money rules', *New York Review of Books*, 7 December 2017.

15 US Census Bureau. Alastair Gee, 'America's homeless population rises for the first time since the Great Recession', *Guardian*, 6 December 2017.

16 Bib Bryan, 'A brutal new analysis shows the GOP tax bill would do little for US economic growth', *Business Insider*, 1 December 2017.

17 See the report by Good Jobs Nation, *The Offshoring of American Jobs Continues*, Washington DC, June 2018.

18 Robert Reich, 'A New Year's update for Trump voters. Have Trump's promises come to fruition?', *Salon*, 1 January 2018.

19 Linda Cox and Kadee Russ, 'Steel Tariffs and US Jobs Revisited', *Econofact*, 6 February 2020.

20 Martin Wolf, 'Trump declares trade war on China', *Financial Times*, 9 May 2018.

21 Jason Beckfield and Nancy Krieger, 'Epi-demos-cracy: Linking Political Systems and Priorities to the Magnitude of Health Inequities – Evidence, Gaps, and a Research Agenda', *Epidemiologic Reviews* 31 (2009), p. 166.

22 Nicholas Timmins, 'The "welfare state" should be something we're proud of. Not a term of abuse', *Guardian*, 2 November 2017; Timmins is the author of *The Five Giants: A Biography of the Welfare State*, William Collins, 2017.

23 Andrew Ellson, 'City traders getting away with abuse of markets. Insider deals by white-collar criminals ignored', *The Times*, 19 January 2018. On tax fraud, see Vanessa Houlder, 'HMRC steps up prosecutions for tax cheating', *Financial Times*, 29 September 2017.

24 Chris Giles, 'PFI discredited by cost, complexity and inflexibility', *Financial Times*, 26 September 2017.

25 Margaret Hodge, 'Labour is right to rule out PFI rip-offs in future', *Guardian*, 26 September 2017.

26 Rajeev Syal, 'Taxpayers to foot £200bn bill for PFI contracts – audit office', *Guardian*, 18 January 2018.

27 'Former Carillion directors branded "delusional" at MPs Q&A', *Guardian*, 6 February 2018.

28 Nick Pratley, 'Entire system failed Carillion, not just directors at the top', *Guardian*, 16 May 2018.

29 See the report by the Centre for Health and the Public Interest, *P.F.I. Profiting From Infirmaries*, 30 August 2017.

30 'NHS hospital trusts to pay out further £55bn under PFI scheme', *Guardian*, 12 September 2019.

31 Chris Ham, Beccy Baird, Sarah Gregory, Joni Jabbal, and Hugh Alderwick, *The NHS Under the Coalition Government: Part One*, The King's Fund, 6 February 2015.

32 'NHS trusts post "unsustainable" £886m third-quarter deficit', *Guardian*, 20 Feb 2017.

33 OECD, *Health at a Glance: Europe 2016. State of Health in the EU Cycle*, November 2016; for hospital beds p. 167, doctors, p. 159; waiting time for surgery, p. 175.

34 Laurent Fabius, *Le Coeur du futur*, CalmanLévy, 1985, p. 207.

35 Pierre-Alain Muet and Alain Fonteneau, *Reflation and Austerity: Economic Policy under Mitterrand*, Berg, 1990, pp. 198–204.

36 Pierre Favier and Michel MartinRoland, *La Décennie Mitterrand, Vol. 1, Les ruptures*, Éditions du Seuil, 1990, p. 114.

37 Pierre Biacabe, 'Les Mésaventures du franc', in Michel Massenet, ed., *La France socialiste. Un premier bilan*, Hachette, 1983, pp. 125–6.

38 Cited in Gérard Grunberg, 'Le cycle d'Épinay', *Intervention* 13 (July–September 1985), p. 83.

39 Alain Touraine, 'Fin de partie', *Intervention* 13 (July–September 1985), p. 17.

40 Nicole Questiaux (ed.), *Les Français et leurs revenus: le tournant des années 80*, Report of Centre d'études des revenus et des coûts, La Documentation française, 1989.

41 Ian Davidson, 'Prudent policies beginning to bear fruit', *Financial Times*, 17 June 1991, p. ii.

42 'German unification: "Thatcher told Gorbachev Britain did not want German unification" (documents from Gorbachev Archive)', Margaret Thatcher Foundation. Source: *The Times*, 11 September 2009.

43 Daniel Vernet, 'Mitterrand, l'Europe et la réunification allemande', *Politique étrangère* 68: 1 (2003), pp. 176–7; Frédéric Bozo, *Mitterrand, la fin de la Guerre froide et l'unification allemande: de Yalta à Maastricht*, Odile Jacob, 2005, p. 417.

44 'The sick man of the euro', *Economist*, 3 June 1999.

45 See the investigation by Francis Beckett, David Hencke, and Nick Kochan, *Blair Inc. The Money, the Power, the Scandals*, John Blake, 2016, p. 87; Edward Malnick, 'Revealed: how Tony Blair makes his millions', *Telegraph*, 18 April 2015; Robert Mendick, 'Tony Blair's £5m deal to advise Kazakh dictator', *Telegraph*, 23 April 2016.

46 Sumi Somaskanda, 'Rich Germany has a poverty problem, *Foreign Policy*, 5 May 2015.

47 Göran Therborn, 'Twilight of Swedish Social Democracy', *New Left Review*, 113 (2018), p. 7.

48 Peter Garpenby, 'The Transformation of the Swedish Health Care System, or the Hasty Rejection of the Rational Planning Model', *Journal of European Social Policy* 2: 1 (1992), pp. 17–31.

49 Survey on Sweden, *Financial Times*, 21 December 1993.

50 William J. Clinton, Address Before a Joint Session of the Congress on the State of the Union, 23 January 1996.

51 Alain, *Propos*, Gallimard Bibliotèque la Pléiade, 1956, p. 983.

52 'En Algérie, Macron qualifie la colonisation de "crime contre l'humanité"', *Le Monde*, 15 February 2017.

53 See the report by the French news network, BFMTV, 'Macron, toujours perçu comme le "président des riches"', 24 October 2017.

54 'L'optimisme post-élection de Macron s'est dissipé', *Le Monde*, 10 July 2018.

55 'Que change la réforme de l'ISF d'Emmanuel Macron?', *Le Monde*, 30 August 2017.

56 'En France, une politique migratoire d'une dureté sans précédent', *Le Monde*, 16 December 2017.

57 Didier Fassin and Anne-Claire Defossez, 'France and the Rise of the Gilets Jaunes', *New Left Review* 115 (2019), pp. 77, 79, 81–2.

58 'La stratégie étriquée de Laurent Wauquiez', *Le Monde*, 27 October 2017.

59 YouGov poll conducted on 31 July 2017.

60 The gap between real achievements and perceptions is examined by Polly Toynbee and David Walker in *Better or Worse? Has Labour Delivered?*, Bloomsbury, 2005.

61 Andrew Hood and Tom Waters, *Living Standards, Poverty and Inequality in the UK: 2017–18 to 2021–22*, Institute for Fiscal Studies, November 2017, p. 19; see also Patrick Butler, 'Child poverty in UK at highest level since 2010, official figures show', *Guardian*, 16 March 2017.

62 Child Poverty Action Group, *Child Poverty Facts and Figures*, updated March 2019.

63 The Joseph Rowntree Foundation Analysis Unit (Helen Barnard), *UK Poverty 2017*, 4 December 2017.

64 Chris Williamson, 'This is how neoliberalism, led by Thatcher and Blair, is to blame for the Grenfell Tower disaster', *Independent*, 4 August 2017.

65 Gordon Brown, Mansion House Speech, 22 June 2006.

66 Gordon Brown, *My Life, Our Times*, Bodley Head, 2017.

67 Robert Shrimsley, 'Boris Johnson's Brexit explosion ruins Tory business credentials', *Financial Times*, 25 June 2018.

68 'Boris Johnson: The EU wants a superstate, just as Hitler did', *Sunday Telegraph*, 15 May 2016.

69 '"In 12 weeks we can turn the tide": now we can ask – was Boris Johnson right?' *Guardian*, 11 June 2020.

70 Hunger in America Study, at feedingamerica.org.

71 Joseph Stiglitz, 'Overselling Globalization', The Paul A. Volcker Prize Lecture, Washington DC, 6 March 2017, p. 19.

4. The Collapse of Established Parties

1 They would have made even more if they had waited a little longer, see Christian Wienberg, 'Goldman missed out on $800 million after selling Dong shares', Bloomberg News, 12 October 2017.

2 Peter Wise and Ben Hall, 'Portugal: a European path out of austerity?', *Financial Times*, 10 April 2019.

3 'How Netanyahu has betrayed the Jews', *Haaretz*, 27 October 2017.

4 Sue Surkes, 'Far-right Austrian party chief visits Israel, tours Yad Vashem', *Times of Israel*, 12 April 2016.

5 Lothar Gall, *Bismarck: The White Revolutionary, Vol. 1, 1815– 1871*, Unwin and Hyman, 1986, p. 83.

6 *Prague Monitor*, 23 October 2017.

7 'Far-right scores surprise success in Czech election', Reuters, 21 October 2017.

8 'Slovakian prime minister says "Islam has no place in this country" – weeks before it takes over EU presidency', *Independent*, 27 May 2016.

9 Party of European Socialists (PES), 'United for secure, tolerant and open societies PES presidency declaration on recent terrorist attacks', 19 November 2015.

10 Gábor Győri, *The Political Communication of the Refugee Crisis in Central and Eastern Europe*, FEPS and Policy Solutions, Brussels 2016, p. 9.

11 European Migration Network, 'Migrant Population and Immigration Statistics in EU Member States'.

12 On the negative economic consequences of austerity policies in Spain as well as in Italy and Portugal, see Philipp Engler and Mathias Klein, 'Austerity measures amplified crisis in Spain, Portugal, and Italy', *DIW Economic Bulletin* 7:8 (2017) pp. 89–93.

13 See Beat Balzli, 'How Goldman Sachs helped Greece to mask its true debt', *Spiegel International*, 8 February 2010.

14 Daniel Finn, 'Erdoğan Cesspit', *New Left Review* 107 (2017), p. 6; and Shadi Hamid, 'How much can one strongman change a country?', *The Atlantic*, 26 June 2017.

15 Kapil Komireddi, 'Five more years of Narendra Modi will take India to a dark place', *Guardian*, 21 May 2019; see also his book *Malevolent Republic: A Short History of the New India*, Hurst, 2019.

16 F. S. Aijazuddin, 'Annual amnesia', *Dawn*, 28 December 2017.

17 Michael Richley, 'Why Japan will lose 20 million people by 2050. Bring in the robots, immigrants, and women!', *Tofugu*, 7 February 2017; see also Robin Harding, 'Japan suffers record decline in population', *Financial Times*, 5 July 2017.

18 'Venezuela's Maduro urges women to have six children', BBC News, 4 March 2020.

19 Gideon Long, 'Alan García joins lamentable list of Peru's former presidents', *Financial Times*, 23 November 2018.

20 'Nicaragua: State repression has reached deplorable levels', Amnesty International, 9 July 2018.

21 Joseph E. Stiglitz, 'When it comes to the economy, Britain has a choice: May's 80s rerun or Corbyn's bold rethink', *Prospect*, October 2017; see also Stiglitz's 'Of the 1%, by the 1%, for the 1%', *Vanity Fair*, May 2011; and his *The Price of Inequality*, Penguin, 2013.

22 Jonathan D. Ostry, Prakash Loungani, and Davide Furceri, 'Neoliberalism: Oversold?', *Finance & Development* 53: 2 (2016), pp. 38–40.

23 Larry Elliott, 'IMF tax stance is music to Labour economists' ears', *Guardian*, 11 October 2017.

24 Bloomberg Billionaire Index; see also 'World's richest 500 see their wealth increase by $1tn this year', *Guardian*, 27 December 2017.

25 OECD Economic Surveys, Sweden, February 2017, Overview, p. 2.

26 *The World Inequality Report 2018*, written and coordinated by Facundo Alvaredo, Lucas Chancel, Thomas Piketty, Emmanuel Saez, and Gabriel Zucman; see esp. p. 7.

27 Danny Dorling, *Do We Need Economic Inequality?*, Polity, 2018, p. 2.

28 Danny Dorling, 'Inequality in Advanced Economies', *The Oxford Handbook of Economic Geography*, Oxford University Press, 2018, p. 44.

29 Dorling, 'Inequality in Advanced Economies', p. 40, quoting T. Cowen, *The Great Stagnations* (2012) and A. Atkinson, *Inequality* (2015).

30 Full text in '"Nasty party" warning to Tories', *Guardian*, 7 October 2002.

31 'Home Office officials destroyed landing cards which could have proved the right of Windrush immigrants to stay in Britain', *Daily Mail*, 17 April 2018.

32 David Cameron's immigration speech, 25 March 2013, at gov.uk.

33 'UK wrongly ordered thousand of foreign students to leave country', *Financial Times*, 2 May 2018.

34 Julian Jackson, *De Gaulle*, Haus Publishing, 2003, p. 65.

35 D. R. Thorpe, *Supermac: The Life of Harold Macmillan*, Random House, 2010, Chapter 16.

36 The speech is immortalised in a YouTube video, 'Peter Lilley speech to Tory conference 1992 – "I have a little list"'.

37 'Flog your private island and pay your staff', *Daily Mail*, 20 March 2020.

38 'Benefit reforms will end "something-for-nothing culture", says Duncan Smith', *Guardian*, 1 October 2013.

39 'Families should only get child benefit for the first two children', *Daily Mail*, 13 January 2013.

40 David Finch, 'It's crunch time for Universal Credit – and big changes are needed', Resolution Foundation, 7 July 2017; see also 'The *Guardian* view on universal credit: brake, don't accelerate', *Guardian*, 29 September 2017.

41 'Anger after Harriet Harman says Labour will not vote against welfare bill', *Guardian*, 12 July 2015.

42 Peter Kellner, 'Why Tessa Jowell is Labour's best hope in London', YouGov, 17 June 2015.

43 The study was conducted by Tim Bale, *Grassroots, Britain's Party Members*, published by the Mile End Institute at Queen Mary University of London, January 2018.

44 Jack Madiment, 'Sir Lynton Crosby's firm "paid £4 million by Conservative Party for 2017 general election campaign"', *Daily Telegraph*, 8 August 2017.

45 Andy Beckett, 'How the Tory election machine fell apart', *Guardian*, 26 June 2017.

46 Craig Brown's review of Tim Shipman's *Fall Out: A Year of Political Mayhem*, in the *Mail on Sunday*, 17 December 2017.

47 Jim Waterson, 'Brexit, cycle lanes and Saudi Arabia: CTF's Facebook campaigns', *Guardian*, 1 August 2019.

48 'Le bilan redistributif du Sarkozysme', *Terra Nova*, 6 March 2012.

49 On the effect on employment, see 'La défiscalisation des "heures sup" a accéléré la hausse du chômage', *Le Monde*, 11 March 2009.

50 Daniel Boffey, 'Polish government widely condemned over morning-after pill law', *Guardian*, 26 June 2017.

51 Irma Allen, 'Solidarity according to Polish women in 2017', openDemocracy, 25 July 2017.

52 'Religious composition by country, 2010–2050', Pew Research Center, 2 April 2015.

53　Neal Ascherson, 'Diary', *London Review of Books*, 19 October 2017.

54　'Warsaw nationalist march draws tens of thousands', BBC News, 11 November 2017.

55　'Poland approves court revamp', Bloomberg News, 8 December 2017.

56　Rick Noak, 'Polish cities and provinces declare "LGBT-free zones" as government ramps up "hate speech"', *Independent*, 20 July 2019; see also Marc Santora, 'Poland's populists pick a new top enemy: gay people', *New York Times*, 7 April 2019; see also Claudia Ciobanu, 'A third of Poland declared "LGBT-Free Zone"', BIRN, the Balkan Investigative Reporting Network, 25 February 2020.

57　Weronika Grzebalska and Andrea Pető, 'The Gendered Modus Operandi of the Illiberal Transformation in Hungary and Poland', *Women's Studies International Forum* 68 (2018), pp. 164–72.

58　Luke Waller, 'Viktor Orbán: the conservative subversive', Politico. eu.

59　On Orbán's 'crony capitalism' see Neil Buckley and Andrew Byrne, 'Orban's oligarchs', *Financial Times*, 22 December 2017.

60　'Viktor Orbán's speech at the 28th Bálványos Summer Open University and Student Camp', at abouthungary.hu.

61　'You, too, can do the shuffle all over George Soros' face!', *Budapest Beacon*, 7 July 2017.

62　Shaun Walker, 'Hungarian leader says Europe is now "under invasion" by migrants', *Guardian*, 15 March 2018.

63　'Aradszki András: Nem, nem, Soros nem egyezik meg a Sátánnal', 24-Hu (an online newspaper), 17 October 2017.

64　'Put pig heads on border fences to deter Muslim refugees, Hungarian MEP suggests', *Independent*, 21 August 2016.

65　Maayan Lubell, 'Why does Israel pour billions into West Bank Jewish settlements?', *Forward*, 24 June 2014.

66　'Israeli anti-corruption police question Netanyahu for fifth time', *Guardian*, 9 November 2017.

67　'Rivlin blasts Netanyahu's dangerous putsch and Likud's profiles in cowardice', *Haaretz*, 24 October 2017.

68　'Young American Jews increasingly turning away from Israel, Jewish Agency leader warns', *Haaretz*, 22 January 2018; see also the Pew report, *A Portrait of Jewish Americans*, 1 October 2013, pp. 81–4.

69　Raphael Ahren, 'Loathed by Jews, Germany's far-right AfD loves the Jewish state', *Times of Israel*, 24 September 2017.

70　Ian Black, 'Why Israel is quietly cosying up to Gulf monarchies', *Guardian*, 19 March 2019.

71　'Sarkozy tells Obama Netanyahu is a liar', Reuters, 8 November 2011.

72 'US, Israel sign 38 billion military aid package', Reuters, 14 September 2016.

73 @JohnBrennan, tweet, 21 December 2017.

74 'Trump praises evangelical pastor who once said Jews can't be saved', *Haaretz,* 22 October 2017.

75 'Jeffress prays "for the peace of Jerusalem" after being attacked for Christian beliefs', CBN News, 14 May 2018.

76 'Avigdor Lieberman roundup: most outlandish public statements', *Huffington Post,* 9 May 2009.

77 'Israeli defense minister: between ISIS and Hamas, Iran remains Israel's biggest threat', *Haaretz,* 18 July 2016.

78 'Lieberman calls Arab MKs who meet with Hamas "collaborators"', *Jerusalem Post,* 4 May 2006.

79 'Avigdor Lieberman roundup', *Huffington Post,* 9 May 2009.

80 Orlando Crowcroft, 'Zion's women of rage: Israel's hardliners who reject the gentle touch', *International Business Times,* 23 May 2015.

81 'Israel's religiously divided society', Pew Research Center, 8 March 2016, p. 148.

82 'A racist, messianic rabbi is the ruler of Israel', *Haaretz,* 1 July 2011.

83 'Controversial rabbi says Paris attacks punishment for Holocaust', *Times of Israel,* 16 November 2015.

84 'Echoing Netanyahu, Labor chief says leftists "forgot what it means to be a Jew"', *Times of Israel,* 19 October 2017.

85 'Party leader Gabbay forces Zionist Union to back expulsion of migrants', *Jerusalem Post,* 20 November 2017.

86 See the report of the independent commission of inquiry established by the UN pursuant to Human Rights Council resolution S-21/1, 23 June 2015, A/HRC/29/CRP.4.

87 *Times of Israel,* 1 March 2020.

88 *Times of Israel,* 5 March 2020.

89 @realDonaldTrump, tweet, 14 July 2019.

90 @SenBobCorker, tweet, 8 October 2017. The quote ('You can't make this … ') is attributed to the former White House press secretary Sean Spicer. The quote from Comey's *A Higher Loyalty* appeared in 'Comey said working with Trump reminded him of the Mob', *Washington Post,* 13 April 2018.

91 Matthew Rosenberg, 'New CIA deputy director, Gina Haspel, had leading role in torture', *New York Times,* 2 February 2017; see also Heather Digby Parton, 'New report on CIA nominee Gina Haspel may rescue her. But it shouldn't', *Salon,* 16 March 2018.

92 'Trump names TV pundit Larry Kudlow as chief economic adviser', *The Times,* 15 March 2018.

93 Charlie Savage, 'What it means: the indictment of Manafort and Gates', *New York Times*, 30 October 2017.

94 'US labour secretary Alex Acosta resigns over Epstein case', BBC News, 12 July 2019.

95 Bob Woodward, *Agenda: Inside the Clinton White House*, Simon & Schuster, 2011, p. 324.

96 'Cabinet ministers believe risk of no-deal Brexit now "very real"', *Guardian*, 21 March 2019.

97 Machiavelli, *The Prince*, Chapter 22.

98 'House Republicans release redacted Russia report', CNN, 28 April 2018.

99 'Russian intervention in American election was no one-off', *New York Times*, 6 January 2017.

100 Robert Shrimsley, 'Alexander Nix, a fake Bond villain obscuring the real mastermind', *Financial Times*, 22 March 2018 – the 'real mastermind' being Mark Zuckerberg; see also William Davies, 'Short Cuts', *London Review of Books*, 5 April 2018, pp. 20–1.

101 See Dov Levin, 'Database tracks history of US meddling in foreign elections', NPR, 22 December 2016; see also Doug Bandow, 'Interfering in democratic elections: Russia against the US, but US against the World', *Forbes*, 22 December 2016.

102 'Barack Obama says Brexit would leave UK at the "back of the queue" on trade', BBC News, 22 April 2016.

103 'Brexit: Nancy Pelosi steps up pressure on UK over Irish border', BBC News, 18 April 2019.

104 'Grenell will Konservative in Europa stärken', *Speigel*, 4 June 2018.

105 'Trump's Brexit blast', *Sun*, 12 July 2018.

106 Nilo Tabrizy, 'Sheldon Adelson's influence on Trump's Israel policy', *New York Times*, 6 December 2017.

107 Reports in the German magazine *Spiegel* and *Bild am Sonntag*, see 'US operates 80 listening posts worldwide', *Daily Telegraph*, 27 October 2013.

108 Data from Edison Research for ABC News, AP, CBS News, CNN, Fox News, NBC News, and 'Reality Check: Who voted for Donald Trump?', BBC News, 9 November 2016; on Trump's support among evangelical Christians see 'Among white evangelicals, regular churchgoers are the most supportive of Trump', Pew Research Center, 26 April 2017.

109 Barnett, *The Lure of Greatness*, p. 14.

110 Michael C. Behrent, 'Un Cyrus américain? Trump contre les Républicains', *Esprit* 440 (2017), p. 16.

111 Sam Rosenfeld, *The Polarizers*, University of Chicago Press, 2018, p. 285.

112 Susanna Barrows, *Distorting Mirrors: Visions of the Crowd in Late Nineteenth-Century France*, Yale University Press, 1981, p. 162.

113 'US public thinks Saddam had role in 9/11', *Guardian*, 7 September 2003.

114 Thomas Frank, 'The media's war on Trump is destined to fail. Why can't it see that?', *Guardian*, 21 July 2017; see also Frank's *Listen, Liberal: or, Whatever Happened to the Party of the People?*, Picador, 2017.

115 The prime minister Georges Pompidou reported, on 19 May 1968, as the student revolt unfolded, that de Gaulle had said 'yes to reform' but 'non à *la chienlit*' (shit-in-bed), an expression hardly ever used.

116 Sources: 'Donald Trumps brags about the size of his penis', You-Tube; 'Two minutes of Trump trashing women', YouTube; 'Trump recorded having extremely lewd conversation about women in 2005', *Washington Post*, 7 October 2016.

117 'Trump derides protections for immigrants from "shithole" countries', *Washington Post*, 12 January 2018.

118 'President Trump has made 1,950 false or misleading claims over 347 days', *Washington Post*, 2 January 2018.

119 For the complete list, see 'People, places and things Donald Trump has insulted on Twitter', *New York Times*, 28 January 2016; see also Peter Barker, 'The Presidency', *New York Times*, 31 December 2017.

120 John McWhorter, 'How to listen to Donald Trump every day for years', *New York Times*, 21 January 2017.

121 See, among others, 'Chirac in quotes', *Daily Telegraph*, 12 March 2007.

122 'Edith Cresson's answer to TV spoof: Hush Puppet!', *LA Times*, 23 July 1991, and 'Anti-Japan din in France softens a bit', *New York Times*, 24 July 1991.

123 'Premiers pas mouvementés de Sarkozy au salon de l'agriculture "casse-toi pauvre", video at leparisien.fr.

124 'Quando Berlusconi diede del Kapò a Schulz', YouTube.

125 On these and more see 'In quotes: Italy's Silvio Berlusconi in his own words', BBC News, 2 August 2013.

126 Public speech at Cabiate, near Como, 26 July 1997, see *La Repubblica*, 23 January 2002.

127 *L'Europeo*, 14 September 1990, cited in Laura Balbo and Luigi Manconi, *Razzismi. Un vocabolario*, Feltrinelli, 1993, p. 44.

128 Henri Deleersnijder, 'La Dérive populiste en Europe centrale et orientale', *Hermès* 2: 42 (2005); and *Libération*, 28 June 2002.

129 'Duterte llama "hijo de puta" y "homosexual" al embajador de EEUU en Filipinas', elperiodico, 10 August 2016.

130 Emily Rauhala, 'Duterte makes lewd threat to female rebels in Philippines', *Washington Post*, 12 February 2018.

131 Hannah Ellis-Petersen, 'Philippine president Duterte needs psychiatric evaluation, says UN chief', *Guardian*, 9 March 2018.

132 Fakir S. Aijazuddin, 'Waiting for Godot', *Dawn*, 5 October 2017. Ishaq Dar, after his indictment, ran away to London.

133 'Fifteen years of Vladimir Putin in quotes', *Daily Telegraph*, 7 May 2015.

134 Oleg Kashin, 'Will Russia's only opposition leader become the next Putin?', *New York Times*, 3 July 2017.

135 'Michael Fallon resigned after allegedly telling Andrea Leadsom: "Cold hands? I know where you can put them"', *Daily Telegraph*, 2 November 2017.

136 'How a racist joke became no laughing matter for Ann Winterton', *Guardian*, 6 May 2002; 'Howard sacks MP for cockle tragedy joke', *Daily Telegraph*, 26 February 2004.

137 'Biden tells factory worker "you're full of s---"', CNBC, 10 March 2020.

138 The term was popularised in a book by the journalists Sergio Rizzo and Gian Antonio Stella, *La casta. Così i politici italiani sono diventati intoccabili* (The Caste: How Italian Politicians Became Untouchable), a bestseller in 2007.

139 Ghita Ionescu and Ernest Gellner (eds), *Introduction to Populism. Its Meaning and National Character*, Weidenfeld and Nicholson, 1969, p. 1.

140 Ana Rita Ferreira, *The Portuguese Government Solution: The 'Fourth Way' to Social-Democratic Politics?* Foundation for European Progressive Studies, Brussels, 2017, p. 52.

141 See the interview with Pablo Iglesias, 'Understanding Podemos', *New Left Review* 93 (2015), p. 12.

142 'Si hay una palabra que defina a nuestra candidatura es "patriotic"', *El Diario*, 6 June 2016.

143 A wider analysis is offered by Donatella della Porta, Joseba Fernández, Hara Kouki, and Lorenzo Mosca, in *Movement Parties Against Austerity*, Polity 2017.

144 Guy Debord, *La Société du spectacle*, Buchet/Chastel, 1967; the opening line of Marx's *Capital* is: 'The wealth of societies in which the capitalist mode of production prevails appears as an immense collection of commodities.'

145 Andy McSmith, 'I'd be proud to follow Blair and Brown's lead, says Burnham', *Independent*, 24 May 2010.

146 'Margaret Beckett: I was moron to nominate Jeremy Corbyn', BBC News, 22 July 2015.

147 Bart Cammaerts, Brooks DeCillia, João Magalhães, and César Jimenez Martínez, *Journalistic Representations of Jeremy Corbyn in the British Press*, Media@LSE Report; see esp. pp. 8 and 12. The Media Reform Coalition's report covered much the same ground and came to similar conclusions: 'The media's attack on Corbyn: research shows barrage of negative coverage', Media Reform, 26 November 2015.

148 See 'The fake news Nazi – Corbyn, Williamson and the anti-Semitism scandal', Media Lens, 6 March 2019.

149 See Jamie Stern-Weiner (ed.), *Antisemitism and the Labour Party*, a free book published by Verso (2019); see also the Jewish Voice for Labour website.

150 Allison Pearson, 'Citizen Corbyn is behaving like a brat', *Daily Telegraph*, 16 September 2015.

151 Martin Amis, 'Amis on Corbyn: undereducated, humourless, third rate', *The Times*, 25 October 2015.

152 'Revealed: the evil monster haunting Jeremy Corbyn's past', *Sunday Express*, 20 September 2015.

153 These nuggets and those that follow are extracted from two brilliant compendiums: Mark Perryman (ed.), *The Corbyn Effect*, Lawrence and Wishart, 2017; and Richard Seymour, *Corbyn: The Strange Rebirth of Radical Politics*, Verso, 2016; see also the long list of anti-Corbyn articles in the *Guardian* in Tony Greenstein's blog: 'The Guardian and Jonathan Freedland's tedious campaign against Corbyn', azvsas.blogspot.com, 21 November 2017.

154 Freedland (*Guardian*, 24 July 2015); Moore (*Guardian*, 16 September); Perkins (*Guardian*, 22 July); Rawnsley (*Observer*, 19 July and 26 July).

155 For many of these quotes see Alex Nunns, 'How the *Guardian* changed tack on Corbyn, despite its readers', Novara Media, 8 January 2017, an extract from his book *The Candidate: Jeremy Corbyn's Improbable Path to Power*, OR Publications, 2016.

156 'Jeremy Corbyn says "overwhelming case" for staying in EU', BBC News, 2 June 2016.

157 Angela Phillips, 'How the BBC's obsession with balance took Labour off air ahead of Brexit', the *Conversation*, 14 June 2016.

158 Tristram Hunt and Alan Lockey, 'English Radicalism and the Annihilation of the "Progressive Dilemma"', *The Political Quarterly* 88: 1 (2017), p. 117.

159 'Ashcroft Model update: potential majorities and seat-by-seat estimates', lordashcroftpolls.com, 6 June 2017.

160 The Conservative Party Manifesto 2017, *Forward, Together. Our Plan for a Stronger Britain and a Prosperous Future*, pp. 9, 18, 36, 49.

161 Theresa May, Speech to the Conservative Party Conference, full text at blogs.spectator.co.uk.

162 William Davies, 'Home Office rules', *London Review of Books*, 3 November 2016.

163 Rafael Behr, 'I knew that many people don't vote. I should have asked why', *Guardian*, 3 January 2018.

164 For another example, see Nick Cohen's article 'It's far easier to be hoodwinked if you really think they're out to get you', *Observer*, 31 March 2019.

165 Peter Oborne, 'I was a strong Brexiteer. Now we must swallow our pride and think again', openDemocracy, 7 April 2019.

166 Laura Kuenssberg, 'The triumph that wasn't', BBC News, 21 June 2017.

167 'Tory-DUP deal: the agreement in full', *Daily Telegraph*, 26 June 2017.

168 'Membership of UK political parties', House of Commons Library, 9 August 2019.

169 Cited in Andy Beckett, 'How the Tory election machine fell apart', *Guardian*, 26 June 2017.

170 Paul Webb, Monica Poletti, and Tim Bale, 'So who really does the donkey work in multi-speed membership parties? Comparing the election campaign activity of party members and party supporters', *Electoral Studies* 46 (2017), p. 67. Grassroots, Britain's Party Members, Mile End Institute at Queen Mary University of London, January 2018.

171 Andrew Rawnsley, 'The Tzu Rule and other iron laws that always apply – until they don't', *Guardian*, 30 July 2017.

172 'Peter Mandelson: I try to undermine Jeremy Corbyn "every single day"', *Guardian*, 21 February 2017.

173 'Crawling back to Corbyn: the Labour rebels eating their words after benefiting from Jeremy Corbyn's popularity', *Daily Telegraph*, 10 June 2017.

174 'Former Danish PM schools husband Labour MP Stephen Kinnock', *Evening Standard*, 21 September 2017.

175 The full quote is 'Nec eventus modo hoc docet – stultorum iste magister est, sed eadem ratio, quae fuit futuraque, donec res eaedem manebunt, immutabilis est' (It is not only experience that guides us, for that is the teacher of fools, but reason too, for reason was and will remain immutable'). *Ab Urbe Condita*, Book 22, Chapter 39.

176 Mike Rustin, 'Are Real Changes Now Possible: Where Next for Corbyn and Labour?, *Soundings* 66 (2017).

177 'Fighting TTIP, defending workers' rights and protecting refugees: Corbyn's EU speech', Labour List, 2 June 2016.

178 See the report compiled by Nick Ritchie and Paul Ingram, *Trident in UK Politics and Public Opinion*, British American Security Information Council, July 2013.

179 On the saga of the East Coast franchise, see Andrew Adonis, 'Chris Grayling's East Coast bailout echoes the errors of New Labour', *Guardian*, 7 February 2018.

180 'Thames Water hit with record £20m fine for huge sewage leaks', *Guardian*, 22 March 2017; 'Thames Water needs to clean up its act after yet more fines', *Guardian*, 15 June 2017; 'Thames Water pays no corporation tax on £1.8bn turnover', *Guardian*, 10 July 2013.

181 Louise Ridley, 'Jeremy Corbyn's policies more popular than the Tories' – but only if they aren't linked to Labour, Poll suggests', *Huffington Post*, 13 October 2016.

182 Gary Younge, 'We were told Corbyn was "unelectable". Then came the surge', *Guardian*, 6 June 2017; see also his thoughtful and lengthy appraisal of the results: 'A shock to the system: how Corbyn changed the rules of British politics', *Guardian*, 16 June 2017.

183 Polly Toynbee, 'Corbyn is rushing to embrace Labour's annihilation', *Guardian*, 19 April 2017, and 'Corbyn's uniting words on Brexit sealed the deal', *Guardian*, 27 September 2017.

184 Rob Merrick, 'Gordon Brown backs Jeremy Corbyn as Labour leader: "People want to see change"', *Independent*, 10 November 2017.

185 Philip Collins, 'What Corbyn shares with Mugabe and Mladic', *The Times*, 24 November 2017.

186 'Former Labour MP Phil Wilson: Jeremy Corbyn lost me my seat', BBC News, 14 December 2019.

187 Costas Douzinas, *Syriza in Power*, Polity, 2017, p. 45.

188 See Yanis Varoufakis, *Adults in the Room: My Battle with Europe's Deep Establishment*, The Bodley Head, 2017, pp. 443–4, 464–70.

189 'Greek finance minister: "It's not about who will blink first"', BBC News, 31 January 2015.

190 'Greece is one of few NATO members to have met defense spending goal', NPR, 9 July 2018.

5. The American Hegemon

1 See Anderson, *The H-Word*, p. 72.

2 Figures from SIPRI Military Expenditures Database, 'World military expenditure grows to $1.8 trillion in 2018', Stockholm International Peace Research Institute, 29 April 2019.

3 Alfred W. McCoy, 'How the heroin trade explains the US–UK failure in Afghanistan', *Guardian*, 9 January 2018.

4 Original text: 'Brzezinski: "Oui, la CIA est entrée en Afghanistan avant les Russes"', *Le Nouvel Observateur*, 15–21 January 1998, p. 76.

5 Marc Lacey, 'Look at the place! Sudan says, "say sorry," but US won't', *New York Times*, 20 October 2005.

6 Christopher Hitchens, 'They bomb pharmacies, don't they?', *Salon*, 23 September 1998.

7 Aidan Hehir, 'How the West built a failed state in Kosovo', the *National Interest*, 31 August 2016.

8 Jeffrey Goldberg, 'The Obama Doctrine', *The Atlantic*, April 2016.

9 'Libya's detention of migrants "is an outrage to humanity," says UN human rights chief', UN News Centre, 14 November 2017.

10 'Yemen's cholera outbreak now the worst in history as millionth case looms', *Guardian*, 12 October 2017.

11 'UN agency chiefs call for immediate lifting of humanitarian blockade in Yemen', UN News, 16 November 2017.

12 'Clinton says US could "totally obliterate" Iran', Reuters, 22 April 2008.

13 Micah Zenko, 'The Big Lie About the Libyan War', *Foreign Policy*, 22 March 2016.

14 William J. Broad, 'Reduction of nuclear arsenal has slowed under Obama, report finds', *New York Times*, 26 May 2016.

15 Jo Becker and Scott Shane, 'Secret "list" proves a test of Obama's principles and will', *New York Times*, 29 May 2012.

16 Kathryn Olmsted, 'Terror Tuesdays: How Obama Refined Bush's Counterterrorism Policies', in Julian E. Zelizer (ed.), *The Presidency of Barack Obama*, Princeton University Press, 2018.

17 Micah Zenko, 'Obama's final drone strike data', Council on Foreign Relations, 20 January 2017.

18 Micah Zenko and Jennifer Wilson, 'How many bombs did the United States drop in 2016?', Council on Foreign Relations, 5 January 2017, on the basis of Pentagon figures.

19 John Haltiwanger, 'Trump has dropped record number of bombs on Middle East', *Newsweek*, 19 September 2017. See also Jennifer

Wilson and Micah Zenko, 'Donald Trump is Dropping Bombs at Unprecedented Levels', *Foreign Policy*, 9 August 2017.

20 United States Air Forces Central Command, Combined Forces Air Component Commander 2013–19 Airpower Statistics, afcent.af.mil.

21 See 'The Mother of All Bombs: How badly did it hurt IS in Afghanistan?', BBC News, 27 April 2017.

22 On the kill rate in Raqqa, see the 'Unprecedented investigation reveals US-led Coalition killed more than 1,600 civilians in Raqqa "death trap"', Amnesty International report, 25 April 2019.

23 On Brazil see the revelations in the leading Brazilian daily *O Globo*, 'Gravação revela que Kennedy pensava em invadir o Brasil', 6 January 2014; more generally see Stephen G. Rabe, *The Most Dangerous Area in the World: John F. Kennedy Confronts Communist Revolution in Latin America*, University of North Carolina Press, 1999.

24 Peter Riddell, 'The crumbling of Camelot', *London Review of Books*, 10 October 1991, reviewing Michael Beschloss's *Kennedy v. Khrushchev: The Crisis Years 1960–63* and Thomas Reeves's *A Question of Character: A Life of John F. Kennedy*; see also Seymour Hersh's effective demolition job, *The Dark Side of Camelot*, HarperCollins, 1998.

25 Inaugural Address of President John F. Kennedy, 20 January 1961, jfklibrary.org.

26 See Ludo de Witte, *The Assassination of Lumumba*, Verso, 2001; as well as Emmanuel Gerard and Bruce Kuklick, *Death in the Congo: Murdering Patrice Lumumba*, Harvard University Press, 2015.

27 Dwight Eisenhower, Speech to the American Society of Newspaper Editors, 16 April 1953, residency.ucsb.edu.

28 Robert S. McNamara, *In Retrospect: The Tragedy and Lessons of Vietnam*, Random House, 1995, p. 33 n.

29 Eliot A. Cohen, 'The Worst Secretary of State in Living Memory', *The Atlantic*, 1 December 2017.

30 Charles Hirshman, Samuel Preston, and Vu Manh Loi, 'Vietnamese Casualties During the American War: A New Estimate', *Population and Development Review* 21: 4 (1995), p. 806.

31 McNamara, *In Retrospect*, p. xvi.

32 Eisenhower–John F. Kennedy Correspondences – Contact Documents, paperlessarchives.com. A scathing indictment of the Kennedy administration and the Vietnam War, so far unsurpassed, is David Halberstam, *The Best and the Brightest*, Barrie & Jenkins, 1972. See also McNamara, *In Retrospect*, p. 37.

33 Department of State, *Foreign Relations of the United States 1964–1968, Volume IV, Vietnam*, 1966.

34 Roxanne Lynn Doty, *Imperial Encounters: The Politics of Representation in North-South Relations*, University of Minnesota Press, 1996, p. 177; for Westmoreland being 'not brilliant' see Halberstam, *The Best and the Brightest*, pp. 465, 549.

35 Max Hastings, *Going to the Wars*, Pan Macmillan, 2012, p. 110; see also his 'Wrath of the centurions', *London Review of Books*, 25 January 2018, reviewing Howard Jones, *My Lai: Vietnam, 1968 and the Descent into Darkness*.

36 Lewis Sorley, *Westmoreland: The General Who Lost Vietnam*, Houghton Mifflin Harcourt, 2011, p. 96; see also Halberstam, *The Best and the Brightest*.

37 McNamara, *In Retrospect*, pp. 238, 243.

38 Halberstam, *The Best and the Brightest*, p. 550.

39 Norman F. Dixon, *On the Psychology of Military Incompetence*, Random House, revised edition 1994 (1st edition 1976), pp. 396–7.

40 Halberstam, *The Best and the Brightest*, p. 665.

41 Louis B. Zimmer, *The Vietnam War Debate: Hans J. Morgenthau and the Attempt to Halt the Drift into Disaster*, Lexington Books, 2011, pp. xxi, 341.

42 There seems to be no satisfactory explanation of why it was not closed. See 'Why Obama has failed to close Guantánamo', *New Yorker*, 1 August 2016.

43 'Here's the full text of Donald Trump's speech in Poland', NBC News, 6 July 2017.

44 'Oprah Winfrey: full transcript of Golden Globes 2018 speech', BBC News, 8 January 2018.

45 See Thomas Lynch, 'President Donald Trump: A Case Study of Spectacular Power', *The Political Quarterly* 4: 88 (2017).

46 Gallup report, *Rating World Leaders 2018. The US vs. Germany, China and Russia*, see pp. 2, 4, 10.

47 'Transcript of Blair's speech to Congress', CNN, 18 July 2003.

48 Niall Ferguson, in *Colossus* (Penguin, 2004), cited in Anderson, *The H-Word*, p. 159.

49 'The US illiteracy rate hasn't changed in 10 years', *Huffington Post*, 6 September 2013.

50 National Institute of Drug Abuse, 'Opioid Overdose Crisis', revised June 2017.

51 'Drug Overdose Deaths in the United States, 1999–2016', US Department of Health and Human Services, Centers for Disease Control and Prevention, National Center for Health Statistics Data Brief No. 294, December 2017.

52 See 'Why is Congress a millionaire's club', CBS News, 27 March 2012. See also, though with different figures, Larry M. Bartels,

Unequal Democracy: The Political Economy of the New Gilded Age, Princeton University Press, 2009, p. 281; Thomas J. Hayes, 'Senators of both parties respond to the preferences of the wealthy, and ignore those of the poorest', LSE US Centre, blog post.

53 'The time when America stopped being great', BBC News, 3 November 2017.

54 Erica L. Smith and Alexia Cooper, *Homicide in the US Known to Law Enforcement, 2011*, US Department of Justice, Bureau of Justice Statistics, December 2013.

55 See gunviolencearchive.org.

56 See the Mexican website seguridadjusticiaypaz.org.mx.

57 Data from *Global Study on Homicide 2013*, United Nations Office on Drugs and Crime, pp. 122–33.

58 @realDonaldTrump, tweet, 6 November 2012.

59 See the full text at 'Opinion of Leon M. Bazile's (January 22, 1965)', *Encyclopedia Virginia*, 25 March 2014.

60 See the report by the Equal Justice Initiative, *Lynching in America: Confronting the Legacy of Racial Terror*, 3rd edition, 2017.

61 See, among others, Daniel Smith, 'A pound a glimpse', *London Review of Books*, 16 November 2017, reviewing *A Smell of Burning: The Story of Epilepsy* by Colin Grant, and *The End of Epilepsy?: A History of the Modern Era of Epilepsy, 1860–2010* by Dieter Schmidt and Simon Shorvon.

62 Takashi Tsuchiya, 'Eugenic Sterilizations in Japan and Recent Demands for Apology: A Report', *Newsletter of the Network on Ethics and Intellectual Disability*, 3: 1 (1997).

63 'Couple charged in Perris torture case', CBS Los Angeles Report, 18 January 2018.

64 Amy Goldstein, 'Worries about medical bills and lost pay may hamper coronavirus efforts in the United States', *Washington Post*, 3 March 2020.

65 Robert Reich, 'America has no real public health system – coronavirus has a clear run', *Guardian*, 15 March 2020.

66 'Donald Trump coronavirus address', CNN, 12 March 2020.

67 Susan Glasser, 'A president unequal to the moment', *New Yorker*, 12 March 2020.

68 See editorial by H. Holden Thorp, 'Do Us a Favor', *Science* 367: 6483 (2020), pp. 1169; see also 'Trump cuts to National Security staff may hurt coronavirus response', NBC News, 26 February 2020.

69 'President Donald J. Trump is devoted to protecting American freedoms and promoting American values', White House fact sheet, 4 February 2020.

6. European Narratives

1   Eric Hobsbawm, *The Age of Revolutions 1789–1848*, New American Library, 1962, p. 163.

2   Credit Suisse Research Institute, *Global Wealth Report*, November 2017, p. 55.

3   Leopold von Ranke, *History of the Latin and Teutonic Peoples*, George Bell & Sons, 1887, p. 5.

4   Larry Wolff, 'Voltaire's Public and the Idea of Eastern Europe', *Slavic Review* 54: 4 (1995), p. 936.

5   Voltaire, *Histoire de l'Empire de Russie sous Pierre le Grand*, in *Œuvres complètes*, Dupont éditeur, 1823, p. 122.

6   Charles de Secondat Montesquieu, *De l'Esprit des lois*, Vol. I, Gallimard, 1995, p. 180.

7   Michael Adas, *Machines as Measures of Men: Science, Technology and Ideologies of Western Dominance*, Cornell University Press, 1989, pp. 79–81.

8   G. W. F. Hegel, *Lectures on the Philosophy of World History*, Vol. 1, *Manuscripts of the Introduction and the Lectures of 1822–23*, edited and translated by Robert E. Brown and Peter C. Hodgson, Clarendon Press, 2011, p. 212.

9   Text in Ssu-yü Teng and John K. Fairbank (eds), *China's Response to the West: A Documentary Survey 1839–1923*, Harvard University Press, 1961, p. 199.

10 'Discours de Jacques Delors devant le Parlement européen (17 janvier 1989)', *Bulletin des Communautés européennes*, 1989, n° Supplément 1/89. Luxembourg: Office des publications officielles des Communautés européennes.

11 Jules Michelet, *Le Peuple*, Calmann Levy, 1877, pp. 277–8.

12 Ernest Lavisse, 'L'Histoire', in *Nouveau Dictionnaire de Pédagogie et d'instruction primaire*, edited by Ferdinand Buisson, Hachette, 1911.

13 'Emmanuel Macron: Le récit national n'est pas un roman totalitaire', France Culture, 9 March 2017.

14 Michael Gove, House of Commons, 9 June 2014, Hansard.

15 Michael Gove, 'All pupils will learn our island story', sayit.my society.org.

16 Ofsted, *School Inspection Handbook*, October 2017.

17 'Full text of Gordon Brown's speech', *Guardian*, 27 February 2007.

18 George Bernard Shaw, 'Common sense about the war', *New York Times*, 15 November 1914.

19 'Paper trail: from Northern Ireland's hooded men to CIA's global torture', Amnesty International, 9 December 2014.

20 See the two reports of the Intelligence and Security Committee of Parliament: *Detainee Mistreatment and Rendition: 2001–2010*, 28 June 2018, and *Detainee Mistreatment and Rendition: Current Issues*, 28 June 2018.

21 Aengus Carroll and Lucas Ramón Mendos, *State Sponsored Homophobia. A World Survey of Sexual Orientation Laws*, 12th edition, Geneva, May 2017.

22 'Rumsfeld steps up Iraq war talk', *Guardian*, 21 August 2002.

23 Hilary Benn, House of Commons, 2 December 2015.

24 House of Commons Defence Committee, *UK Military Operations in Syria and Iraq*, Second Report of Session 2016–17, pp. 22, 62, 19, 49.

25 James Wharton, 'I was the army's gay "trailblazer", but this recruitment campaign is a gross distortion of soldiering', *Daily Telegraph*, 11 January 2018.

26 'Iraq and allies violated international law in Mosul battle: Amnesty', Reuters, 11 July 2017; see also 'US admits Mosul airstrikes killed over 100 civilians during battle with Isis', *Guardian*, 25 May 2017.

27 Jared Malsin, 'The Islamic State is gone. But Raqqa lies in pieces', *Time* magazine (n.d.).

28 'Syria: Raqqa in ruins and civilians devastated after US-led "war of annihilation"', Amnesty International, 5 June 2018.

29 Mark Hookham, 'Major-General Rupert Jones lays bare grim cost of beating Isis', *Sunday Times*, 24 September 2017.

30 Nobel Lecture by Barack H. Obama, Oslo, 10 December 2009.

31 Iain Duncan Smith, 'The Nazis, Maggie, the euro … our business bosses always get it wrong', *Daily Mail*, 28 June 2018.

32 Madeline Albright, *Fascism: A Warning*, HarperCollins, London 2018.

33 'Saudi Crown Prince: Iran's supreme leader "makes Hitler look good"', *The Atlantic*, 2 April 2018.

34 On the dire economic situation of Cornwall, see the report *Cornwall's Vital Issues 2017* by the Cornwall Foundation.

35 On Du Maurier's *Rule Britannia* see 'Did Daphne du Maurier predict Brexit?', BBC News, 17 August 2016.

7. Europe Imploding?

1 'Coronavirus: arrivati in Italia dalla Cina 9 medici specializzati', *La Repubblica*, 13 March 2020; Elisabeth Braw, 'The EU is Abandoning Italy in Its Hour of Need', *Foreign Policy*, 14 March 2020.

2 Karl Marx, *Capital*, Vol. 1, Progress Publishers, 1965, p. 176.

3 'Citigroup tops list of banks who received federal aid', CNBC, 16 March 2011.

4 Frank Rich, 'The brightest are not always the best', *New York Times*, 6 December 2008.

5 Jonathan Steele and Suzanne Goldenberg, 'What is the real death toll in Iraq?', *Guardian*, 18 March 2008.

6 Carter Malkasian, *Illusions of Victory: The Anbar Awakening and the Rise of the Islamic State*, Oxford University Press, 2017, p. 29, citing an Oxford Research International poll in March 2004.

7 Malkasian's *Illusion of Victory*; and Emma Sky's *Unraveling: High Hopes and Missed Opportunities in Iraq*, PublicAffairs, 2015.

8 Jonathan Steele, 'Chilcot Report: Foreign Office', *Political Quarterly* 87: 4 (2016), p. 484; see also in the same issue, Emma Sky, 'Chilcot Report: Post-Invasion Planning'.

9 Brown, *My Life, Our Times*, p. 250.

10 'Outrage at "old Europe" remarks', BBC News, 23 January 2003.

11 Robert Kagan, *Of Paradise and Power: America and Europe in the New World Order*, Knopf Doubleday, 2007, p. 3. The formula was not original: in 1992 the self-help guru John Gray had published his bestselling *Men Are from Mars and Women Are from Venus*.

12 Kagan, *Of Paradise and Power*, pp. 3–4.

13 The original quote is: 'I suppose it is tempting, if the only tool you have is a hammer, to treat everything as if it were a nail.' Abraham Maslow, *The Psychology of Science*, Harper and Row, 1966, p. 16.

14 'Ukraine crisis: transcript of leaked Nuland-Pyatt call', BBC News, 7 February 2014.

15 Eurostat, 'Monthly minimum wages – bi-annual data', 2018 figures.

16 At least according to the evangelical Christian polling firm Barna, based in California, and reported by Albert Mohler, 'The scandal of biblical illiteracy: it's our problem', *Christian Headlines*, 29 June 2004.

17 *Cultures croisées*, Département des études, de la prospective et des statistiques, culture.gouv.fr.

18 European Commission, *Public opinion in the European Union*, Standard Eurobarometer 86, Autumn 2016.

19 See the YouGov poll 'How Britain voted at the Brexit referendum', 27 June 2016; for more Brexit data, see Matthew Goodwin and Oliver Heath, 'A tale of two countries: Brexit and the "left behind" thesis', LSE blog, 25 July 2016.

20 'EU Referendum result: 7 graphs that explain how Brexit won', *Independent*, 24 June 2016.

21 'How to make sense of those pesky Brexit forecasts', BBC News, 30 January 2018.

22 Global Future report, *Too High a Price? The Cost of Brexit – What the Public Thinks*, April 2018.

23 See David Marquand, 'Blair for EU? Nonsense from start to finish', openDemocracy, 6 November 2009.

24 David Butler and Uwe Kitzinger, *The 1975 Referendum*, Macmillan, 1976, p. 176.

25 Alan Watkins, *A Conservative Coup: The Fall of Margaret Thatcher*, Duckworth, 1991, p. 142.

26 Margaret Thatcher, Debate in the House of Commons, 30 October 1990, Column 873, publications.parliament.uk.

27 Geoffrey Howe, Debate in the House of Commons, 13 November 1990, Hansard, Vol. 180 cc461–5.

28 Stephen Castle, 'Major says three in Cabinet are bastards', *Independent*, 24 July 1993.

29 'Blair's speech: full text', *Guardian*, 10 May 2007.

30 Stiglitz, 'Overselling Globalization', p. 8.

31 Gordon Brown, Speech to the Lord Mayor's Banquet, 16 November 2009, cited in Pauline Schnapper, 'The Labour Party and Europe from Brown to Miliband: Back to the Future?', *Journal of Common Market Studies* 1: 53 (2015), pp. 157–73.

32 Gordon Brown, Speech to the Lord Mayor's Banquet, 12 November 2007.

33 Brown, *My Life, Our Times*, pp. 174–5.

34 This is the constant element in the history of the Conservative Party, according to its historian, himself a Conservative, John Ramsden. See his *An Appetite for Power: A History of the Conservative Party Since 1830*, HarperCollins, 1998.

35 David Davis, 'Trade deals. Tax cuts. And taking time before triggering Article 50. A Brexit economic strategy for Britain', Conservative Home, 11 July 2016.

36 Jim Pickard, 'Brexit secretary admits there are no impact papers', *Financial Times*, 6 December 2017.

37 'Liam Fox says the Brexit deal will be the "easiest thing in human history"', *Independent*, 20 July 2017.

38 David Davis, Secretary of State update to the House of Commons on EU negotiations, 5 September 2017.

39 Daniel Boffey, 'Irish report shows lack of respect in EU for UK's handling of Brexit', *Guardian*, 23 November 2017.

40 BBC, *Newsnight*, 28 October 2015.

41 See johnredwoodsdiary.com, 17 July 2016.

42 John Redwood, 'Time to look further afield as UK economy hits the brakes', *Financial Times*, 3 November 2017.

43 See @theresa_may, tweet, 13 January 2018, and Blanchflower's response at @D_Blanchflower.

44 'Theresa May's government: divided they drift', *Guardian*, 26 January 2018.

45 Peter Mair, 'Ruling the Void?', *New Left Review* 42 (2006), p. 26.

46 Ibid., p. 36.

47 Filip Kostelka, 'The State of Political Participation in Post-Communist Democracies', *Europe-Asia Studies* 66: 6 (2014).

48 World Bank, *World Development Report: Governance and the Law*, 2017, p. 228.

49 Enoch Powell, *Joseph Chamberlain*, Thames and Hudson, 1977, p. 151.

8. Lost Hopes?

1 Machiavelli, *Le Opere*, Editori Riuniti, 1973, *Istorie fiorentine*, pp. 417–21, originally Book III, Chapter 5.

2 Joseph S. Nye, Philip Zelikow, and David C. King (eds), *Why People Don't Trust Government*, Harvard University Press, 1997.

3 Gallup News, 'In depth: trust in government', gallup.com.

4 'Public trust in government remains near historic lows as partisan attitudes shift', Pew Research Center, 3 May 2017.

5 'Many unhappy with current political system', Pew Research Center, 16 October 2017.

6 'Politicians are still trusted less than estate agents, journalists and bankers', Ipsos Mori, 22 January 2016.

7 Claire Malone, 'Americans don't trust their institutions anymore', FiveThirtyEight, 16 November 2016.

8 Gallup report, *What Happiness Today Tells Us About the World Tomorrow*, 2017, esp. pp. 3, 8–9.

9 Statistics Finland, 'Finland among the best in the world', at stat. fi; on Finland being the 'happiest country in the world', see John F. Helliwell, Richard Layard, and Jeremy Sachs, *World Happiness Report 2018*, New York: Sustainable Development Solutions Network, 2018.

10 Helliwell et al., *World Happiness Report 2018*.

11 Office of National Statistics, *Methodology: Personal Well-being Frequently Asked Questions*, 26 September 2018.

12 Office of National Statistics, *Personal Well-being in the UK: April 2016 to March 2017*, 26 September 2017.

13 Richard Stone, 'Counting the Cost of London's Killer Smog', *Science* 298: 5601 (2002), pp. 2106–7.

14 See Benjamin Coghlan, Richard J. Brennan, Pascal Ngoy, David

Dorasa, et al., 'Mortality in the Democratic Republic of Congo: A Nationwide Survey', *The Lancet* 367 (2006); and the BBC report questioning the higher figure: 'DR Congo war deaths exaggerated', BBC News, 20 January 2010.

15 Karl Marx and Friedrich Engels, *The German Ideology*, International Publishers, 1970, p. 53.

16 'Obama's pastor: God Damn America, US to blame for 9/11', ABC News, 7 May 2008.

17 From 'Front Rouge', by Louis Aragon, originally published in 1931 in *Littérature de la Révolution mondiale*, by the Central Organ of the International Union of Revolutionary Writers, Moscow. The issue was seized by the French police and Aragon was charged with incitement to anarchist violence, risking five years in prison. After a campaign by intellectuals, the charges were dropped.

18 Joseph Stiglitz, 'The Coming Great Transformation', *Journal of Policy Modeling* 39: 4 (2017), p. 627.

19 Martin Wolf, 'Davos 2018: the liberal international order is sick', *Financial Times*, 23 January 2018.

Index of Names